PEAK TO PEAK

COLORADO FRONT RANGE SKI TRAILS

GUIDEBOOK AND MAP

Revised Edition

Harlan N. Barton

Front Range Publishing
889 Forest Ave.
Boulder, Colorado 80304
(303) 449-4296

To Weaugen

ISBN: 0-9624606-1-3

Printed by Quality Press, Englewood, Colorado

All photographs by author

Front cover photograph: Sawtooth Mountain from Coney Flats

Back cover photograph: Traverse below Clayton Lake

TABLE OF CONTENTS

PART ONE—USING THIS BOOK AND MAP

PART TWO—GENERAL INFORMATION

PART THREE—TRAIL INFORMATION

Illustrations

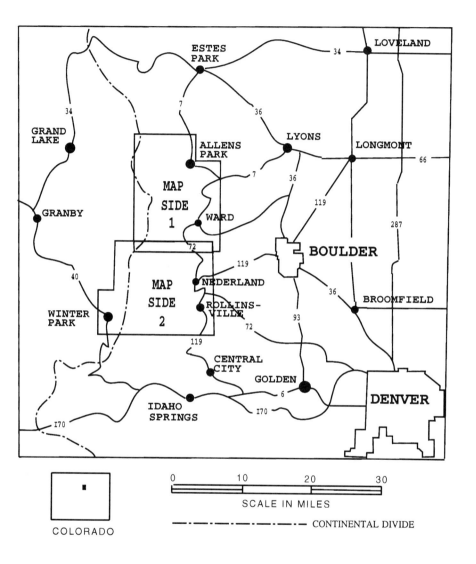

Figure 1. Location of the area covered by Side 1 (North Half) and Side 2 (South Half) of the accompanying folded trail map relative to the cities, towns, and highways of the surrounding area.

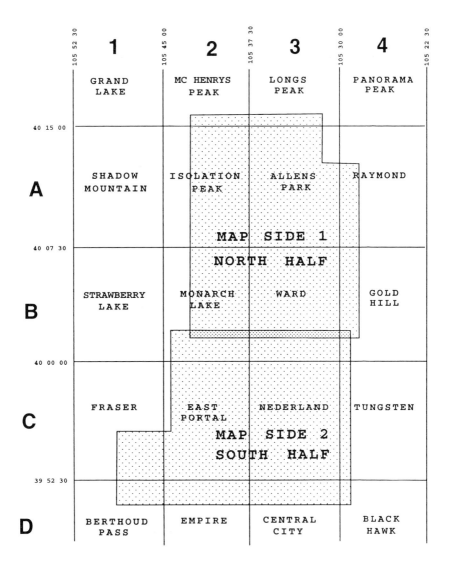

Figure 2. Area covered by Side 1 (North Half) and Side 2 (South Half) of accompanying folded trail map, shown on a mosaic of USGS 7 ½' quadrangles. Letters and numbers along margins are combined to give abbreviations used in trail summary table for USGS quadrangle names, i.e. Ward is abbreviated B3.

PART ONE—USING THIS BOOK AND MAP

Introduction

The 85 trails and routes described in this book form a unique two hundred mile network of trails extending from the southern slopes of Mt. Meeker and Longs Peak, thirty miles south along the eastern slope of the Front Range to James Peak. They are bounded by the Peak to Peak Highway on the east and, except for several routes to Winter Park, by the crest of the Front Range which forms the continental divide on the west.

The area is readily accessible from the Denver-Boulder area, with none of the trailheads more than a pleasant one hour drive from Boulder and more importantly, without the heavy traffic frequently encountered on week end trips to western slope skiing, via Interstate Highway 70.

State highways and county roads, on easy routes west into the mountains, ascend the valleys of Middle and South St. Vrain Creeks, Left Hand Creek, Middle and South Boulder Creeks, and Coal Creek. These roads end at the north-south *Peak to Peak Highway* (an assemblage of Highways 7, 72, and 119) which links the mountain communities of Estes Park, Allens Park, Raymond, Peaceful Valley, Ward, Nederland, Rollinsville, and Central City. From 19 trailheads located along this highway, or on short spur roads to the west, a web of ski trails extends westward toward the continental divide.

On this network of trails, in addition to out and back trips, numerous combinations of trails of all levels of difficulty can joined into loop trips or skied from one trailhead to another. A note of caution however, many of the routes connecting adjacent trailheads cross from one drainage to another. These are consequently not as easy, nor do they offer snow conditions as good as trails confined to the valley bottoms.

Trail altitudes range from 8,300 feet at Wild Basin to 12,200 feet where several routes cross the divide near Rogers Pass, north of James Peak. Altitudes along the continental divide in the area range from 11,671 feet at Rollins Pass to above 13,500 feet at North Arapaho Peak and at Chiefs Head Peak. The eastern side of the divide is precipitous with cirques at the head of glacial valleys along much of the divide. The western side has gentler tundra covered slopes, especially near the southern end of the area considered here.

Heavy forest extending to about 11,000 feet provides shelter from the frequent strong winds out of the west. Above this, the tundra slopes and rock cliffs are exposed to the west wind which transports snow into cornices and hard wind slab, difficult to ski and prone to avalanche, while leaving the windward faces stripped of snow.

9

Surveying the route

Most of the area is administered by federal agencies, although there are islands of private land, some of which are open to skiing. Roosevelt National Forest, administered by the U. S. Forest Service, comprises most of the area. Within Roosevelt National Forest and the adjacent Arapaho National Forest to the west, the Indian Peaks Wilderness takes in most of the higher ground on both sides of the continental divide from Rocky Mountain Park south to Rollins Pass. The Toll Ranch property above East Portal has been purchased by the Forest Service, and could become part of a James Peak Wilderness.

Wild Basin is within Rocky Mountain National Park and is administered by the National Park Service. The City of Boulder controls the drainage of North Boulder Creek west of Rainbow Lakes Road from Niwot Ridge south to the east ridge of South Arapaho Peak. Entry is prohibited, except to city employees and officials, purportedly to protect the water supply.

Location of information in this book

Part One defines terms and explains the format used in the trail descriptions, tables, and maps.

Part Two presents general information.

Part Three presents information on trails. Text descriptions of 19 trailheads and 85 trails are supplemented by a summary table, twenty page-size trail maps, and a folded large scale trail map.

Trailheads

Directions for driving to each of the nineteen trailheads from the nearest of four mountain towns in the area (Allens Park, Ward, Nederland, or Rollinsville) are given in a separate trailhead section in Part Three.

Trail descriptions

The 85 trail descriptions and the trail summary table both present information on access, difficulty and other trail characteristics in a standardized format that facilitates access to specific information. The following paragraphs explain some of the conventions and definitions used in both.

Trail numbers

Trail numbers indicate the classification of a trail as a main trail (no suffix) or as a sub-trail (A, B, C, etc. suffix). Of the 85 trails, 45 are classified as main trails and 40 are classified as sub-trails. The distinction is somewhat arbitrary, generally a main trail is one that would constitute a ski trip by itself while sub-trails may be spurs off a main trail, extensions of a main trail, connections between trails, or alternates to a main trail. Trails are, in general, numbered from north to south.

Trail names

These were selected to conform as nearly as possible with those shown on USGS topographic maps, Forest Service maps, other publications, and trail signs. There are unfortunately, numerous contradictions among these.

Some other names for the named trails of this book are as follows:

Wapiti Trail . . . . Baptiste-Wapiti Trail
Lefthand Ski Trail . . . . Left Hand Park Reservoir Road
Mt Audubon Ski Trail . . . . Beaver Creek Trail
Long Lake Ski Trail . . . . Pawnee Pass Trail
Forest Access Trail . . . . Jenny Creek Trail
Moffat Road . . . . Giants Ladder Railroad Grade
Moffat Road . . . . Rollins Pass Route

Where no trail name existed, a name was originated for this book which incorporated the name of a nearby topographic or cultural feature. Trail names commonly include the term *Trail,* implying that a recognizable trail exists. When *Route* is used as part of the name, no definite path exists. Routes represent a general line of travel from one point to another. A ridge, drainage, direction, or a line on a map may represent a route. In a few cases, *Road* may be part of the trail name and in one instance, *Railroad Grade.*

Difficulty ratings, numerical and descriptive

A consistent set of terms is used in the trail descriptions to classify trails for overall difficulty. The more specific skills or abilities appropriate for a given trail (skiing ability, endurance, and routefinding skill) are similarly described with a consistent set of terms, as are the expected trail conditions (snow quality, exposure to wind, gradient or steepness, and amount of use).

The trail summary table presents similar information, but uses numerical ratings on a scale of 1 to 5. The terms used in the trail descriptions and the corresponding numerical ratings used in the trail summary table are given in the following index.

INDEX OF DESCRIPTIVE TERMS
AND CORRESPONDING NUMERICAL RATINGS

Classification for
overall difficulty
1. Easy
2. Moderate
3. Moderate-difficult
4. Difficult
5. Very difficult

Skiing ability, Routefinding
1. Novice
2. Beginner
3. Intermediate
4. Advanced
5. Expert

Endurance
1. Very easy
2. Easy
3. Moderate
4. Strenuous
5. Very strenuous

Snow quality
1. Very Poor
2. Poor
3. Medium
4. Good
5. Excellent

Amount of use
1. Nearly unused
2. Very light
3. Light
4. Moderate
5. Heavy

Gradient/steepness
1. Nearly flat
2. Slight
3. Moderate
4. Steep
5. Very steep

Classification for overall difficulty

A one/two word or numerical classification, it gives a general summary rating of the difficulty of a trail. Its meaning however, is an oversimplification unless a trail is rated the same (easy, moderate, or difficult) for all the trail characteristics and the special skills appropriate to ski it. Where these differ, the overall rating becomes only an average and trails with the same overall rating may differ markedly. Specific ratings, which allow a better understanding of a trail's character, are discussed in the following paragraphs.

Skiing ability indicates what technical skill is necessary to ski the trail or route with the expected snow conditions. It does not consider distance, total altitude gain or loss, weather, or remoteness from trailheads. Snow conditions can have a major influence on the skiing ability required.

Endurance rating is influenced by both the length of the trail and the altitude gain and loss. Of consideration also, is the expected snow quality, the probability of having to break trail, and the length of the connecting trails which provide access.

Routefinding skill is a appraisal of the skill and equipment (maps, compass, altimeter, etc.) which may be necessary to follow the route. It varies from simply following tracks on a blazed trail through closely spaced trees to traveling untracked routes above or below timberline in bad weather and reduced visibility.

Telemarker's delight

Survival and mountaineering skill is a measure of the difficulty of the terrain, altitude, remoteness from the trailhead, amount of use on the route, expected snow conditions, and probable exposure to adverse weather. It is, in addition to a measure of recommended skill, an indication of preparation, equipment, and clothing which is appropriate. It is given in the trail summary table only.

Both the overall rating and the specific ratings discussed above are for skiing an entire route or trail. Frequently the beginning part is easier and should be considered if one is looking for a shorter and less difficult trip.

Snow conditions is an estimate of the quality of the snow pack that would normally be encountered during midwinter. It is subjective, based on the author's experience in skiing most of the trails a number of times. Those trails with a higher rating, in addition to offering better snow under normal conditions, have a longer season.

Wind exposure is presented in the trail summary table as an estimate of the percentage of a trail that is exposed to significant wind. Trail descriptions point out wind exposed localities.

13

Tracks in deep powder

Gradient or steepness is given in the trail summary table for both the steepness which is frequently encountered and for the maximum steepness encountered. Trail descriptions locate steep sections.

Amount of use is an estimate of the relative number of people to be encountered. It may also be an indicator of the probability of your breaking trail. One of the benefits hopefully to be derived from this guide book, is to discover some less used but interesting trails with good snow. Other ways of avoiding crowded conditions are to get an early start and to ski further from the trailhead.

Skiing time estimate, is given for an intermediate skier at a moderate pace without allowance of time for stops. A rough approximation of the sustained speed of an intermediate skier with a day pack, over mountainous terrain of different gradients is:

Up	steep gradient	1.2 mi/hr
Up	moderate gradient	1.7 mi/hr
—	level gradient	2.0 mi/hr
Down	moderate gradient	2.7 mi/hr
Down	steep gradient	3.5 mi/hr

Altitude gain and loss in both the text descriptions and trail summary table are in feet and are cumulative for gain and loss. Commonly, gain and loss pertain to a trip outbound from a trailhead. For a trip from one trailhead to another, refer to the direction of travel given either in the text route description or trail summary table.

14

USGS maps

USGS Maps, 7 ½ minute, (scale 1:24,000) are referenced in the text by both the quadrangle name and by a letter/number abbreviation from which the position of a map relative to adjacent maps is apparent. Only the abbreviation is used in the trail summary table. Figure 2 shows the configuration of USGS quadrangles and gives both quadrangle names and abbreviations.

By way of example, the USGS Nederland quadrangle map is abbreviated as C3, Ward is B3, East Portal is C2. With familiarity with the system, it can be deduced without need for reference to Figure 2 that Map B3 is north of Map C3 or that Map C1 is west of Map C2, etc.

Trail summary table

A Trail summary table (page 202) allows rapid scanning and comparison of trail characteristics. Information is abbreviated or presented in numerical format. Abbreviations are defined on pages immediately following the table. The correspondence of numerical ratings to descriptive terms is given in the preceding table, *Index of Descriptive Terms and Corresponding Numerical Ratings*.

Page-size trail maps

An array of twenty, page-size maps (pages 208-227) shows detailed traces of the 85 trails. They duplicate much of the information shown on the accompanying folded trail map and serve as a backup, should it not be available. The coverage of the array, on a background of USGS quadrangles, is shown in figure 4. Each map is a reproduction of a quarter of a USGS 7 ½' quadrangle. North is at the top of all maps and all are at the same scale (1:43,000). Numbers (with or without letter suffixes) appearing alongside the trails designate trail numbers. Names and a letter abbreviation designate trailheads. The magnetic declination averages 13 ½ degrees east.

Trail map

The topographic base for the accompanying folded trail map was reproduced from a mosaic of all or part of, 17 USGS 7 ½' quadrangle maps shown in Figure 2. Scale was reduced from 1:24,000 to 1:37,500, yielding a map 22 X 28 inches. Side 1 is the north half (from the Mountain Research Station Trailheads north to Longs Peak). Side 2 is the south half (from the same trailheads south to James Peak).

A coordinate system (labeled with blue numbers) is provided for giving locations to the nearest kilometer. Trail locations are specified in the individual trail descriptions and in the trail summary table in this manner. By way of example, the grid location for Brainard Lake is 51/36. The easting coordinate is given first, followed by the northing coordinate (READ RIGHT UP). This is an abbreviated Universal Transverse Mercator (UTM) grid coordinate described in more detail in the section in Part Two, *Global Position System (GPS)*.

Latitude and longitude ticks at 2 ½' intervals are labeled in red. Latitude and longitude scales are provided for interpolation.

Most trails are identified by name on the map. Where space is too small, the trail is identified with a number and the corresponding trail name is given in the legend on the same side of the map.

Additional or replacement maps are available from the author/publisher.

Figures

Small scale sketch maps show the coverage of the two sides of the accompanying folded trail map, and of the twenty, page-size trail maps.

Figure 1 shows the location of the area covered by the two sides of the accompanying folded trail map relative to the cities, towns, and highways of the surrounding area.

Figure 2 shows the location of the area covered by the two sides of the accompanying folded trail map relative to the USGS 7 ½' quadrangle maps.

Figure 3 shows the coverage of the twenty page-size trail maps on a mosaic of USGS 7 ½' quadrangles.

PART TWO—GENERAL INFORMATION

Reporting emergencies

Search and rescue is the responsibility of the county sheriff. Most of the area covered in this book is in Boulder County, except for trails along South Boulder Creek in Gilpin County, and the trails to Winter Park west of the continental divide in Grand County. After requests for aid are processed by the sheriffs department, mountain rescue is generally performed by Rocky Mountain Rescue Group. Located in Boulder, this volunteer organization was founded in 1947.

To report emergencies: (1) call the sheriff, (2) describe the problem and ask that a Rescue Group mission leader call you back, (3) remain at the telephone so that the mission leader can speak with you directly.

Call the following numbers to reach the Boulder County sheriff from:

>   Allens Park, Raymond, Peaceful Valley ..747-2538
>   Ward 441-4444
>   Boulder, Nederland 911

Call the following number to reach the Gilpin County sheriff from:

>   Nederland, Rollinsville 572-0750

16

Pay telephones (listed from north to south) are at the following locations: (1) In Allens Park, ½ block east of the post office. (2) In Raymond, at the fire station across the road from the Raymond store. (3) At the Millsite Inn, 0.3 miles north of Ward on the Peak to Peak Highway. (4) In Nederland, at the main bus stop in Wolftounge Square. (5) At Eldora Ski Area, in the lodge. (6) In Rollinsville, at both the Stage Stop Inn and at the liquor store. All are outside except (5).

Emergency telephones (free, in yellow boxes on posts) are located at: (1) Allens Park fire station/Boulder County Sheriff Department building, 100 yards north on Highway 7 from the north exit to Allens Park. (2) Glacier View Overlook, approximately half way between Peaceful Valley and Allens Park. It is ¼ mile east on Highway 7 from the junction with Highway 72. (3) Peaceful Valley Trailhead, on the east side of the highway. (4) On the Peak to Peak Highway (east side), 1.3 miles north of the road to the University of Colorado Mountain Research Station. (5) The east end of Brainard Lake, 150 yards south of the bridge on the wind scoured unplowed road. (6) Eldora town, 100 yards east on the main road from the four way stop in the town center.

Weather, avalanche, and road condition information sources

Toll free recorded messages may be heard from a number of sources. The U. S. Forest Service's Colorado Avalanche Information Center at 275-5360 provides information on weather, snow conditions, and avalanche hazards. The Colorado State Patrol at 639-1111 presents information on road conditions. Colorado Ski Country at 831-7669 reports information at downhill ski areas, including new snow, depth of base, surface conditions, and weather. Eldora ski area at 440-8800 provides snow and weather conditions. The National Weather Service at 398-3964 provides a weather forecast for the Denver area. Boulder's Daily Camera newspaper infocall at 938-9090 provides a Boulder County weather forecast (category 8900) and downhill ski conditions (categories 4767 and 4754). The Weather Channel (Channel 45 on Boulder Cable) reports continuously on local, regional, national, and global weather conditions and forecasts.

Organized groups, clubs

Several organizations conduct ski tours led by persons familiar with the area. The most active is the Colorado Mountain Club (CMC) with large groups in Boulder and Denver, smaller groups in nearby Loveland, Longmont, Fort Collins, and Estes Park, and in other locations throughout the state. On a typical weekend the Boulder group will conduct about four ski tours, with many located in the area described by here. The Denver group will have probably twice that number but scattered in a larger area. The club also schedules snowshoe trips and extensive hiking and climbing activities, summer and winter. Information may be obtained by calling the state and Denver group offices at 279-3080 or the Boulder group at 449-1135.

The Flatirons Ski Club in Boulder places more emphasis on downhill skiing, but also schedules cross country trips.

Deep snow at Arestua Hut

The Sierra Club chapter in Boulder also schedules cross country ski trips in the area.

Public transportation

The Denver-Boulder public transit system (RTD) provides bus service to Eldora Ski Area from Boulder. The regional fare from Boulder or Denver is $2.50 for the 1994-5 season.

Return transportation to Denver from an across the divide trip to Winter Park can be by bus or train. Call Greyhound at 1-800-231-2222 for up to date fare and schedule information. Currently the eastbound bus leaves Winter Park at 6:15 p.m. and arrives in Denver at 8:00 p.m. The one way fare is $10.

The ski train from Denver Union Station to Winter Park runs on Saturdays and Sundays. Call Southern Pacific Line 296-4754 for information, reservations, and tickets.

Huts, cabins

Two huts are operated by the Boulder Group of the Colorado Mountain Club. A cabin near Brainard Lake is available for overnight use by members of any group of the CMC and their guests for a fee. The cabin is locked and reservations are required. All persons are welcome to stop for a rest and hot drink for a small fee when the cabin is hosted on week ends. The Arestua Hut near the top of Guinn Mountain is open without reservations. Cooking with backpacking stoves is not allowed in either hut due to the disastrous consequences of what might start as a minor fire. Cooking can be done on the wood burning stoves in each.

The Estes Park Group of the CMC serves hot drinks on week ends at a warming hut near the Wild Basin Trailhead.

The Tennessee Mountain Cabin operated by the Eldora Ski Area is on their fee trail system.

Safety

Serious or life threatening situations in backcountry skiing are largely from two sources, avalanche and hypothermia.

Avalanche statistics place Colorado as the most dangerous state, recording 103 deaths from avalanche in a 37 year period beginning in 1950. This is more than twice that of second place Washington, according to Knox Williams, director of the Colorado Avalanche Information Center. Avalanche avoidance is a matter of education, awareness, and prudence so that areas likely to run are avoided during periods of instability. Avalanche rescue rests almost entirely upon the resources of a backcountry ski group. Avalanche transceivers operating on 457 kHz, shovels, and a party large enough to effect an immediate search and rescue effort are necessary. A solitary skier has virtually no chance of surviving burial in an avalanche.

Hypothermia can result from being forced to bivouac due to any one or a combination of several reasons— becoming lost, equipment failure, physical injury, or deteriorating weather coupled with poor judgement about capabilities. Becoming lost can be avoided by learning better routefinding skills, having maps and compass, and most of all, by giving the necessary attention to routefinding. The consequences of equipment failure can usually be avoided by carrying repair and replacement tools and equipment. A reliable headlamp can at times enable one to avoid a bivouac by skiing out in darkness. Equipment repair and headlamps are discussed in the equipment section.

Survival in a bivouac situation may well depend on the clothing and bivouac equipment carried and on having informed a reliable person about your plans. This person should have been instructed to call the county sheriff at a specified time on your failure to return and have been provided with information identifying the car used, where it would be parked, the planned route along with possible alternatives, and the expected time of return. Given this information, the chances of rescue that night or the following day are good in most cases.

Skiing alone decreases the ability to deal with some hazards, such as avalanche rescue or the ability to send for help in case of physical injury. Skiing with companions is not a cure-all however. It may only to make the party less decisive.

Light frostbite of the face, common when exposed to wind, can be avoided or minimized by periodically checking each other's faces for white spots and warming these by hand.

Litter

Few people today participating in cross country skiing discard the conventional litter of orange peels, plastic bags, or toilet tissue. Some, unthinkingly leave sticky wax scrapings in the trail. A few leave brightly colored flagging or surveyors tape to mark a trail. Trail markings are not allowed in wilderness areas and flagging doesn't seem to be necessary elsewhere with the majority of trails well marked with tree blazes or otherwise apparent. Leave something to discover for those who follow. I pick up this unsightly flagging the same as other litter.

Private property

Private property restrictions are noted in each trail description where they were encountered. Restrictions and postings change with time however, and the absence of restrictions mentioned herein does not, of course, constitute permission to ski on private property.

Dogs

Dogs are not allowed on trails in Rocky Mountain National Park, on the Waldrop (North), CMC South, and Little Raven Trails from Red Rock Trailhead to Brainard Lake, and on the access trail through Eldora Ski Area to Jenny Creek.

Equipment

For skiing trails or routes classified as difficult or very difficult special equipment and clothing aids in adapting to conditions of steep terrain, difficult snow conditions, high wind, severe weather, high altitude, long trail distances, and remote location. Maps, compass, and altimeter are discussed in the section *Navigation aids: compass, altimeter, miscellaneous.*

Travelers above timberline or along open meadows or lakes should have face protection readily accessible for use. Long gaiters keep snow out of boots and off socks when breaking trail. Special aids to skiing difficult conditions include metal edged skis, heavy duty boots, climbing skins affixed with adhesive, and a pack with ski carrying slots in the event walking becomes necessary.

Avalanche rescue equipment includes avalanche transceivers, ski pole avalanche probes, and shovels. To be compatible with rescue groups, transceivers should operate on 457 kHz. Transceivers operating on the old frequency of 2.275 kHz are of use within the group if all members have this capability. Shovels are useful for digging snow shelters in addition to recovering avalanche victims.

Material and tools to repair or replace broken poles, bindings, torn or separated boots, and lost baskets should be carried. These include nylon alpine cord, wire, duct tape, nylon strapping tape, spare basket, binding parts, selected screws and small bolts and nuts, swiss army knife and small pliers or leatherman tool. Split sections of plastic pipe and hose clamps make a repair kit for poles. A second water bottle for long trips is advisable as is foam insulation to prevent its contents from freezing. Plastic trash bags are a lightweight aid in keeping dry in a snow bivouac.

A headlamp can allow one to continue skiing after dark instead of huddling in a snow shelter. No trip of more than a few miles should be undertaken without one. An excellent but heavy headlamp is powered with four alkaline D cells. Modification may be necessary to insure that good electrical contact is maintained even when subjected to shaking. Accidental turn on in the pack should be prevented by modification or reversing batteries. Steel wool for cleaning contacts and a spare bulb should be carried. Used only when necessary and with use on the trail shared with companions, the four alkaline D cells will last an incredible time. When a lighter headlamp with less battery capacity is used, spare batteries should be routinely carried.

Skiing difficult conditions

Much of the eastern slope offers snow of excellent quality. Weather conditions characteristic of the eastern slope of the Rockies in comparison to the western slope however, include higher temperatures, less snowfall, and most importantly, high winds. These can combine to produce difficult to ski snow conditions on exposed steep slopes.

Mastery of the advanced techniques of cross country skiing, telemark and parallel, aids in the enjoyable skiing over steep terrain of a variety of snow conditions; deep powder, heavy wet snow, wind slab, and variable breakable crust. Instruction in these advanced techniques is available from ski schools or through organizations such as the Colorado Mountain Club.

Less aesthetic snow plow and step turns are however, still valuable techniques for steep packed trails. Unscrupulous methods to cope with or even avoid difficult conditions should not be overlooked. Falling may be part of the process of learning advanced technique but excessive falling and the resultant struggle to regain ones feet is exhausting. Each fall then contributes to additional falls.

Techniques of controlling speed include dragging ski pole baskets in the loose snow on the side of the trail and, for the fearless, straddling poles with the points dug in on hard packed snow. Climbing skins can be used for slowing the descent although this results in the loss of edge control and contributes significantly to their wear. Using them backward for really steep descents is, unfortunately, only a wishful myth.

Skiing with one or both skis in the unpacked snow along the edge of a packed trail aids in controlling speed while maintaining good form. On an untracked steep trail, the first person down goes the slowest but those following have the advantage of

High ridge crossing

seeing where the bumps are. Steep icy trail sections may sometimes be detoured by gentle traverses through the trees linked by kick turns. For snowplowing narrow steep packed trails across a slope, hold the upper ski straight ahead and the lower ski at an extreme angle. Short steep sections of a packed trail may be descended more quickly by sideslipping or sidestepping than recovering from a fall.

Extremely hard windslab above timberline, either smooth or sculptured by the wind into sastrugi can sometimes be negotiated better by walking than skiing. The practicality depends on the extent of the hardpacked snow. The same is true for hard or icy sections of trail with exposed rocks at lower altitudes. Trails should not be walked however, where the snow is not strong enough to prevent post holing.

Rotation of the lead in breaking trail aids in conserving the strength of the group. It is accomplished without interrupting progress by the leader stepping aside after an interval of leading, waiting for the entire group to pass, and falling in at the end of the line.

Particularly unfavorable snow conditions, especially the mixed conditions found near or above timberline can sometimes be more easily dealt with on snowshoes. Although lacking the speed and thrill of the descent of skis, modern snowshoes and bindings are marvels of reliability and effectiveness for these conditions.

Finally one can try to ski the best snow available. The main criteria are simple: trees, altitude, and north facing. Trees, large and dense enough to provide shelter from sun and wind, are probably the most important factor affecting snow quality on the eastern slope. Nearly as important and interrelated, is altitude. Without the protection of trees, above timberline slopes are, except immediately following a snowfall, exposed to the deleterious effects of wind. Slopes on the windward side of ridges are blown clear of snow which is deposited as cornices and hard wind slab snowfields on the leeward side. The snow surface may sculptured by the wind into sastrugi.

The best snow will be high and with good tree cover. Snow from 10,000 feet to timberline is always better than that found lower. There is generally more snowfall at the higher altitude and temperatures remain lower. Although mitigated by good tree cover, the effect of sun on a south facing slope degrades the snow more rapidly than on a north facing one. Finally, if other conditions are equal, a trail with less traffic will have better snow.

Weather forecasting hints

Most ski trips in the front range are short and weather prediction is not normally necessary if a forecast has been obtained prior to starting the trip. Telephone numbers for obtaining this information are given in the *Information Sources* section. The following rules of thumb however, may add to ones skill in short range forecasting and enjoyment. They are from the CompuServe Outdoor Forum, a public domain source and were reprinted in Newsletter vol. 1, #3, of the Tenth Mountain Trail Association.

1. Steadily falling barometric pressure usually means an approaching storm while steadily rising pressure signals clearing weather. An altimeter allows you to evaluate this and number 2.

2. There is little chance of precipitation continuing when the barometric pressure is more than 30.10.

3. When the temperature during a storm drops to less than 5 degrees F, snowfall will rapidly diminish.

4. Cirrus clouds can precede a storm by 24 hours or more. A ring around the moon is caused by thin cirrus.

5. Mountain wave clouds and snow plumes on ridges, indicate high winds at mountain top levels.

6. Frontal passage (the end of a storm) is often indicated by the lowest point of the barometric pressure curve, a wind shift, and a sudden appearance of heavily rimed snow crystals or graupel.

7. If the wind direction changes clockwise with time (for example, wind out of the south changing to the west), expect mostly fair weather; low pressure is passing to the north. If the wind direction turns counterclockwise (northwest becoming southwest), expect poor weather; low pressure is passing to the south.

8. Current weather reports on radio, especially NOAA Weather Radio on VHF band (162.55 MHz, Denver) are your best sources for accurate forecasts while skiing.

Routefinding

The necessity for routefinding, navigation or orienteering skills in backcountry ski touring varies greatly. Little skill is required to follow a tracked distinct trail cut through stands of closely spaced trees blazed with blue diamond markers, compared to that necessary to follow an indistinct route above timberline or one through thick timber in a white out or darkness. Even the seemingly foolproof technique of following tracks can pose problems, there is no guarantee that solitary tracks are a trail. They may mean only that an off trail skier wandered this way. Tracks are also at times very temporary, being subject to obliteration in a few minutes by wind or in little more time by new snowfall. A skier can be deprived of even his own tracks for a return route.

Other indicators of an established trail are more permanent. Tree clearing and trimming of branches is apparent in dense timber but less so in more widely spaced trees. The traditional inverted "!" tree slash or the flattened metal can nailed to a tree mark some trails but these are being replaced by the more visible blue diamond trail markers. Contrary to their meaning at downhill ski areas, they indicate nothing about the difficulty rating of the trail. Trails in Rocky Mountain Park are often marked with orange square blazes. Trails within the Indian Peaks Wilderness are unmarked except for old and frequently indistinct tree slashes.

Trail signs are surprisingly impermanent. They suffer the effects of weathering, nibbling horses, vandalism, and souvenir seekers. Another form of trail marking is the use of cairns above timberline. The Rollins Pass route is marked part of the way by an abandoned telegraph pole line. Flagging, the brightly colored surveyors tape has been discussed in the section on litter. Its only justifiable use is in an emergency or to mark a route temporarily. Then it should be tied shoe lace fashion, so that it may be removed with a single pull on the return trip.

Maps, USGS & Forest Service

U.S. Geological Survey 7½ minute quadrangle maps at a scale of 1:24,000 and in six colors are the most detailed maps available. Reproductions in commercial maps printed on waterproof paper and in guidebooks often at a reduced scale do not offer the same quality of detailed information. Four of these maps (Allens Park, Ward, Nederland, and East Portal) cover the majority of the trails discussed in this book.

A consistent system of folding maps has advantages in storage and use, in addition to lessening the damage from folding in many different places. To aid in seeing the continuity of terrain features across map boundaries when holding a map next to the adjacent one, trim or fold back half of the margins (top and left on each map) to the neat line. After trimming the right boundary to near the neat line but retaining the marginal information and folding the bottom margin under, a single vertical fold down the center followed by accordion folds into four sections yields a map which can be viewed in its entirety with a folded size of six by nine inches, small enough to fit into a parka pocket, map case or fanny pack. An accessible map which can be consulted readily, especially during adverse weather conditions, is of far greater value than a map buried in a pack. A plastic map cover, trimmed to size and open on two sides, provides protection from both snow and from crumpling in the pocket or pack, while allowing easy access to change the accordion section viewable.

Smaller scale USGS topographic maps for the area are the 1:50,000 Boulder, Grand, and Gilpin County maps and the 1:100,000 metric Estes Park and Denver West 30 by 60 minute quadrangles. All are available, over the counter, at the USGS map sales office, Building 810, at the Federal Center in Lakewood.

Forest Service maps are particularly useful for information on trails, roads, and land ownership. The Roosevelt National Forest map includes the adjacent Arapaho National Forest on the west side of the continental divide.

Navigation aids: compass, altimeter, miscellaneous

A simple compass with a rectangular transparent body having provision for an attachment cord and with a graduated rotating azimuth ring is well suited for winter use. Map orientation and the ability to follow a selected compass course by centering the needle over an arrow are the major uses. Like the map, it should always be accessible even though clothing changes may have to be made to accommodate to changing weather conditions. It may be attached with a neck loop or to clothing with a cord and alligator clamp. Once a compass direction has been established, shadows if present, may be used to maintain a given direction with sufficient precision for most situations.

An altimeter can be extremely useful in determining one's position along a linear terrain feature such as a valley, trail or ridge when visibility is restricted by trees, snow, or darkness. It should be reset frequently to minimize the transfers of distance, altitude and time. Notes made prior to a trip of altitudes of key points along the route assist in gauging progress toward them and facilitates resetting the altimeter as they are passed. The altimeter may also be used as a barometer to assist in weather prediction.

Other useful aids are a watch, pocket size notebook, and pencil. The usefulness of information such as time traveled on various segments of the trip as well as landmark information is usually not recognized until later in the trip. Then it often isn't possible to be accurately recalled unless it was recorded. A wood pencil is reliable and avoids the hassle of trying to write with a frozen ball point pen or load a mechanical pencil with freezing fingers.

Global Position System (GPS)

Handheld GPS units using precisely timed radio signals from satellites to determine positions are available for as little as three hundred dollars. The Magellan is typical

Consulting guidebook and notes

of several on the market. Weighing 14 ounces and operating on three AA batteries, it will give its position with an accuracy of 100 meters in two minutes from turn on. Direction and distance to a previously visited point or to a destination whose location has been entered as coordinates (usually determined by map measurement) are calculated and displayed. While not necessary for skiing in the area, those who have them for more far flung adventures may want to practice their use while cross country skiing. Two grids on the accompanying folded map facilitate the use of GPS.

Latitude/longitude ticks at 2 ½ minute intervals are labeled in red, near the map borders. Graphic scales for measuring up to 150 " latitude or longitude are provided in the legend as are relationships of map distance to latitude and longitude. The change in the longitude scale with latitude is negligible for most purposes, changing 0.55 percent over the north-south range of the map.

Universal Transverse Mercator (UTM) 1 km grid ticks (labeled in blue) are shown at 10 km spacings. The area is in UTM Zone 13. Leading digits (small superscript numbers on USGS maps) are **4** for the easting coordinate and **44** for the northing.

As an example of both systems, the location of the Red Rock Trailhead can be measured on the map to be 40°05'21"N latitude, 105°32'05"W longitude. Complete UTM coordinates are Zone 13, 454417 meters E, 4436681 meters N. Within a given 100 km square, a shorthand method omits the zone and leading digits and the coordinate shortens to 54417 E, 36681 N. If the location is known with less precision, say to the nearest 100 meters, only the significant numbers are given. The spacing between the east and north components may be eliminated and the entire coordinate becomes 544367. The easting component is written first and both components have the same number of digits. See the margin of the USGS Ward 7 ½' quadrangle map for the source of Zone and leading digits in this example.

GPS users will find it convenient to draw lines connecting tick marks for both latitude/longitude and UTM coordinates to facilitate plotting locations.

Handheld amateur radios

Lightweight handheld transceivers operating on the 2-meter amateur radio band (144.5 to 148 Mhz) can reach most of the unmanned repeater stations which are typically located on mountain tops in the area. Messages are automatically rebroadcast at higher power and are receivable over a much larger area. One can talk with other licensed amateur radio operators in the mountains or in the Denver-Boulder area. Since these repeater frequencies are routinely monitored by local amateur radio operators, a request for assistance in an emergency could be relayed. A modern handheld radio weighs less than a pound including battery and costs from $200 to $500. Most can receive the NOAA weather on 162.55 MHz. One must pass a test to obtain the license issued by the Federal Communications Commission. Use of these radios in the mountain environment is described by Dick Kiefer in the 11/89 and 2/92 issues of *Trail & Timberline* published by the Colorado Mountain Club.

Repeaters which can be reached from trailhead locations are shown below:

Trailhead or locality	1	2	3	4	5	6	7	8	9	10	11
Sandbeach	-	*	-	*	*	*	*	*	*	-	-
Wild Basin	-	*	-	*	*	*	*	*	*	-	-
Allens Park	-	*	-	*	*	*	-	*	*	*	-
Rock Creek	-	*	-	*	*	*	*	*	*	*	-
Peaceful Valley	-	*	-	*	*	*	-	*	*	*	*
Beaver Reservoir North	-	*	*	*	*	*	*	*	*	*	-
Beaver Reservoir East	-	*	*	*	*	*	*	*	*	*	-
Tahosa Bridge	-	*	*	*	*	*	-	-	*	-	-
Red Rock	*	*	*	*	*	*	*	*	-	*	*
Brainard Lake	-	*	*	*	*	*	*	*	*	-	*
Mountain Research Station East	-	*	*	*	*	*	*	*	*	*	-
Mountain Research Station West	-	*	*	*	*	*	*	*	*	*	-
Caribou	-	*	*	*	*	*	*	*	*	*	*
Eldora	-	*	-	*	*	-	-	*	-	-	-
Eldora Ski Area	-	-	-	*	*	*	*	-	-	-	-
Jenny Lind Gulch	-	*	-	*	*	-	*	*	-	-	-
Tolland	-	*	-	*	*	*	*	*	-	-	-
Giants Ladder	-	*	-	*	*	-	-	*	-	-	*
East Portal	-	*	-	*	-	*	-	*	-	-	*
Ward	*	*	*	*	*	*	*	*	*	*	-
Boulder	*	*	*	*	*	-	*	*	*	-	-

Symbols used in table: (-) repeater not reached; (*) repeater reached.

27

The frequency in MHz, offset, affiliation and location for the repeaters in the above table are:

1 146.70 - BARC, Boulder Amateur Radio Club
2 146.27 + WB0Z Longmont
3 145.385 - Blue Mountain
4 145.31 - Colorado Connection, Mt Thorodin
5 145.46 - Colorado Repeater Assoc, Lee Hill
6 145.145 -   "   "   " , Squaw Mtn
7 147.225 +   "   "   " , Conifer Mtn
8 146.94 - RMRL, Rocky Mtn Radio League, Squaw Mtn
9 146.76 - RMVHFS, Rocky Mtn VHF Society, Boulder
10 145.475 - IRG, Winter Park
11 146.82 - GCRA, Winter Park

PART THREE— TRAIL INFORMATION

Trailheads

Each of the 85 trails described in this book begins at one of the 19 trailheads listed here or branches from trails that do. Directions to the start of a given trail are presented in the *Access* section of that trail description and consist of a reference to one of the trailheads identified by name and a letter abbreviation. Access is further described where necessary, by identifying connecting trails and the distance skied from the trailhead. Trailhead information is presented in an abbreviated form in the trail summary table where the trailhead is identified only by the letter abbreviation.

Directions on how to reach each trailhead from the nearest of four towns are given here. The towns — Allens Park, Ward, Nederland, and Rollinsville are familiar to most residents of the Denver-Boulder area or can be located with a road map. Mileage from Allens Park is given from the northernmost of the two exits from Highway 7. From Ward, mileage is given from the junction of the Left Hand Canyon road with Highway 72. Mileage from Nederland, unless specified differently is from the RTD bus stop in Wolftongue Square in the center of town. Mileage from Rollinsville is from the junction of the East Portal road with Highway 119. Map N refers to Side 1 (North half) of the accompanying folded map, Map S refers to Side 2 (South half).

A. Sandbeach Trailhead. (Alt. 8,360 ft., Map N) From Allens Park, drive north 2.1 miles on Highway 7, turn left (west) onto a loop road toward the Wild Basin Ranger Station. Drive 0.4 miles to the parking area on the right side of the road, about 100 yards beyond the Wild Basin Lodge.

B. Wild Basin Trailhead. (Alt. 8,380 ft., Map N) From Allens Park, drive north 2.1 miles on Highway 7, and turn left as for Sandbeach Trailhead. Drive 1.4 miles from the highway to the winter closure gate where there is parking for about 15 cars.

C.   Allens Park Trailhead.   (Alt. 8,900 ft., Map N)   Exit Highway 7 at the northernmost of the two Allens Park exits, drive south one block to the corner with both the Allens Park Community Church and post office, and turn right onto the road heading west.   At 0.8 miles from the highway take the left (more prominent) fork and continue on the curving, climbing road.   At 1.4 miles turn right onto Meadow Mountain Drive and continue 200 yards to a summer parking lot at the boundary of Rocky Mountain Park.   The trailhead is marked with a sign *Allens Park Trail Parking*.

D.   Rock Creek Trailhead.   (Alt. 8,580 ft., Map N)   Exit Highway 7 at the northernmost of the two Allens Park exits, drive south one block to the corner with both the Allens Park Community Church and post office, turn left to go east one block and turn right at the road sign *Ski Road, County Road 107*.   Drive south 1.4 miles to a sign *Roosevelt National Forest Boundary*.   Here snow conditions generally make further driving inadvisable.   Park at the edge of the road.

E.   Peaceful Valley Trailhead.   (Alt. 8,520 ft., Map N)   From Ward, drive north 5.8 miles on Highway 72.   Park on the plowed loop road on the west side or on the edge of the highway where it makes a curve to the west to cross Middle St. Vrain Creek.   An emergency telephone is located here on the east side of the highway.

From Lyons, drive west on Highway 7 up the canyon of South and Middle St. Vrain Creeks 13.9 miles to the junction with Highway 72, then south on Highway 72, 3.9 miles.

F.   Beaver Reservoir North Trailhead.   (Alt. 9,190 ft., Map N)   From Ward, drive north 2.5 miles on Highway 72, turn west onto the forest access road, pass Camp Tahosa, and continue to Beaver Reservoir.   Follow the road around the lake, across a concrete spillway to the trail sign at 2.6 miles from the highway turnoff.

G.   Beaver Reservoir East Trailhead.   (Alt. 9,140 ft., Map N)   The directions are the same as for Beaver Reservoir North, but stop 2.0 miles from the highway turnoff, or 300 yards before the lake, where trail signs are visible on both sides of the road.

H.   Tahosa Bridge Trailhead.   (Alt. 8,740 ft., Map N)   From Ward, drive north 2.5 miles on Highway 72 and turn west onto the same forest access road as for Beaver Reservoir North and East.   Cross a bridge and park on the far side near the trail sign for the South St. Vrain Trail.

J.   Red Rock Trailhead.   (Alt. 10,060 ft., Map N)   From Ward, drive north on Highway 72 200 yards, turn west on the Brainard Lake road and continue 2.6 miles to the end of the plowed road.   The trailhead area has a winter closure vehicle gate, numerous trail signs, and parking along the road.

K. Brainard Lake Trailhead. (Alt. 10,345 ft., Map N) This is not a true trailhead as it is not accessible by vehicle. For convenience, it is treated as a trailhead in the trail descriptions and in the trail summary table because it is the starting point for several trails which go beyond it. Access to it is by any of several trails.

From Red Rock Trailhead, ski west on the CMC South Trail (15), 2.0 miles to Brainard Lake. Add 0.5 miles to ski to the west side of the lake on the Brainard Loop Road (14 A) and an additional 0.4 miles to reach either the Mitchell or Long Lake trails by the Mitchell Lake Road Spur (14 B) or Long Lake Road Spur (14 C).

Brainard Lake may also be reached from Red Rock Trailhead by either the Waldrop North Trail (13), Brainard Lake Road (14), or Little Raven Trail (16) with only a slight increase in distance traveled.
An emergency telephone is located at the east end of Brainard Lake, 150 yards south of the bridge on the wind scoured unplowed road.

L. Mountain Research Station East Trailhead. (Alt.9210 ft., Map N,S) From Ward, drive south on Highway 72, 4.7 miles to a sign *University of Colorado Mountain Research Station.* Drive west on this road to a sign marking the Sourdough Trail at 0.5 miles. There is parking here along the road for about 12 cars.

An emergency telephone is on the east side of Highway 72, 1.3 miles north of the highway turnoff. This is at the junction with County Road 52 to Gold Hill.

The turnoff from the highway may also be reached by driving north from Nederland 7.0 miles on Highway 72.

M. Mountain Research Station West Trailhead. (Alt.9290 ft., Map N,S) Drive past the Mountain Research East Trailhead to a fork 0.9 miles from the highway. The unplowed left fork with a winter closure barrier is the Rainbow Lakes Road (25). The plowed right fork continues 0.4 miles to the research station.

N. Caribou Trailhead. (Alt. 9,990 ft., Map S) From the junction of Highways 72 and 119 in Nederland, start northbound on Highway 72 and at 0.4 miles, turn left at a sign for Caribou. Drive 5.4 miles west from this junction, past the turnoffs to the Cross Mountain and Caribou Silver Mines and past the stone building ruins marking the townsite of Caribou. The road becomes rocky and steeper for the final climb to the saddle and trailhead.

I have always found this road plowed and passable with a passenger car. The county road department does not maintain it for passenger cars nor provide snow removal. One should not depend on it being plowed to get out if heavy snowfall or high winds occur.

P. Eldora Trailhead. (Alt. 8,810 ft., Map S) From Nederland, start southbound on Highway 72 and at the edge of town, turn off to the right at the sign for Eldora Ski Area. Follow this paved road west, past a turn off to the ski area at 1.4 miles from the highway, and continue up the valley bottom through Eldora to the end of the plowed road at the far edge of town at 3.9 miles. Park along the designated side of the road.

R. Eldora Ski Area Trailhead. (Alt. 9,360 ft., Map S) From Nederland, start southbound on Highway 72 and at the edge of town, turn right at the ski area sign. Take the left fork at 1.4 miles from the highway. This road climbs out of the valley to the ski area at 4.2 miles from the highway. Park in the first parking lot, near the base of a wide beginners slope with a short chair lift and the ski area's Nordic Center.

RTD, the Denver-Boulder metropolitan area public transit system, has bus service to the ski area. A one way fare from Boulder or Denver is $2.50 for the 1994-5 season.

S. Jenny Lind Gulch Trailhead. (Alt. 8,800 ft., Map S) From Rollinsville, drive west on the road, paralleling and to the north of the railroad, toward East Portal. Parking at the trailhead is designated by signs along the road at 3.8 miles.

T. Tolland Trailhead. (Alt. 8,920 ft., Map S) From Rollinsville, drive west on the road, paralleling and to the north of the railroad, toward East Portal. Pass Jenny Lind Gulch trailhead and continue 0.1 miles past Tolland, to where unplowed Forest Service Road 176 to Apex forks off uphill to the left at 5.2 miles. Park at the edge of the road.

U. Giants Ladder Trailhead. (Alt. 9,190 ft., Map S) From Rollinsville, drive west toward East Portal, passing the Jenny Lind Gulch and Tolland trailheads. The trailhead is at a junction with the old railroad grade on the right at 7.2 miles. A sign reads *Snowmobile Route to Rollins Pass, Winter Park*. Park at the edge of the road.

W. East Portal Trailhead. (Alt. 9,210 ft., Map S) From Rollinsville, drive west on the road, paralleling and to the north of the railroad. Continue 8.0 miles to the end of the road at East Portal and the Moffat Tunnel. A designated area for parking is about 200 yards from the tunnel.

TRAIL NO. 1

SANDBEACH LAKE TRAIL

SUMMARY

This infrequently skied summer hiking trail nearly always offers excellent snow for the ascent out of Wild Basin onto the forested southern slopes of Mt. Meeker. First you must climb a steep, south facing slope from the trailhead to the top of Copeland Moraine. This slope may be without snow due to the effects of sun and wind at low altitude. Thereafter the trail is protected and the gradient generally moderate. Unobstructed views from Sandbeach Lake reveal the distant Indian Peaks beyond the rim of Wild Basin as well as nearby massive Mt. Meeker.

CLASSIFICATION Difficult

ALTITUDE (feet)
- Starting 8,360
- Highest 10,330
- Cumulative gain 2,010
- Cumulative loss 40

TIME (hours)
- Westbound, up 3.2
- Eastbound, down 1.7

TRAIL MAP Side 1 (North)

MAP COORDINATES 52/52

PAGE-SIZE MAP No.3

USGS 7 ½' QUADRANGLES
Allens Park (A3)

DISTANCE (one way)
4.2 miles

ACCESS

At Sandbeach trailhead (A).

ROUTE DESCRIPTION (westbound)

From a large sign at the trailhead parking area, the unblazed trail climbs 150 yards northeast to switchback left onto a long climbing traverse west through massive ponderosa pines, interrupted by a 30 yard switchback. Orange square blazes at 100 to 400 yard intervals mark the trail after the initial 0.4 miles.

The crest of Copeland Moraine, 700 feet above the trailhead, is gained at 1.2 miles. A sign here marks a junction with a trail originating at Meeker Park. Continuing west, the trail passes a single orange square blaze as it stays near the top of the moraine and then moves onto a bench to traverse the side of Lookout Mountain. On descending slightly to Campers Creek, look to the left to find an orange blaze at the creek crossing where the trail is indistinct.

The trail swings south for 200 yards to climb out of Campers Creek. Between here and Hunters Creek the nearly level trail is marked by two orange blazes as it crosses

Snow conditions improve dramatically beyond here on this long, generally protected and moderate trail to the source of North St. Vrain Creek. The isolation and grandeur of snow plumed peaks and the ridge of the continental divide at the head of the valley affirm this is fittingly named Wild Basin.

CLASSIFICATION Difficult

ALTITUDE (feet)
Starting 8,380
Highest 10,600
Cumulative gain 2,220
Cumulative loss 0

TIME (hours)
Westbound 4.4
Eastbound 2.4

TRAIL MAP Side 1 (North)

MAP COORDINATES 48/51

PAGE-SIZE MAP No.3

USGS 7 ½' QUADRANGLES
Allens Park (A3)
Isolation Peak (A2)

DISTANCE (one way)
7.1 miles

ACCESS
At Wild Basin Trailhead (B).

ROUTE DESCRIPTION (westbound)
Ski or walk, as conditions dictate, west on the main road up the valley bottom to cross the creek to the south side and pass the sign-marked Finch Lake trailhead at 0.8 miles. Continue on the road as it turns left after crossing the creek again and pass through a parking area for the summer trailhead with a large sign at 1.0 miles. A warming hut operated by volunteers from the Enos Mills group of the Colorado Mountain Club in Estes Park is generally open on weekends in the Wild Basin ranger station 150 yards north of here.

The trail continues west along the north side of North St. Vrain Creek to cross the creek on a substantial log footbridge at 2.4 miles. Log steps may be icy on this well defined section with little altitude gain. The burned area on Meadow Mountain to the south is visible from here. Beyond the bridge, the character of the trail changes abruptly, with steep grades, sharp turns, ice, and protruding rocks and logs on the narrow twisting trail. On the return if poor snow conditions exist, descent of the entire section may be most easily done by walking.

Calypso Cascades is at 2.7 miles. About 200 yards beyond, a burned area is entered. Ouzel Falls with an outhouse, frozen waterfall, and log footbridge is reached at 3.4 miles. A pair of switchbacks at 3.7 miles marks the end of the tedious obstacles. The trail is nearly level past a sign-marked junction with a trail to Ouzel and Bluebird Lakes at 4.2 miles and on to a footbridge crossing of North St. Vrain Creek at 4.6 miles. There, a steady moderate climb for the remainder of the trail begins.

Thunder Lake patrol cabin

A switchback at 4.9 miles affords views of Meadow and St. Vrain Mountains to the southeast and Mt. Copeland to the southwest. The sign-marked junction with a trail to Lion Lakes is reached at 5.4 miles. Orange square tree blazes start at a pair of switchbacks at 5.7 miles and continue for the remainder of the trail. On rounding a windy corner at 5.9 miles a spectacular view of the continental divide from Isolation Peak to Mt. Alice unfolds.

Cross a footbridge over the creek from Lion Lakes at 6.6 miles. Depart from the orange square-blazed route to head west northwest on a slight climb to Thunder Lake and the patrol cabin at 7.1 miles and 10,580 feet. The steeper blazed summer trail leads to an outhouse and camping area, 200 feet higher and north of the patrol cabin.

ADDITIONAL CONNECTING TRAIL INFORMATION
The Calypso Cascades Cutoff Trail (2A) junction is at 2.7 miles. This trail connects to the Allens Park-Finch Lake-Pear Reservoir Trail (3).

SKILLS RECOMMENDED
Skiing ability— Advanced. The first two and a half miles to the bridge are novice. The section to Calypso Cascades and Ouzel Falls is intermediate as there are tedious obstacles and ice on a narrow twisting trail. Beyond here, there are no particularly difficult sections and the gradient is moderate and the snow commonly excellent but untracked. An intermediate to advanced level of skiing however, must be maintained over a long trip.

Endurance— Very strenuous. This is a very long day of 14.2 miles round trip and 2,220 feet altitude gained and lost. The lower part of it will probably be on poor snow and the upper on untracked powder.

Routefinding skill— Intermediate. Only beginner skills are required as far as Ouzel Falls. The trail beyond is almost entirely in trees, with most of it blazed with widely spaced orange squares.

Longs Peak from Thunder Lake Trail

SNOW CONDITIONS
Snow conditions are usually poor as far as Ouzel Falls due to the relatively low altitude. Near Calypso Cascades, ice from freezing of water seeps is frequently encountered. Beyond, snow conditions improve steadily with altitude except for a few minor windblown localities. Conditions are excellent in the upper reaches.

WIND EXPOSURE
In the initial, low altitude segment of the trail in the valley bottom, tree cover is widely spaced and interspersed with long clearings so the effect of the wind is appreciable. Thereafter the trail is well sheltered by trees, with the exception of a wind swept corner where the valley and trail turn northwest.

GRADIENT OR STEEPNESS
The gradient for the first mile is nearly flat, from there to the crossing of the Creek at 2.4 miles, slight. Thereafter the trail climbs steeply through icy switchbacks for 0.3 miles to Calypso Cascades. After a moderate climb to Ouzel Falls, the next

mile to another crossing of the creek is nearly flat. The remainder of the trail climbs moderately.

AMOUNT OF USE
Light as far as Ouzel Falls at 3.4 miles and beyond there, very light.

VIEWS
Views of the spectacular peaks at the head of Wild Basin are a highlight of the trip. Mt. Meeker, Longs Peak, and Pagoda Mountain are visible from the burned area at 2.8 miles. Ouzel Falls at 3.4 miles is of special interest when festooned with ice climbers. A switchback at 4.9 miles (9,740 feet altitude) affords views to the south across Wild Basin, of Meadow and St. Vrain Mountains and Mt. Copeland. Rounding a windy corner at 5.9 miles (10,240 feet altitude) reveals a splendid panorama of the continental divide north from Isolation Peak to Eagles Beak, The Cleaver, Tanima Peak, Boulder-Grand Pass, Pilot Mountain, and Mt. Alice. Boulder-Grand Pass and Chiefs Head Peak are viewed close up from Thunder Lake.

PRIVATE PROPERTY AND OTHER RESTRICTIONS
The entire trail is in Rocky Mountain Park. Dogs are not permitted on the trails. The patrol cabin at Thunder Lake is not open for public use.

* * * * *

TRAIL NO. 2A

CALYPSO CASCADES CUTOFF TRAIL

SUMMARY
This infrequently skied summer hiking trail may be used as a connecting link from the lower part of Wild Basin up to the Allens Park-Finch Lake-Pear Reservoir trail. From the junction, one can contour on that trail around Meadow Mountain, either west into Cony Creek drainage toward Elk Tooth or east to Allens Park.

CLASSIFICATION Moderate-difficult

ALTITUDE (feet)

Starting	9,150
Highest	9,720
Cumulative gain	570
Cumulative loss	0

TIME (hours)

Up, eastbound	0.7
Down, westbound	0.5

TRAIL MAP Side 1 (North)

MAP COORDINATES 51/49

PAGE-SIZE MAP No.2

USGS 7 ½' QUADRANGLES
Allens Park (A3)

DISTANCE (one way)
1.5 miles

ACCESS
Ski the Thunder Lake Trail (2) west from the Wild Basin Trailhead (B), 2.7 miles to the sign-marked trail junction at Calypso Cascades.

ROUTE DESCRIPTION (uphill, eastbound)
From the junction at Calypso Cascades, the orange square-blazed trail climbs eastward through four switchbacks, up the steep south side of Wild Basin. A sign-marked four way trail junction is reached at 1.5 miles as the steepness of the slope lessens.

ADDITIONAL CONNECTING TRAIL INFORMATION
The upper or east end of this trail connects with the Allens Park-Finch Lake-Pear Reservoir Trail (3) at mile 1.6. Also at this junction is an unblazed trail to the Finch Lake trailhead near the Wild Basin ranger station.

SKILLS RECOMMENDED
Skiing ability— Intermediate. This is a steep narrow trail with sharp switchbacks to negotiate. Done only uphill as part of a loop trip, it is beginner level.

Endurance— Easy.

Routefinding skill— Novice. There are no route finding problems on this well defined trail through dense trees with trail signs at both ends.

SNOW CONDITIONS
Snow conditions here reflect the influence of altitude, ranging from medium at the bottom to good at the top. The narrow trail is sheltered from wind and sun by trees and a north facing slope.

WIND EXPOSURE
The entire trail is protected from the wind by the dense forest.

GRADIENT OR STEEPNESS
The entire trail is steep, gaining 570 feet altitude in 1.5 miles with four switchbacks.

AMOUNT OF USE
Nearly unused. Steep switchbacks discourage its use as ski trail.

VIEWS
Mt. Meeker is seen occasionally through the trees.

PRIVATE PROPERTY AND OTHER RESTRICTIONS
All of the trail is within Rocky Mountain Park and subject to park regulations. Dogs are not allowed on the trails.

TRAIL NO. 3

ALLENS PARK-FINCH LAKE-PEAR RESERVOIR TRAIL

SUMMARY

A marked change in both snow quality and amount of use are encountered as this trail climbs from the edge of Allens Park village, around the north side of Meadow Mountain, to the far reaches of Wild Basin and the edge of the forest near the base of the lofty cliffs bounding Mt. Copeland. The low altitude beginning sees moderate to heavy use and generally has only medium quality snow, whereas the deep powder at the high isolated far end is ordinarily untracked.

CLASSIFICATION Difficult

TRAIL MAP Side 1 (North)

ALTITUDE (feet)

Starting	8,900
Highest	10,600
Cumulative gain	1,950
Cumulative loss	250

MAP COORDINATES 48/47

PAGE-SIZE MAP No.3

USGS 7 ½' QUADRANGLES
Allens Park (A3)
Isolation Peak (A2)

TIME (hours)

Westbound	3.4
Eastbound	2.0

DISTANCE (one way)
5.8 miles

ACCESS

At Allens Park Trailhead (C). Here at a summer parking lot at the eastern boundary of Rocky Mountain Park, the beginning of the trail is marked with a sign *Allens Park Trail*.

ROUTE DESCRIPTION (westbound)

This well defined, orange square-blazed trail climbs through a forest of moderately spaced trees to circle to the north side of Meadow Mountain. Pass a junction at 0.7 miles, where a trail branches off to the right, and continue on to a sign-marked, four way junction at 1.6 miles. Bear left here as directed by signs, toward Finch Lake and Pear Reservoir on a trail marked with orange square blazes. Cross a 500 yard wide burned area with standing dead trees and widely spaced orange square blazes at 2.0 miles. The trail levels off and crosses a drainage on a log footbridge with a handrail at 3.3 miles, and then descends a steep 200 feet via four switchbacks, to the north end of Finch Lake at 3.8 miles.

The now less distinct trail goes around the north end of the lake and heads southwest, staying near the shoreline through a summer camping area, and passes the last two orange blazes. After passing a sign *Pear Creek, Pear Lake*, it crosses the outlet creek of Finch Lake and then crosses Coney Creek at a log bridge. Although now unblazed and probably untracked, the trail is distinct enough to follow without too much difficulty. It climbs through the forest of large trees, passing to the right of a pond at 4.8 miles, and on to a sign marking Pear Creek at 5.4 miles. Here it heads up the left (south) side of the drainage 600 yards to the site of the former rock dam at Pear Reservoir and the base of Mount Copeland (5.8 miles).

ADDITIONAL CONNECTING TRAIL INFORMATION
The unblazed trail at 0.7 miles, usually untracked, goes to the Wild Basin Ranger Station. At the sign-marked, four way trail junction at 1.6 miles, the first trail to the right goes northeast to Wild Basin Ranger Station and is unblazed. A second trail to the right goes west to Wild Basin Ranger Station, via the Calypso Cascades Cutoff Trail (2A), and is marked with orange square blazes.

An unmarked junction with the North Gully of St. Vrain Mountain Route (5A) is at the creek crossing at 3.3 miles. It is near a log foot bridge with a handrail.

SKILLS RECOMMENDED
Skiing ability— Intermediate. Short difficult steep sections are at 1.0 miles, and at the switchbacks east of Finch Lake at 3.6 miles. The most difficult part is the steep section beyond Finch Lake, which will probably have deep powder.

Endurance— Very strenuous. Twelve miles round trip and 2000 vertical feet are gained and lost. Probably four miles and 700 feet of this will be in untracked deep powder snow. Take some friends to break trail.

Routefinding skill— Advanced skill is required beyond Finch Lake. Novice or beginner skills are adequate for the easily followed trail to there.

SNOW CONDITIONS
Medium snow conditions, characteristic of the relatively low altitude at the beginning, improve as altitude is gained to become excellent beyond Finch Lake. Deep untracked powder snow here can make short steep sections laborious to climb but easy to descend.

WIND EXPOSURE
The entire route is in the protection of trees, with the exception of a 500 yard wide burned area midway, and the final 600 yards to Pear Reservoir.

GRADIENT OR STEEPNESS
Moderate overall. A short steep section at 1.0 miles gains about 100 feet. Steep sections are also encountered in the deep powder beyond Finch Reservoir, and again as the crossing of Pear Creek below Pear Reservoir is approached.

AMOUNT OF USE
Usage varies from moderate at the beginning to very light beyond Finch Lake.

VIEWS

Glimpses of Mt. Meeker to the northwest, Twin Sisters to the east, and Mt. Alice to the west are seen through the trees in the first two miles. At the burned area at 2.0 miles, Chiefs Head, Pagoda Mountain, Longs Peak, and Mt. Meeker are visible four miles to the northwest across Wild Basin.

Finch Lake offers unobstructed views of Mt. Copeland and Elk Tooth.

Pear Reservoir is situated at the base of cliffs soaring up toward Mt. Copeland. Elk Tooth is visible at the head of the valley to the west southwest.

PRIVATE PROPERTY AND OTHER RESTRICTIONS

All of the trail is within Rocky Mountain Park and subject to park regulations. Dogs are not allowed on the trails.

* * * * *

TRAIL NO. 4

ROCK CREEK TRAIL

SUMMARY

An easy mile and a half along a wide road following the gentle valley bottom leads to the abandoned Rock Creek ski area. Snow conditions, frequently poor at this low altitude, improve steadily on the ascent of the steepening, north facing slope. The old logging road ultimately becomes difficult to follow, and is not generally tracked all the way to the saddle on the east ridge of St. Vrain Mountain.

CLASSIFICATION Moderate-difficult

ALTITUDE (feet)
Starting 8,580
Highest 10,680
Cumulative gain 2,100
Cumulative loss 0

TIME (hours)
Up, southwestbound 2.4
Down, northeastbound 1.2

TRAIL MAP Side 1 (North)

MAP COORDINATES 53/45

PAGE-SIZE MAP No.6

USGS 7 ½' QUADRANGLES
Allens Park (A3)

DISTANCE (one way)
3.1 miles

ACCESS

At Rock Creek Trailhead (D).

ROUTE DESCRIPTION (up, southwestbound)

Ski the wide road south, passing a sign at 0.3 miles, *St. Vrain Mountain Trailhead ½ mile*, which marks a road to the west. Continue south on the road, along the valley bottom to the old ski area, where the valley turns west at 1.4 miles. The wide, easily recognized road/trail now climbs more steeply, with occasional switchbacks, up the south side of the valley through dense trees. A few dead end logging spurs branch off to the north. If in doubt, take the left branch. The slope lessens and the trail becomes less distinct in the more widely spaced trees as the 10,600 foot saddle on the east ridge of St. Vrain Mountain is approached at 3.1 miles. An alternative to following the road where it becomes indistinct, is to simply head uphill for the ridge on the easy terrain. The ridge may be skied eastward to Point 10,810 by going between rock outcrops on the ridge top.

ADDITIONAL CONNECTING TRAIL INFORMATION
The St. Vrain Mountain Trail (5) branches off at a sign- marked junction at 0.3 miles.

A cairn-marked junction with the Rock Creek Saddle Route (8B) is at 2.3 miles and 9680 feet.

The East Ridge St. Vrain Mountain Route (4A) continues on from the end of the trail.

SKILLS RECOMMENDED
Skiing ability— If snow conditions are good, the terrain below the ski area is suitable for novice skiers. Above, beginner and eventually intermediate skills are advisable.

Endurance— Moderate, but could be strenuous if a lot of trail has to be broken near the saddle.

Routefinding skill— Beginner. There are few problems in following this distinct road. Even at the top, where the road becomes indistinct, the ridge is nearby and not difficult to find.

SNOW CONDITIONS
Snow quality improves with distance and altitude along the trail. Below the old ski area, it may be very poor due to low altitude, exposure to sunlight, and the effect of vehicles sometimes driven onto the snowpacked road. Higher, on the north facing slope, it improves to good.

WIND EXPOSURE
I haven't experienced much wind here, even in the lower part where the sparse trees offer little protection. The north-south orientation of the valley may diminish the effect of the wind.

GRADIENT OR STEEPNESS
Moderate overall, although the first part to the ski area is slight. Thereafter it increases with altitude until lessening near the saddle at the end.

AMOUNT OF USE

Moderate as far as the old ski area, above there it decreases progressively to light and very light near the saddle.

VIEWS

The nearby slopes of St. Vrain and Meadow Mountains, to the west and northwest, block views in those directions. From the ridge line at 3.1 miles, Twin Sisters Peaks are visible to the north northeast and Sawtooth Mountain, Paiute Peak, and Mt. Audubon are visible to the southwest, across the valley of Middle St. Vrain Creek. The bench route followed by the Coney Flats Trail (10) from Beaver Reservoir to Coney Flats is visible across the valley to the south.

PRIVATE PROPERTY AND OTHER RESTRICTIONS

None.

* * * * *

TRAIL NO. 4A

EAST RIDGE ST. VRAIN MOUNTAIN ROUTE

SUMMARY

This unmarked and probably untracked route climbs above timberline on the exposed eastern slopes of St. Vrain Mountain, to connect the Rock Creek Trail (4) with the St. Vrain Mountain Trail (5) and the North Gully St. Vrain Mountain Route (5A). Loop trips around the head of Rock Creek and around Meadow Mountain can be done with this route as the high link.

CLASSIFICATION Difficult

ALTITUDE (feet)
Starting 10,680
Highest 11,330
Cumulative gain 650
Cumulative loss 130

TIME (hours)
Up, northwestbound 1.2
Down, southeastbound 0.8

TRAIL MAP Side 1 (North)

MAP COORDINATES 52/45

PAGE-SIZE MAP No.5

USGS 7 ½' QUADRANGLES
Allens Park (A3)

DISTANCE (one way)
1.5 miles

ACCESS

From the Rock Creek Trailhead (D), ski 3.1 miles to the end of the Rock Creek Trail (4).

ROUTE DESCRIPTION (up, northwestbound)

From the end of the Rock Creek Trail (4), head west up the ridge, first through

44

widely spaced trees and then above timberline, on a climb of 600 feet to where the ridge levels out. Follow the ridge to the northwest and traverse across the eastern spur of St. Vrain Mountain to the saddle between it and Peak 11,478. Continue the traverse north across the west side of this knob to the saddle between it and Meadow Mountain at 1.5 miles.

ADDITIONAL CONNECTING TRAIL INFORMATION
An unmarked junction with both the North Gully St. Vrain Mountain Route (5A) and the St. Vrain Mountain Trail (5) is at the saddle at the end of the route.

SKILLS RECOMMENDED
Skiing ability— Advanced. The difficulties are likely more with snow conditions than terrain.

Endurance— Very strenuous, particularly in breaking trail up the ridge.

View across Wild Basin to Mt. Alice

Routefinding skill— Advanced routefinding skills are advisable to make any of the loop trips of which this route is part.

SNOW CONDITIONS
Snow conditions on this untracked route are good to excellent in the shelter of the trees at the lower altitudes but deteriorate to poor or very poor above timberline due to the effect of the wind. Wind slab, sastrugi, and bare tundra are likely.

WIND EXPOSURE
Very severe, most of the route is above timberline.

GRADIENT OR STEEPNESS
A constant moderate to steep gradient is maintained until timberline is reached at 11,200 ft. Thereafter the gradient is nearly flat.

AMOUNT OF USE
Nearly unused.

VIEWS
In addition to the views obtained lower from the Rock Creek Trail (4), the view to the west and north, previously blocked by Meadow Mountain is now unobstructed. Elk Tooth, Ogalalla Peak, Mt. Copeland, Isolation Peak, Mt. Alice, Chiefs Head Peak, Pagoda Mountain, Longs Peak, and Mt. Meeker are seen across Wild Basin.

PRIVATE PROPERTY AND OTHER RESTRICTIONS
None.

* * * * *

TRAIL NO. 5

ST. VRAIN MOUNTAIN TRAIL

SUMMARY
This trail climbs a vigorous 2600 feet, in three and a half miles, to a high saddle between Meadow Mountain and St. Vrain Mountain. There, one can continue 900 feet to the summit of St. Vrain Mountain or 400 feet to the top of Meadow Mountain. Descent from the saddle can be by either the East Ridge St. Vrain Mountain Trail (4A) or North Gully St. Vrain Mountain Route (5A), both giving challenging loop trips. The high saddle is an superb vantage point for views across Wild Basin of peaks on the continental divide.

CLASSIFICATION Difficult

ALTITUDE (feet)
Starting	8,580
Highest	11,200
Cumulative gain	2,620
Cumulative loss	0

TIME (hours)
Up, westbound	3.0
Down, eastbound	1.4

TRAIL MAP Side 1 (North)

MAP COORDINATES 53/46

PAGE-SIZE MAP No.6

USGS 7 ½' QUADRANGLES
Allens Park (A3)

DISTANCE (one way)
3.5 miles

ACCESS
From Rock Creek Trailhead (D), ski 0.3 miles south on the Rock Creek Trail (4) to a sign-marked junction.

ROUTE DESCRIPTION (up, westbound)
From the junction at 0.3 miles on the Rock Creek Trail (4), head west on the road identified with the sign *St. Vrain Mountain Trailhead ½ mile*, as it climbs on a curving route to a sign-marked summer trailhead and end of the road at 0.5 miles. From here, the unblazed but distinct trail climbs steadily through aspen and evergreen trees and angles into the tributary drainage to Rock Creek, as an open treeless bowl comes into view ahead. The summer trail stays to the right of the drainage with several switchbacks, but the snow may be better in the drainage. Switchback to the left at 10,200 feet and climb 500 yards through scattered trees, then switchback right to cross above the steepest part of the bowl. Proceed up the right side of the now less steep drainage, through scattered low trees to the 10,200 foot saddle between Meadow Mountain and Peak 11,478, to the end of the route at 3.5 miles.

ADDITIONAL CONNECTING TRAIL INFORMATION
Unmarked junctions with the North Gully St. Vrain Mountain Route (5A) and East Ridge St. Vrain Mountain Route (4A) are at the 10,200 saddle.

SKILLS RECOMMENDED
Skiing ability— Advanced skills are required to descend the 2600 feet of steep terrain.

Endurance— Strenuous, for both climbing and descending 2600 feet.

Routefinding skill— Intermediate. You probably won't find this route tracked, and it may be difficult to stay on the summer trail, but the terrain is uncomplicated.

SNOW CONDITIONS
Poor to medium conditions can be expected at the bottom, improving to medium to good as one gains altitude, but deteriorating to poor above timberline. If snow conditions are unstable due to recent heavy snowfall or wind deposition, stay out of this bowl because of avalanche danger. The East Ridge St. Vrain Mountain route (4A) is a safer alternative.

WIND EXPOSURE
Very exposed, especially at the above timberline saddle and in the open bowl on the ascent. The widely spaced trees are too small to offer much shelter.

GRADIENT OR STEEPNESS
Unremittingly steep for nearly the entire route.

AMOUNT OF USE
Very light.

Mt. Copeland from Meadow Mountain

VIEWS

From the west side of the saddle, one has a spectacular vista across Wild Basin of (left to right) Elk Tooth, Ogallala Peak, Copeland Mountain, Isolation Peak, Tanima Peak, Mt. Alice, Chiefs Head Peak, Pagoda Mountain, Longs Peak, and Mt. Meeker.

PRIVATE PROPERTY AND OTHER RESTRICTIONS

None.

* * * * *

TRAIL NO. 5A

NORTH GULLY ST. VRAIN MOUNTAIN ROUTE

SUMMARY

This off trail route makes a 1100 foot descent of a steep drainage between Meadow and St. Vrain Mountains into Wild Basin. When linked with the Allens Park-Finch Lake-Pear Reservoir Trail and the St. Vrain Mountain Trail, it forms a circular route from Allens Park around Meadow Mountain. It is not recommended for uphill travel.

CLASSIFICATION Very difficult   **TRAIL MAP** Side 1 (North)

ALTITUDE (feet)	MAP COORDINATES 50/47

ALTITUDE (feet)
Starting 11,200
Highest 11,200
Cumulative gain 0
Cumulative loss 1,100

MAP COORDINATES 50/47

PAGE-SIZE MAP No. 5

USGS 7 ½' QUADRANGLES
Allens Park (A3)

TIME (hours)
Down, northwestbound 0.7
Up, southeastbound 2.0

DISTANCE (one way)
1.3 miles

ACCESS

From Rock Creek Trailhead (D), ski the Rock Creek Trail (4) and then the East Ridge St. Vrain Mountain Route (4A) to the 11,200 foot saddle where this trail begins, a total distance of 4.6 miles.

Alternatively, the St. Vrain Mountain Trail (5) provides a 3.8 mile access to the saddle.

ROUTE DESCRIPTION (down, northwestbound)

From the 11,200 foot saddle between Meadow Mountain and Peak 11,478, head west northwest to enter the drainage on a gentle slope, through widely spaced trees. As the trees become more closely spaced, the slope steepens and one is forced into the gully by steep side slopes. Both the side slopes and the general stream gradient lessen before the end of the route is reached at a junction with the Allens Park-Finch Lake-Pear Reservoir Trail (3) at 10,100 feet altitude and 1.3 miles. Aids to recognizing this trail if it is untracked, are widely spaced orange square trail blazes and a log footbridge with a handrail, where it crosses one of several stream channels in the vicinity of the junction.

ADDITIONAL CONNECTING TRAIL INFORMATION

Unmarked junctions with the East Ridge St. Vrain Mountain Route (4A) and the St. Vrain Mountain Trail (5) are at the 11,200 foot saddle, at the beginning of the route. An unmarked junction with the Allens Park-Finch Lake-Pear Reservoir Trail (3) is at the north end (bottom) of the route.

SKILLS RECOMMENDED

Skiing ability— Expert skills are required to descend the steep gully with dense trees and deep powder snow.

Endurance— Very strenuous. This route has to be linked with other routes that give access to it. It would be extraordinarily strenuous to ascend the steep 1100 feet of untracked deep powder snow.

Routefinding skill— Advanced skills are required to link this route with the routes that give access and exit. At the north end, one can easily fail to recognize the Allens Park-Pear Reservoir Trail if it is untracked. An altimeter is helpful here.

View up Cony Creek to Elk Tooth, Ogallala Peak

SNOW CONDITIONS
High altitude, a north facing slope, and protection by trees all combine to make excellent snow for a descent but exhausting deep snow for climbing.

WIND EXPOSURE
None, except at the above timberline beginning of the route.

GRADIENT OR STEEPNESS
Overall very steep, but moderate at the top and nearly flat at the bottom.

AMOUNT OF USE
Nearly unused.

VIEWS
None other than at the start. These are listed in the trail descriptions for the connecting routes, the St. Vrain Mountain Trail (5) and the East Ridge St. Vrain Mountain Route (4A).

PRIVATE PROPERTY AND OTHER RESTRICTIONS
Part of the trail is within Rocky Mountain Park, dogs are not permitted.

TRAIL NO. 6

MIDDLE ST. VRAIN ROAD

SUMMARY
Although used by snowmobilers, this is a pleasant road up the valley bottom of the Middle St. Vrain Creek. It provides easy access to the Indian Peaks Wilderness from the Peak to Peak highway at Peaceful Valley, a distance of nearly five miles. Paralleling the Buchanan Pass Trail (7), it usually has better snow. It is the easier and faster route for the downhill return.

CLASSIFICATION Moderate

ALTITUDE (feet)
Starting	8,520
Highest	9,600
Cumulative gain	1,080
Cumulative loss	0

TIME (hours)
Westbound	2.0
Eastbound	1.5

TRAIL MAP Side 1 (North)

MAP COORDINATES 55/42

PAGE-SIZE MAP No.6

USGS 7 ½' QUADRANGLES
Allens Park (A3)

DISTANCE (one way)
4.7 miles

ACCESS
At Peaceful Valley Trailhead (E).

ROUTE DESCRIPTION (westbound)
Ski west on the road up the valley bottom, passing a trail sign for the Buchanan Pass Trail (7) in 200 yards at a vehicle bridge, where our road crosses to the north side of the valley. At 0.8 miles the road crosses back over the creek to pass through the Camp Dick summer campground. From here the road climbs steadily west along the bottom of the straight valley. At 2.6 miles, a four post barrier to vehicular crossing of the creek can be seen at the side of the road. Pass a sign-marked junction, where the Coney Flats-Middle St. Vrain Trail (10B) descends into the valley at 4.6 miles, and continue another 220 yards to the end of the road. Here, at a footbridge with a handrail, a sign marks the wilderness boundary at 4.7 miles.

ADDITIONAL CONNECTING TRAIL INFORMATION
At 0.3 miles, the Park Creek Trail (8) turns back sharply and uphill on the Bunce School Road.

The Buchanan Pass Trail crosses our road at a sign-marked junction at 1.1 miles and continues to parallel it.

The Buchanan Pass Trail can be easily reached at the four post barrier at 2.6 miles. It is only 100 yards to the north, across the creek and a clearing.

Yet another junction with the paralleling Buchanan Pass Trail is at the end of the route at 4.7 miles and across the foot bridge.

SKILLS RECOMMENDED
Skiing ability— Novice at beginning, beginner if extended to the upper part.

Endurance— Moderate, if the entire route is done.

Routefinding skill— Novice.

SNOW CONDITIONS
Poor at beginning, improving to good to excellent at far end. Except for the first mile, the road stays near the shaded south side of the valley. The snowmobile traffic may help the snow conditions in the lower section by providing a packed base.

WIND EXPOSURE
Slight, the road is generally in trees but there are a few clearings in the lower part where this protection is lacking.

GRADIENT OR STEEPNESS
The overall gradient is slight and there are no steep sections. A gradual 1,080 feet is gained in 4.7 miles.

AMOUNT OF USE
Moderate at beginning, light at far end. Snowmobiles use the road.

VIEWS
Sawtooth Mountain and Buchanan Pass, to its right, are visible at the head of the valley throughout most of the trip. Ogalalla Peak and Elk Tooth appear as the valley turns northwest.

PRIVATE PROPERTY AND OTHER RESTRICTIONS
None.

* * * * *

TRAIL NO. 7

BUCHANAN PASS TRAIL

SUMMARY
The straight, steadily rising valley floor of the Middle St. Vrain is followed west nearly five miles, from the Peaceful Valley Trailhead to a junction with the end of

the paralleling Middle St. Vrain Road at the Indian Peaks Wilderness boundary. The trail then continues up the valley as it turns to the northwest another mile and a half, to link with the St. Vrain Glacier Trail.

CLASSIFICATION Moderate-difficult	**TRAIL MAP** Side 1 (North)

ALTITUDE (feet)

Starting 8,520

Highest . . . . 9,910 **PAGE-SIZE MAP** No.6

Cumulative gain 1,390

Cumulative loss . . . . 0 **USGS 7 ½' QUADRANGLES**
Allens Park (A)

MAP COORDINATES 55/42

TIME (hours)

Westbound . . . . 3.4 **DISTANCE** (one way)

Eastbound . . . . 2.7 6.3 miles

ACCESS
From Peaceful Valley Trailhead (E), ski west 200 yards on the Middle St. Vrain Road (6) to the sign-marked trail junction at a vehicle bridge.

ROUTE DESCRIPTION (westbound)
From the vehicle bridge, the blue diamond-blazed trail heads up the south side of the valley through dense trees. A sign-marked junction with the North Sourdough Trail (9) is passed at 0.7 miles. At 1.2 miles the trail crosses the Middle St. Vrain Road (6) and then crosses the creek on a footbridge. Continuing up the northern side of the valley, a short climb leads to sign-marked Timberline Falls, on a rocky ledge at 3.1 miles.

Stay on the right side of the valley on entering a wind swept treeless area, near a major right turn of the valley. Continue past a distinctive slender 15 foot high gneissic boulder, 340 yards to a blue diamond blaze on a post. Turn left and cross the valley bottom 50 yards to a junction at 4.8 miles with the Middle St. Vrain Road (6), at a footbridge over the creek.

Continue up the broad open valley on the unblazed jeep road. The road enters the shelter of trees near signs marking the Red Deer Cutoff and St. Vrain Mountain summer trails and the wilderness boundary at 5.4 miles. After passing through an area of dead trees, a sign-marked junction is reached at 6.3 miles. The summer Buchanan Pass Trail crosses the creek on a footbridge with a handrail, to switchback and climb south on the side of the valley toward the pass. The St. Vrain Glacier Trail (7A) continues up the valley, and the Buchanan Pass Trail as described here, ends.

ADDITIONAL CONNECTING TRAIL INFORMATION
A sign-marked junction with the North Sourdough Trail (9) is at 0.7 miles. The parallel Middle St. Vrain Road (6) is crossed at 1.1 miles and a junction at its far

end is reached at 4.8 miles. The St. Vrain Glacier Trail (7A) starts at the end of this trail at 6.3 miles.

SKILLS RECOMMENDED

Skiing ability— Beginner. The tight turns and narrowness of this summer hiking trail are trying.

Endurance— Moderate. It's all very easy skiing, but lengthy.

Routefinding skill— Beginner. The only problem might be in finding the junction with the Middle St. Vrain Road at 4.8 miles. Visibility here is frequently impaired by blowing snow.

SNOW CONDITIONS

Poor at the beginning due to the low altitude and exposure to sunlight on the north side of the valley, but improving to good. The section where the valley turns northwest at 4.8 miles is usually poor.

WIND EXPOSURE

The treeless section near the wilderness boundary where the valley turns northwest is extremely windy.

GRADIENT OR STEEPNESS

The gradient is slight but steady, gaining 1400 feet in 6.8 miles.

AMOUNT OF USE

Light at the beginning, decreasing to very light at the upper end.

VIEWS

Sawtooth Mountain is visible at the head of the valley (Middle St. Vrain) for much of the trip. As the turn of the valley is approached, Paiute Peak emerges from behind the bulk of Mt. Audubon and can be seen to the southwest up the tributary Coney Creek. After the turn, Elk Tooth and Ogalalla Peak can be seen up valley to the northwest.

PRIVATE PROPERTY AND OTHER RESTRICTIONS

Beyond the turn of the valley at 4.8 miles, the trail is within the Indian Peaks Wilderness.

TRAIL NO. 7A

ST. VRAIN GLACIER TRAIL

SUMMARY

The head of this secluded valley in the Indian Peaks Wilderness lies in a glacial cirque, nestled beneath the rock buttresses and snow couloirs of Elk Tooth on one side, and the St. Vrain Glaciers on the other. Reached by an off trail and little used route over easy terrain, up the Middle St. Vrain valley from the end of the Buchanan Pass Trail, it lies a total of eight miles from the Beaver Reservoir North Trailhead and a mile more from Peaceful Valley.

CLASSIFICATION Difficult

ALTITUDE (feet)
Starting 9,910
Highest 10,900
Cumulative gain 990
Cumulative loss 0

TIME (hours)
Westbound 2.4
Eastbound 1.2

TRAIL MAP Side 1 (North)

MAP COORDINATES 47/45

PAGE-SIZE MAP No.5

USGS 7 ½' QUADRANGLES
Allens Park (A3)
Isolation Peak (A2)

DISTANCE (one way)
2.4 miles

ACCESS

From Beaver Reservoir North Trailhead (F), ski 3.2 miles to the end of the Coney Flats Trail (10) at Coney Flats. Descend 230 feet into the valley on the 0.6 mile Coney Flats-Middle St. Vrain Trail (10B), to a junction with the Middle St. Vrain Road (6). Follow this road west 0.1 mile to a junction with the Buchanan Pass Trail (7), which is followed 1.5 miles to its end. A total distance of 5.4 miles. Although it is troublesome to descend on an outward overall climb, this route saves 220 feet of climbing and is 0.9 miles shorter than the access routes from Peaceful Valley described next.

From Peaceful Valley Trailhead (E), ski 6.3 miles to the end of the Buchanan Pass Trail (7). The parallel Middle St. Vrain Road (6) is faster and may be substituted for the initial 4.8 miles.

ROUTE DESCRIPTION (westbound)

Continue up the bottom of the valley, following the jeep road to where it turns left to cross the creek at 0.7 miles. Pick a route on the easy terrain through the widely spaced tall trees along the right side of the valley floor. Pass a boulder field at 1.1

St. Vrain Glacier Trail

miles and continue to the above timberline lake at the base of Elk Tooth, 2.7 miles and 10,900 feet.

ADDITIONAL CONNECTING TRAIL INFORMATION
The trail begins at the end of the Buchanan Pass Trail (7) as described here. Here the summer Buchanan Pass Trail turns left to cross a footbridge and climb back up the side of the valley.

SKILLS RECOMMENDED
Skiing ability— Only beginner skills are necessary.

Endurance— Very strenuous due to the long access and the likelihood of breaking trail.

Routefinding skill— Advanced, the off trail route follows the valley bottom but it is nearly unused and remote.

SNOW CONDITIONS
Good, but expect to break trail.

WIND EXPOSURE
Low. The route is generally among widely space tall trees. Only on the road near the beginning and on the upper part, where the valley floor climbs above timberline, is the route exposed.

Elktooth Mountain from St. Vrain Glacier Trail

GRADIENT OR STEEPNESS
Slight.

AMOUNT OF USE
Nearly unused.

VIEWS
Elk Tooth is visible near the head of the valley throughout the trip. From the upper part of the route, Ogallala Peak is seen to its left. The St. Vrain Glaciers descend from cirques along the continental divide on the left side of the valley.

PRIVATE PROPERTY AND OTHER RESTRICTIONS
The entire route is within the Indian Peaks Wilderness.

* * * * *

TRAIL NO. 8

PARK CREEK TRAIL

SUMMARY
This pleasant and infrequently traveled forest trail offers good snow at a relatively low altitude. In series with the Rock Creek Saddle Trail, it forms the only connecting link of the northern trails, in the Rock Creek drainage and Wild Basin, with those of the Middle St. Vrain valley.

CLASSIFICATION Moderate-difficult	**TRAIL MAP** Side 1 (North)

ALTITUDE (feet)

Starting 8,560

Highest 9,760

Cumulative gain 1,200

Cumulative loss 0

TIME (hours)

Up, northwestbound 2.7

Down, southeastbound 1.4

MAP COORDINATES 56/43

PAGE-SIZE MAP No.6

USGS 7 ½' QUADRANGLES
Allens Park (A3)

DISTANCE (one way)
3.3 miles

ACCESS
From Peaceful Valley Trailhead (E), ski west 0.3 miles on the Middle St. Vrain Road (6) to the Bunce School Road. A sign identifying this road is currently missing. It is 300 yards past the bridge.

ROUTE DESCRIPTION (up, northwestbound)
From the turn off on the Middle St. Vrain Road (6), climb north through two switchbacks 200 feet onto a bench. Turn left at 1.0 miles, off the main road onto a jeep road. This is 70 yards past the second slight rise after reaching the bench and is 340 yards past the second switchback.

Follow this jeep road north as it crosses to the north side of Park Creek. It then follows the creek west past a rock quarry at 1.5 miles. At 1.7 miles take the left fork, cross Park Creek, and follow the trail upstream. At a 100 yard diameter clearing at 2.1 miles, the trail turns right, traverses, then climbs toward the rocky outcrop of Peak 10,583 and makes another right turn in a 70 yard clearing. Switchback to the left after 200 yards onto a climbing traverse to the northwest.

Turn right at a five foot tall red-brown stump at 2.8 miles and 9,360 feet altitude. Switchback left in 100 yards onto a 500 yard near level traverse, then switchback right 100 yards to where the trail turns uphill to end at 3.3 miles and 9,760 feet.

ADDITIONAL CONNECTING TRAIL INFORMATION
The Logging Road Spur (8A) branches off at the rock quarry at 1.5 miles.

The Rock Creek Saddle Route (8B) continues on from the end of this trail.

SKILLS RECOMMENDED
Skiing ability— Beginner.

Endurance— Moderate, but expect to break trail.

Routefinding skill— Advanced, this route description is complex.

SNOW CONDITIONS
Medium overall. Starting snow conditions are very poor on the south facing slope, but improve greatly at Park Creek.

WIND EXPOSURE
None except at the beginning.

GRADIENT OR STEEPNESS
Slight overall, with a moderate gradient at the end.

AMOUNT OF USE
Nearly unused.

VIEWS
Mt. Audubon and Sawtooth Mountain are visible to the west, from the upper part of the trail.

PRIVATE PROPERTY AND OTHER RESTRICTIONS
None.

* * * * *

TRAIL NO. 8A

LOGGING ROAD SPUR

SUMMARY
This short, infrequently traveled, low altitude, sheltered trail through the trees near Peaceful Valley is an interesting addition to the overcrowded easy trails of the area. It's a good trail for the neophyte skier to gain experience in breaking trail and routefinding.

CLASSIFICATION Moderate

ALTITUDE (feet)
Starting 8,870
Highest 9,220
Cumulative gain 350
Cumulative loss 0

TIME (hours)
Up, southbound 0.7
Down, northbound 0.4

TRAIL MAP Side 1 (North)

MAP COORDINATES 56/43

PAGE-SIZE MAP No.6

USGS 7 ½' QUADRANGLES
Allens Park (A3)

DISTANCE (one way)
1.0 miles

ACCESS
From Peaceful Valley Trailhead (E), ski west up the valley 0.3 miles on the Middle

St. Vrain Road (6), then north out of the valley 1.5 miles on the Park Creek Trail (8). A total distance of 1.8 miles.

ROUTE DESCRIPTION (up, southbound)
From the junction at the rock quarry at 1.5 miles on the Park Creek Trail (8), ski south on a jeep road which winds among the large trees before heading uphill to end at 1.0 miles in a wind swept clearing cluttered with logging cable.

ADDITIONAL CONNECTING TRAIL INFORMATION
None.

SKILLS RECOMMENDED
Skiing ability— Beginner.

Endurance— Very easy.

Routefinding skill— Beginner.

SNOW CONDITIONS
Generally poor due to the low altitude, but definitely better than the Park Creek Trail switchbacks used to gain access. The best snow is on the lower part.

WIND EXPOSURE
The lower part is well sheltered by trees, the upper is less so.

GRADIENT OR STEEPNESS
Generally slight, increasing to moderate at the upper end.

AMOUNT OF USE
Nearly unused.

VIEWS
None.

PRIVATE PROPERTY AND OTHER RESTRICTIONS
None.

* * * * *

TRAIL NO. 8B

ROCK CREEK SADDLE ROUTE

SUMMARY
An off trail route through a 10,100 foot saddle that, in conjunction with the Park Creek Trail, connects the trails in Rock Creek and Wild Basin with those in the Middle St. Vrain valley and further south.

CLASSIFICATION Difficult

ALTITUDE (feet)
Starting 9,760
Highest 10,140
Cumulative gain 380
Cumulative loss 460

TIME (hours)
Northwestbound 1.5
Southeastbound 1.5

TRAIL MAP Side 1 (North)

MAP COORDINATES 54/44

PAGE-SIZE MAP No.6

USGS 7 ½' QUADRANGLES
Allens Park (A3)

DISTANCE (one way)
1.8 miles

ACCESS

South end. From Peaceful Valley Trailhead (E), ski 0.3 miles on the Middle St. Vrain Road (6), then 3.3 miles to the end of the Park Creek Trail (8). A total distance of 3.6 miles.

North end. From the Rock Creek Trailhead (D), ski the Rock Creek Trail (4) 2.3 miles to a cairn-marked junction at 9680 feet.

ROUTE DESCRIPTION (northwestbound)

From the end of the Park Creek Trail (8), proceed on a moderate climbing traverse to the west, on easy terrain through widely spaced trees. As the slope lessens, bear more to the right (north) to pass through the gentle saddle at 0.6 miles, with a low rock outcrop on your right. This is the saddle between Park Creek and the unnamed tributary to Middle St. Vrain Creek to the west.

Continue on a level traverse to the north, across a steep west facing slope with poor snow and exposed logs and boulders, to the 10,100 foot saddle between the Middle St. Vrain and Rock Creek drainages at 0.9 miles. Follow a faint flagged trail, that descends on a gentle traverse northwest, to a junction with the Rock Creek Tail (4) at 1.8 miles and 9680 feet.

Should the flagging not be found, either bushwhack on a descending traverse to the left to intercept the Rock Creek Trail or with good downhill skill, descend the slope to the old downhill ski area.

ADDITIONAL CONNECTING TRAIL INFORMATION
None.

SKILLS RECOMMENDED

Skiing ability— Advanced skill is required to handle the short steep descents on untracked snow through closely spaced trees.

Endurance— Moderate.

Routefinding skill— Advanced routefinding skills are necessary to follow the southern part of the route through the two saddles. The route north from the saddle is flagged, but be prepared to find your way if these are not locatable.

SNOW CONDITIONS
Expect medium snow quality for the southernmost section, on the climb toward the saddle. Snow quality, where the route traverses the steep side slope leading into the saddle, is very poor and may require walking. Snow quality north of the saddle is good.

WIND EXPOSURE
Some minor exposure at the saddle, but generally well protected by trees.

GRADIENT OR STEEPNESS
Moderate on the south side. The north side is moderate but has two steep sections.

AMOUNT OF USE
Nearly unused.

VIEWS
Mt. Audubon, Sawtooth Mountain, and Buchanan Pass are visible to the west, from the southern end of the route to the pass. Longs Peak and Mt. Meeker come into view, to the north through the pass.

PRIVATE PROPERTY AND OTHER RESTRICTIONS
None.

* * * * *

TRAIL NO. 9

NORTH SOURDOUGH TRAIL

SUMMARY
The northernmost of the three segments of the Sourdough Trail, it climbs steeply out of the Middle St. Vrain Valley on a switchbacked course through dense trees. Peaceful Valley Trailhead and the trails of Middle St. Vrain valley are thereby linked with those of the upland pediment at Beaver Reservoir.

CLASSIFICATION Moderate-difficult

ALTITUDE (feet)
Starting 8,600
Highest 9,160
Cumulative gain 540
Cumulative loss 0

TRAIL MAP Side 1 (North)

MAP COORDINATES 56/41

PAGE-SIZE MAP No.6

USGS 7 ½' QUADRANGLES
Allens Park (A3)
Ward (B3)

TIME (hours)

Southbound 1.3

Northbound 1.0

DISTANCE (one way)

2.0 miles

ACCESS

North end. From Peaceful Valley Trailhead (E), ski 0.1 mile west on the Middle St. Vrain Road (6), then 0.7 miles on the Buchanan Pass Trail (7). A total distance of 0.8 miles.

South end. At Beaver Reservoir East Trailhead (G).

ROUTE DESCRIPTION (southbound)

From a junction at 0.7 miles on the Buchanan Pass Trail (7), marked with a sign *Beaver Reservoir*, the blue diamond-blazed trail climbs up the steep side of the Middle St. Vrain valley, through four switchbacks, as it crosses and recrosses a steep gully. Switchback to the left, at the sign-marked junction with the Beaver Reservoir Cutoff Trail (9A) at 0.6 miles, onto a climbing traverse to the east. After a steep switchback to the right (south) at 0.8 miles, the gradient lessens. At 1.0 miles the trail divides, with both forks blue diamond-blazed. Either is okay as they rejoin in about 0.3 mile. The westernmost is slightly shorter but steeper. Distances beyond here are calculated using it. Cross Beaver Creek at a footbridge with a log railing, at 1.5 miles and contour around the hill to the Beaver Reservoir East Trailhead (G) at 2.0 miles.

ADDITIONAL CONNECTING TRAIL INFORMATION

The Middle Sourdough Trail (12) continues to the south from the end of this trail.

SKILLS RECOMMENDED

Skiing ability— Intermediate skill for southbound or uphill travel, advanced for travel in the other direction.

Endurance— Easy.

Routefinding skill— Beginner, the route is blue diamond-blazed but may be untracked. It is generally an easy to follow, distinct trail through trees.

SNOW CONDITIONS

Medium conditions are the product of a north facing slope, with dense tree cover but at a relatively low altitude.

WIND EXPOSURE

None, protected by trees.

GRADIENT OR STEEPNESS

The climb out of the valley is initially steep, gaining 300 feet in 0.4 mile, but moderate thereafter.

AMOUNT OF USE

Very light.

VIEWS

Good views of Mt. Audubon and Sawtooth Mountain are to be had from anywhere in the vicinity of Beaver Reservoir. From the overlook at 0.4 miles, Elk Tooth and Ogalalla Peak are seen at the head of the Middle St. Vrain valley. St. Vrain Mountain and Meadow Mountain are to the north across the valley.

To the southwest, the tips of Kiowa, Navajo, Apache, and Shoshoni Peaks are seen above the tree covered east ridge of Mt. Audubon.

PRIVATE PROPERTY AND OTHER RESTRICTIONS

None.

* * * * *

TRAIL NO. 9A

BEAVER RESERVOIR CUTOFF TRAIL

SUMMARY

A short trail through the woods east of Beaver Reservoir, it connects the North Sourdough Trail with the Beaver Reservoir North Trailhead. Loop trips by way of Beaver Reservoir, Coney Flats, and Peaceful Valley are practical, using this as a connecting link.

CLASSIFICATION Moderate

TRAIL MAP Side 1 (North)

ALTITUDE (feet)

Starting	8,990
Highest	9,190
Cumulative gain	300
Cumulative loss	0

MAP COORDINATES 56/41

PAGE-SIZE MAP No.8

USGS 7 ½' QUADRANGLES
Allens Park (A3)
Ward (B3)

TIME (hours)

Southwestbound, up	0.6
Northeastbound, down	0.4

DISTANCE (one way)
0.8 miles

ACCESS

Southwest end. At Beaver Reservoir North Trailhead (F).

Northeast end. From Peaceful Valley Trailhead (E), ski 0.1 mile west on the Middle St. Vrain Road (6), 0.7 miles on the Buchanan Pass Trail (7), and 0.6 miles on the North Sourdough Trail (9). A total distance of 1.4 miles.

Northeast end. From Beaver Reservoir East Trailhead (G), ski 1.4 miles north on the North Sourdough Trail (9).

ROUTE DESCRIPTION (southwestbound, up)
Start at the northeast end, at the junction with the North Sourdough Trail (9). Ski west on the blue diamond-blazed and easy to follow trail on a moderate climb to the sign-marked junction with the Coney Flats Trail (10). This is 70 yards north of the Beaver Reservoir North Trailhead (E).

ADDITIONAL CONNECTING TRAIL INFORMATION
None.

SKILLS RECOMMENDED
Skiing ability— Beginner.

Endurance— Very easy.

Routefinding skill— Beginner, the trail however may not be tracked.

SNOW CONDITIONS
Medium.

WIND EXPOSURE
Very little.

GRADIENT OR STEEPNESS
Moderate.

AMOUNT OF USE
Nearly unused.

VIEWS
None.

PRIVATE PROPERTY AND OTHER RESTRICTIONS
None.

CONEY FLATS TRAIL

SUMMARY

This popular trail follows a jeep road west from Beaver Reservoir over gently sloping forested terrain on the eastern flank of Mt. Audubon. The moderately long climb to the Indian Peaks Wilderness boundary ends at wind swept Coney Flats.

CLASSIFICATION Moderate

ALTITUDE (feet)

Starting	9,190
Highest	9,790
Cumulative gain	600
Cumulative loss	0

TIME (hours)

Westbound	1.9
Eastbound	1.3

TRAIL MAP Side 1 (North)

MAP COORDINATES 53/42

PAGE-SIZE MAP No.8

USGS 7 ½' QUADRANGLES
Allens Park (A3)
Ward (B3)

DISTANCE (one way)
3.2 miles

ACCESS

At Beaver Reservoir North Trailhead (F).

ROUTE DESCRIPTION (westbound)

From the Beaver Reservoir Trailhead (F), ski the easily followed blue diamond-blazed jeep road west. At 1.3 miles, take the right fork at a junction, which is marked with a sign directing vehicles left and skiers right. Pass through private property marked with a sign and three cabins at 1.7 miles. At 2.6 miles, again stay right at a sign directing vehicles left and skiers right. Stay to the right of steeper slopes as the trail becomes more difficult to follow where it enters an area of stunted trees and drifts. Pass a large sign *Coney 4WD Route* at 3.0 miles and continue west 270 yards more to the Indian Peaks Wilderness boundary and a sign *Coney Flats Trailhead*, at 3.2 miles.

ADDITIONAL CONNECTING TRAIL INFORMATION

Junctions with the Four Wheel Drive Trail (10A) are at 1.3 and 2.6 miles.

SKILLS RECOMMENDED

Skiing ability— Beginner.

Endurance— Moderate.

Routefinding skill— Beginner. The wide jeep road is easy to follow until an area of stunted trees and drifted snow is reached at about three miles.

Sawtooth Mountain

SNOW CONDITIONS
Medium.

WIND EXPOSURE
Medium forest cover generally provides adequate protection from the wind. The last 400 yards are however, fully exposed to the frequent westerly gales.

GRADIENT OR STEEPNESS
Slight.

AMOUNT OF USE
Moderate.

VIEWS
The massive bulk of Mt. Audubon is to the southwest. Sawtooth Mountain, Buchanan Pass, and Elk Tooth are in view at the head of Middle St. Vrain valley to the west. St. Vrain Mountain is across the valley to the northwest.

PRIVATE PROPERTY AND OTHER RESTRICTIONS
Stay on the trail where it passes through private property at 1.7 miles.

* * * * *

TRAIL NO. 10A

FOUR WHEEL DRIVE TRAIL

SUMMARY
An alternate to the Coney Flats Trail, it allows one to make a solitary, below timberline loop near Coney Flats. In addition, it provides access to the Firebreak Cutoff Route and a shortcut to the north end of the Beaver Creek Route.

CLASSIFICATION Moderate-difficult

ALTITUDE (feet)

Starting	9,590
Highest	9,880
Cumulative gain	290
Cumulative loss	100

TIME (hours)

Westbound	1.2
Eastbound	0.9

TRAIL MAP Side 1 (North)

MAP COORDINATES 52/41

PAGE-SIZE MAP No.6

USGS 7 ½' QUADRANGLES
Allens Park (A3)
Ward (B3)

DISTANCE (one way)
1.8 miles

ACCESS
East end. From Beaver Reservoir North Trailhead (F), ski 1.3 miles west on the Coney Flats Trail (10).

West end. From Beaver Reservoir North Trailhead (F), ski 2.6 miles west on the Coney Flats Trail.

ROUTE DESCRIPTION (westbound)
At 1.3 miles on the Coney Flats Trail (10), take the left fork at a sign directing vehicles and motorbikes left and hikers and skiers right. This junction is 500 yards east of the private cabins at mile 1.7 on the Coney Flats Trail.

At 0.4 miles the easily followed jeep road switchbacks right as the second and larger of two ponds is passed on your left, and becomes less distinct as it climbs to the west. At 1.3 miles and 9850 feet altitude, take the right fork onto a near level route which then descends to a junction with the Coney Flats Trail (10) at 1.8 miles.

ADDITIONAL CONNECTING TRAIL INFORMATION
A junction with the Firebreak Cutoff Trail (21B) is at the switchback at 0.4 miles.

The junction at the west end is 0.6 miles east of the lake at Coney Flats. It is marked with a sign directing hikers to the lower Coney Flats Trail and vehicles to the higher Four Wheel Drive Trail.

SKILLS RECOMMENDED

Skiing ability— Intermediate at the west end, beginner at the east.

Endurance— Strenuous, because you will probably break trail. The total distance for the loop from Beaver Reservoir is 5.7 miles.

Routefinding skill— Intermediate.

SNOW CONDITIONS

Good, but probably untracked.

WIND EXPOSURE

The trail is well sheltered by trees from wind.

GRADIENT OR STEEPNESS

Moderate.

AMOUNT OF USE

Nearly unused.

VIEWS

Nothing in addition to those for the Coney Flats Trail (10).

PRIVATE PROPERTY AND OTHER RESTRICTIONS

None.

* * * * *

TRAIL NO. 10B

CONEY FLATS-MIDDLE ST. VRAIN TRAIL

SUMMARY

This short, moderately steep trail descends from the wind swept meadow at Coney Flats to the tall trees and deep powder of the upper Middle St. Vrain valley. The western end of the Coney Flats Trail, on the upland pediment east of Mt. Audubon, is thereby connected to the paralleling Middle St. Vrain Road and Buchanan Pass Trail in the glacial valley below.

CLASSIFICATION Moderate-difficult   **TRAIL MAP** Side 1 (North)

69

ALTITUDE (feet)

Starting 9,790

Highest 9,820

Cumulative gain 30

Cumulative loss 230

TIME (hours)

Down, northbound 0.3

Up, southbound 0.5

MAP COORDINATES 51/43

PAGE-SIZE MAP No.5

USGS 7 ½' QUADRANGLES
Allens Park (A3)

DISTANCE (one way)
0.6 miles

ACCESS

South (upper) end. From the Beaver Reservoir North Trailhead (F), ski the Coney Flats Trail (10),3.2 miles to its end at the wilderness boundary and Coney Flats trailhead signs.

North (lower) end. From the Peaceful Valley Trailhead (E), ski the Middle St. Vrain Road (6), 4.6 miles to a sign-marked junction.

ROUTE DESCRIPTION (down, northbound)

Head directly north from the wilderness boundary and Coney Flats trailhead signs, across the wind swept meadow, to locate the path of the jeep road cut into the low trees. The road becomes much more distinct as it enters larger trees to descend to the valley bottom and a junction with the Middle St. Vrain Road (6) at 0.6 miles.

ADDITIONAL CONNECTING TRAIL INFORMATION

None.

SKILLS RECOMMENDED

Skiing ability— Beginner

Endurance— Strenuous, because of the distance from trailheads.

Routefinding skill— Beginner, the only problem could be locating the indistinct jeep road at Coney Flats when visibility is reduced by blowing snow.

SNOW CONDITIONS

Poor, where exposed to the wind at Coney Flats, but good to excellent lower, in the shelter of trees.

WIND EXPOSURE

Very exposed in the open meadow at Coney Flats, well protected by trees lower.

GRADIENT OR STEEPNESS

After crossing a nearly flat bench, the trail descends moderately to the valley bottom.

Very light.

None other than those for the Coney Flats Trail.

None.

*****

TRAIL NO. 11

SOUTH ST. VRAIN TRAIL

SUMMARY
A wide variety of snow and weather conditions can be encountered in following this venerable pack trail as it climbs 1700 feet on its five and a half mile course up South St. Vrain Creek, from the Peak to Peak Highway to Brainard Lake.

CLASSIFICATION Moderate-difficult

ALTITUDE (feet)

Starting	8,740
Highest	10,480
Cumulative gain	1,730
Cumulative loss	70

TIME (hours)

Westbound	3.0
Eastbound	2.0

TRAIL MAP Side 1 (North)

MAP COORDINATES 57/38

PAGE-SIZE MAP No.9

USGS 7 ½' QUADRANGLES
Ward (B3)
Gold Hill (B4)

DISTANCE (one way)
5.6 miles

ACCESS
East end. At Tahosa Bridge Trailhead (H).

West end. From the Brainard Lake Trailhead (K), ski the Mitchell Lake Road Spur (14B) 0.3 miles to the sign-marked trailhead.

Middle. From Red Rock Trailhead (J), ski the Middle Sourdough Trail (12) north 1.3 miles to the sign-marked junction at 2.9 miles.

ROUTE DESCRIPTION (westbound)
From the Tahosa Bridge Trailhead (H), ski the well defined blue diamond-blazed trail, up the west side of South St. Vrain Creek. At 0.9 miles, the trail climbs away from the stream, past a pond and up an aspen covered slope. At 1.6 miles pass a log shelter, and at 1.9 miles return to the creek at a low vehicle bridge and an unmarked junction with a road.

71

Follow the road upstream along the north side of the creek to its end at the buildings of the Baptist Camp at 2.6 miles. Beyond the camp, the narrower trail climbs more steeply through thick trees, past the sign-marked junction with the Church Camp Cutoff Trail (12B) at 2.7 miles, and on to a sign-marked junction with the Middle Sourdough Trail (12) at 2.9 miles.

Trail through aspen grove

The coincident trails are blue diamond-blazed where they follow the north side of the creek west to a sign-marked junction at 3.9 miles. Here, the blue diamond-blazed Middle Sourdough Trail heads north uphill, and the South St. Vrain Trail crosses a tributary creek and heads west along a lateral moraine, staying south of a large meadow. The widely spaced blue diamond blazes continue to 4.6 miles, but are visible only for westbound travel. A sign-marked junction with the Waldrop (North) Trail (13), and blue diamond blazes again, is reached at 4.9 miles.

Cross a stream gorge, steep on the west side, 100 yards beyond the junction and continue past a sign-marked junction with the Brainard Bridge Cutoff Trail (13A) at 5.0 miles. At 5.5 miles, the trail emerges from the dense trees. A post marks where the Waldrop (North) trail jogs south across the clearing on a blue diamond-blazed route. The unblazed South St. Vrain Trail continues west along the north side of the clearing, 300 yards to a sign-marked junction with the Mitchell Lake Road Spur (14B) at 5.6 miles.

ADDITIONAL CONNECTING TRAIL INFORMATION
A summary of the junctions with other trails and routes is as follows:
   (1) Private road to Chipmunk Gulch (closed) at 1.9 miles.
   (2) Church Camp Cutoff Trail (12B) at 2.7 miles.
   (3) Middle Sourdough Trail (12) at 2.9 miles.
   (4) Middle Sourdough Trail (12) at 3.9 miles.
   (5) Waldrop (North) Trail (13) at 4.9 miles.
   (6) Brainard Bridge Cutoff Trail (13 A) at 5.0 miles.
   (7) Waldrop (North) Trail (13) at 5.5 miles.
   (8) Audubon Cutoff Route (21A) at 5.5 miles.
   (9) Mitchell Lake Road Spur (14B) at 5.6 miles.

Skiing ability— Intermediate.

Endurance— Strenuous.

Routefinding skill— Intermediate.

SNOW CONDITIONS
Conditions at the lower end can be very poor. The upper part will likely be good, except in the long meadow at the west end, where it is often blown clear.

WIND EXPOSURE
The trail is for the most part, well protected by trees. The 0.7 mile section of road east of the Baptist Camp is exposed to wind, and the final 300 yards in the open meadow at the west end is exposed to strong winds.

GRADIENT OR STEEPNESS
The overall grade is slight, with a few short moderate segments.

AMOUNT OF USE
Light.

VIEWS
The Indian Peaks seen from the open meadow at the west end of the trail are (left to right): Kiowa Peak (above Niwot Ridge), Navajo Peak, Apache Peak, Shoshoni Peak, Pawnee Peak, Mount Toll, the tip of Paiute Peak, and Mt. Audubon.

PRIVATE PROPERTY AND OTHER RESTRICTIONS
The 0.7 mile section from the vehicle bridge at 1.9 miles to the Baptist Camp passes through private property.   The west end of the trail is in the Indian Peaks Wilderness.

* * * * *

TRAIL NO. 12

MIDDLE SOURDOUGH TRAIL

SUMMARY
The center section of the long, north-south Sourdough Trail, it parallels the Peak to Peak Highway, one to two miles to the east.   An intermediate blazed trail, it traverses undulating forested terrain between the Brainard Lake Road at Red Rock Trailhead and Beaver Reservoir.

Passage may be shortened two miles by use of the Church Camp Cutoff. An alternate mile longer route, uses the Baptiste-Wapiti Trail.

CLASSIFICATION Moderate-difficult

ALTITUDE (feet)
Starting 10,060
Highest 10,120
Cumulative gain 600
Cumulative loss 1,620

TIME (hours)
Northbound 3.1
Southbound 3.5

TRAIL MAP Side 1 (North)

MAP COORDINATES 55/38

PAGE-SIZE MAP No.8

USGS 7 ½' QUADRANGLES
Ward (B3)

DISTANCE (one way)
6.3 miles

ACCESS

North end. At Beaver Reservoir East Trailhead (G).

South end. At Red Rock Trailhead (J).

ROUTE DESCRIPTION (northbound)

Find the trail sign at the north side of the road, 120 yards east of the large roofed sign at the center of the Red Rock Trailhead. Ski to the blue diamond tree blaze visible across a meadow 100 yards to the east, and then 100 yards north to a large sign. Enter the trees on a well defined trail and descend 400 feet through two switchbacks to cross South St. Vrain Creek on a footbridge. At a sign-marked junction 50 yards beyond (1.3 miles), the trail merges with the South St. Vrain Trail (11). The common trail climbs first gently and then more steeply west, to a sign-marked junction at 2.4 miles, where the South St. Vrain Trail continues west.

The Sourdough Trail climbs to the north, then turns east to descend a steep 100 feet to a level area at 3.0 miles. The trail follows the north perimeter of a flat area, passing through stunted aspen trees, close to the low hill to the north. Sign-marked junctions with the Baptiste-Wapiti and Church Camp Cutoff Trails are passed at 3.4 and 3.7 miles. The trail continues east along the north side of a 300 yard diameter bog (Fresno Lake) at 3.9 miles.

Turning north, the trail descends 160 feet to a sign-marked junction with the Baptiste Trail from the southeast, at 4.3 miles. Continue north to a sign-marked junction at 4.6 miles, where the Baptiste-Wapiti Trail (12C) continues straight and the Sourdough switchbacks east and downhill. Another sign-marked junction is encountered in 430 yards (4.8 miles). Both forks here are blue diamond-blazed and the sign is confusing. The Sourdough Trail follows the right or easternmost fork, dropping into a shallow valley to an unmarked crossing of an unplowed road at 5.2 miles (Beaver Reservoir Road Cutoff (12A)), and continues north to the Beaver Reservoir East Trailhead (G) at 6.3 miles.

The left fork at 4.8 miles is the Sourdough Cutoff Trail, which rejoins the Sourdough at mile 5.6. It is 350 yards shorter and avoids the loss of 140 feet.

ADDITIONAL CONNECTING TRAIL INFORMATION

Turn east at the sign-marked junction with the South St. Vrain Trail (11) at 1.3 miles, to use the Church Camp Cutoff Trail (12B) and shorten the trip by 1.9 miles.

The junction at 3.4 miles is the southwest end of the Baptiste-Wapiti Trail (12C). Turn north to use this alternate trail which lengthens the route 1.0 miles.

SKILLS RECOMMENDED

Skiing ability— Intermediate.

Endurance— Strenuous.

Routefinding skill— Intermediate.

Winter wonderland

SNOW CONDITIONS

Conditions vary considerably along the trail, primarily with altitude. The southern portion, from Red Rock Trailhead down to and along South St. Vrain Creek and about 0.4 miles beyond to where it drops below 10,000 feet altitude, has good snow. From there to the switchback at 9,400 feet (4.6 miles), it is likely of medium quality, and the final 1.7 miles, below 9,400 feet, are frequently poor.

WIND EXPOSURE

The trail is well protected, except near the pond at 3.4 miles, and at Fresno Lake at 3.9 miles.

GRADIENT OR STEEPNESS

Moderate gradients are interspersed with less steep and nearly flat sections. The steepest is the descent from Red Rock Trailhead to South St. Vrain Creek.

AMOUNT OF USE

Expect light usage from Red Rock Trailhead down to and along the South St.Vrain Creek. Very light further north.

VIEWS

Niwot Mountain is visible to the south from the level bench near 3.5 miles.

Beaver Reservoir is visible one mile to the north, from the switchback at 4.6 miles.

Mt. Audubon, Sawtooth Mountain, Ogallala Peak, Elk Tooth, and St. Vrain Mountain are visible from the ridge crossed at 4.9 miles.

PRIVATE PROPERTY AND OTHER RESTRICTIONS

The Baptiste Trail at 4.3 miles continues southeast into private property.

* * * * *

TRAIL NO. 12A

BEAVER RESERVOIR ROAD CUTOFF

SUMMARY

This short, easy jeep road gives access to the middle section of the Sourdough Trail from the Beaver Reservoir Road. It is useful when the access road is not driveable all the way to the Beaver Reservoir East Trailhead.

CLASSIFICATION Easy

TRAIL MAP Side 1 (North)

ALTITUDE (feet)

Starting	8,920
Highest	9,160
Cumulative gain	240
Cumulative loss	0

MAP COORDINATES 56/40

PAGE-SIZE MAP No.8

USGS 7 ½' QUADRANGLES
Ward (B3)

TIME (hours)

Southwestbound	0.4
Northeastbound	0.3

DISTANCE (one way)
0.7 miles

ACCESS

From the Tahosa Bridge Trailhead (H), drive west on the Beaver Reservoir Road 1.3 miles. Park near the curves where a jeep road is visible to the west. It is marked with a sign, *Forest Service Road 113A* and has a vehicle closure gate 50 yards beyond.

ROUTE DESCRIPTION (southwestbound)
Ski the jeep road up the north side of South Fork of Beaver Creek to the unmarked junction with the Middle Sourdough Trail (12) at 0.7 miles.

ADDITIONAL CONNECTING TRAIL INFORMATION
The junction with the Middle Sourdough Trail is at mile 5.2 of that trail and is 1.1 miles south of the Beaver Reservoir East Trailhead (G).

SKILLS RECOMMENDED
Skiing ability— Novice.

Endurance— Very easy.

Routefinding skill— Novice.

SNOW CONDITIONS
Usually very poor, but probably good if the road on to Beaver Reservoir is undriveable due to a excess of snow.

WIND EXPOSURE
Moderate due to the thin tree cover.

GRADIENT OR STEEPNESS
Slight.

AMOUNT OF USE
Nearly unused.

VIEWS
Mt. Audubon and Sawtooth Mountain.

PRIVATE PROPERTY AND OTHER RESTRICTIONS
None.

* * * * *

TRAIL NO. 12B

CHURCH CAMP CUTOFF TRAIL

SUMMARY
A rough shortcut of the big bend of the Middle Sourdough Trail, it saves two miles.

77

CLASSIFICATION Moderate-difficult

ALTITUDE (feet)

Starting 9,640
Highest 9,720
Cumulative gain 80
Cumulative loss 0

TIME (hours)

Northbound 0.3
Southbound 0.2

TRAIL MAP Side 1 (North)

MAP COORDINATES 55/38

PAGE-SIZE MAP No.8

USGS 7 ½' QUADRANGLES
Ward (B3)

DISTANCE (one way)
0.3 miles

ACCESS

South end. From the sign-marked junction at mile 1.3 on the Middle Sourdough Trail (12)(50 yards north of the bridge over Middle St. Vrain Creek), ski east on the South St. Vrain Trail (11), 400 yards to a sign-marked junction. This is at mile 2.7 of the South St. Vrain Trail, 200 yards west of the Baptist Camp.

North end. At a sign-marked junction at mile 3.7 of the Sourdough Trail, 300 yards west of a 300 yard diameter bog at mile 3.9.

ROUTE DESCRIPTION (northbound)

From the sign-marked junction at mile 2.7 on the South St. Vrain Trail (11), ski north up the blue diamond-blazed, initially steep, confined, rocky trail. This soon levels out and joins the Middle Sourdough Trail (12) at a sign-marked junction at 0.3 miles.

ADDITIONAL CONNECTING TRAIL INFORMATION

None.

SKILLS RECOMMENDED

Skiing ability— Intermediate.

Endurance— Moderate.

Routefinding skill— Beginner.

SNOW CONDITIONS

Poor, on a south facing slope.

WIND EXPOSURE

Very little.

GRADIENT OR STEEPNESS

Moderate at the south end, less steep further north.

Nearly unused.

None.

None.

* * * * *

TRAIL NO. 12C

BAPTISTE-WAPITI TRAIL

SUMMARY

A more lengthy alternative to the center section of the Middle Sourdough Trail, it approaches the privately owned Stapp Lakes on a near level traverse to the northwest from the Middle Sourdough Trail. After a sharp turn to the south, it climbs steeply to pass through a saddle to rejoin the Sourdough Trail. A loop trip, accessible by the Sourdough Trail from either Beaver Creek East or Red Rock Trailheads, is feasible including this little used intermediate trail.

CLASSIFICATION Moderate-difficult

ALTITUDE (feet)

Starting 9,400
Highest 9,920
Cumulative gain 580
Cumulative loss 200

TIME (hours)

Counter clockwise (NE to SW) 1.5
Clockwise (SW to NE) 1.0

TRAIL MAP Side 1 (North)

MAP COORDINATES 54/39

PAGE-SIZE MAP No.8

USGS 7 ½' QUADRANGLES
Ward (B3)

DISTANCE (one way)
2.2 miles

ACCESS

Northeast end. From Beaver Reservoir East Trailhead (G), ski south on the Middle Sourdough Trail (12), 1.7 miles to a sign-marked junction at a switchback.

Southeast end. From the north end of the Church Camp Cutoff Trail (12B), ski 600 yards west on the Middle Sourdough Trail (12) to a sign-marked junction.

ROUTE DESCRIPTION (counter clockwise, NE to SW)

From the sign-marked junction with the Middle Sourdough Trail (12) marking the northeast end of this trail, ski northwest on a blue diamond-blazed, near level traverse through the forest. The trail climbs slightly to a sign at 0.7 miles, the most northern point of the trail. Here it turns a sharp corner to the left or south and

79

climbs a steep 500 feet to a 9920 foot saddle at 2.0 miles. It then descends 120 feet to a sign-marked junction at mile 3.4 of the Middle Sourdough Trail.

ADDITIONAL CONNECTING TRAIL INFORMATION
None.

SKILLS RECOMMENDED
Skiing ability— Intermediate, advanced if the descent from the saddle is to the north.

Endurance— Moderate, a moderately long access from Beaver Reservoir East or Red Rock trailhead is required.

Routefinding skill— Intermediate, the trail is well marked but may be untracked.

SNOW CONDITIONS
Medium overall, but poor for the fourth of a mile on the south facing slope south of the saddle.

WIND EXPOSURE
None.

GRADIENT OR STEEPNESS
The 0.7 mile leg running northwest toward Stapp Lake is nearly flat. The climb south to the saddle is steep.

AMOUNT OF USE
Very light.

VIEWS
None.

PRIVATE PROPERTY AND OTHER RESTRICTIONS
Exit to the north from the northernmost corner at mile 0.7 is blocked by private land near Stapp Lakes.

* * * * *

TRAIL NO. 13

WALDROP (NORTH) TRAIL

SUMMARY
One of the classic trails from Red Rock Trailhead to Brainard Lake, the small but steep gullies encountered on the straight line course of the abandoned telephone line add a bit of excitement not found on the other analogous trails. Coupled with the

CMC South or Little Raven Trails, it makes a pleasant loop tour of several hours over dependably good snow with a possible warming stop at the Colorado Mountain Club Brainard Cabin. As with the other trails to Brainard, it provides access to the far reaching skiing beyond.

CLASSIFICATION Moderate

ALTITUDE (feet)
Starting 10,120
Highest 10,420
Cumulative gain 520
Cumulative loss 230

TIME (hours)
Westbound 1.4
Eastbound 1.0

TRAIL MAP Side 1 (North)

MAP COORDINATES 53/37

PAGE-SIZE MAP No.8

USGS 7 ½' QUADRANGLES
Ward (B3)

DISTANCE (one way)
2.8 miles

ACCESS
At Red Rock Trailhead (J).

ROUTE DESCRIPTION (westbound)
From the parking alongside the Brainard Lake Road, ski west on the road 80 yards past the winter closure gate to the sign-marked trailhead, on the north side of the road at the first curve. The blue diamond-blazed trail makes a wide loop to the north before crossing the outlet creek from Red Rock Lake at 0.6 miles. A three quarter mile straight section west relentlessly follows the route of an abandoned telephone line without regard for contours as it crosses four gullies.

Ski 300 yards past a six foot boulder in the middle of the trail to a 100 yard diameter clearing at 1.5 miles. A sign marks the junction with the connecting trail to the Brainard Lake Road (14). To continue on the Waldrop (North) Trail, ski across the meadow, descending slightly, to cross South St. Vrain Creek at 1.7 miles. Climb to a sign-marked junction with the South St. Vrain Trail (11) at 2.1 miles and continue 100 yards more to cross a stream gorge, steeper on the far side. Forty yards beyond the top of the climb out is a sign-marked junction with the Brainard Bridge Cutoff Trail (13A) at 2.2 miles. Continue west on a gentle climb and emerge from the dense trees at 2.7 miles to an area of stunted trees and wind sculptured drifts, where a sign marks the separation of the Waldrop and South St. Vrain trails. Turn left (south) to cross the wind swept area. The blue diamond blazes are widely separated and tracks are quickly obscured here by the high winds. Enter the trees again and follow the trail west through the trees past the cabin of the Boulder group of the Colorado Mountain Club (CMC), 60 yards to a junction with the Mitchell Lake Road Spur (14B) at 2.8 miles.

The CMC cabin is usually hosted on weekends during the winter and offers a hot drink and warm resting place to both members and non-members for a small fee.

81

Mt. Toll, Mt. Audubon from Waldrop (North) Trail

The wide loop to the northeast near the eastern end may be shortcut by bushwhacking 100 yards to or from the road. This is through dense trees anywhere between the stream crossing at 0.6 miles and the top of the slight rise near 0.8 miles.

ADDITIONAL CONNECTING TRAIL INFORMATION

A blue diamond-blazed trail from the sign at 1.5 miles leads about 200 yards to the Brainard Lake Road (14).

Sign-marked junctions with the South St. Vrain Trail (11), are at 2.1 miles, 100 yards before a stream gorge, and at 2.7 miles, at the entrance to a wind swept meadow. Between these two points, the trails are coincident.

A sign-marked junction with the Brainard Bridge Cutoff Trail (13A), is at 2.2 miles, 60 yards west of the top of the stream gorge.

An unmarked junction with the Audubon Cutoff Route (21A), is at 2.7 miles.

SKILLS RECOMMENDED

Skiing ability— Intermediate, the gullies can be challenging for the beginner.

Endurance— Easy.

Routefinding skill— Novice, the well traveled trail is distinct and blazed with blue diamonds. Look closely to stay on the trail at the wind swept area at 2.7 miles.

SNOW CONDITIONS
Medium at the east end, improving to good at the west.

WIND EXPOSURE
Generally well protected by trees, a 100 yard clearing near the mid-point of the trail, where the junction to the short connecting trail to the road is located, is exposed to the wind. A second clearing, near the west end where the trail splits away from the South St. Vrain Trail, is exposed to the high winds common here.

GRADIENT OR STEEPNESS
Slight overall but with steep gradients at four small gullies crossed by the straight section following the telephone line, and at the larger drainage further west.

AMOUNT OF USE
Moderate.

VIEWS
Longs Peak and Mt. Meeker are visible to the north from a clearing near the stream crossing at 0.6 miles.

The Indian Peaks seen from open areas near the west end of the trail are (left to right): Kiowa Peak (above Niwot Ridge), Navajo Peak, Apache Peak, Shoshoni Peak, Pawnee Peak, Mount Toll, the tip of Paiute Peak, and Mt. Audubon.

PRIVATE PROPERTY AND OTHER RESTRICTIONS
Dogs are not allowed on the trail.

* * * * *

TRAIL NO. 13A

BRAINARD BRIDGE CUTOFF TRAIL

SUMMARY
This short, easy, and well protected cutoff trail from the Waldrop (North) and South St. Vrain Trails, ends at the east end of Brainard Lake near the bridge. It avoids the wind swept meadow they both encounter further west.

CLASSIFICATION Easy   **TRAIL MAP** Side 1 (North)

Mt. Toll, Mt. Audubon from east of Boulder

ALTITUDE (feet)

Starting 10,300

Highest 10,380

Cumulative gain 80

Cumulative loss 40

TIME (hours)

Southwestbound 0.3

Northeastbound 0.3

MAP COORDINATES 52/37

PAGE-SIZE MAP No.7

USGS 7 ½' QUADRANGLES
Ward (B3)

DISTANCE (one way)
0.5 miles

ACCESS

East end. From Red Rock Trailhead (J), ski 2.2 miles to the sign-marked junction.

West end. Brainard Lake Trailhead (K), at the northwest end of the bridge.

ROUTE DESCRIPTION (southwestbound)

The northeast end of the trail, at the junction with the Waldrop (North) (13) and South St. Vrain (11) Trails, is marked with a sign *Brainard Lake*. This is 60 yards west of the top of the stream gorge at mile 2.2 on the Waldrop (North) Trail.

Blue diamond blazes mark the trail to the northwest end of the bridge over the outlet stream, at the east end of Brainard Lake. The trail junction here is marked with a sign *Waldrop Trail 1 mile*.

None.

SKILLS RECOMMENDED

Skiing ability— Novice.

Endurance— Easy.

Routefinding skill— Beginner.

SNOW CONDITIONS

Good.

WIND EXPOSURE

Well protected except at the lake.

GRADIENT OR STEEPNESS

Nearly flat.

AMOUNT OF USE

Very light.

VIEWS

Views are the same as those described for the west end of the Waldrop (North) (13) and South St. Vrain (11) trails.

PRIVATE PROPERTY AND OTHER RESTRICTIONS

None.

* * * * *

TRAIL NO's. 14, 14A, 14B, 14C

BRAINARD LAKE ROAD (14)
BRAINARD LAKE ROAD LOOP (14A)
MITCHELL LAKE ROAD SPUR (14B)
LONG LAKE ROAD SPUR (14C)

SUMMARY

The Brainard Lake Road continues west past the winter closure gate at the Red Rock Trailhead, two miles to Brainard Lake. A nearly flat, wide paved road, stretches of it are frequently blown clear of snow. It can serve as an emergency escape route from the Brainard Lake area as it can probably be followed at night or in ground blizzards when traveling downwind (east). Much of it could probably be done without skis.

The loop road circles the lake and the spur roads connect with trails extending west.

An emergency telephone is located on the west side of the road 150 yards south of the bridge at the east end of Brainard Lake.

CLASSIFICATION Easy

ALTITUDE (feet)
Starting 10,120
Highest 10,500
Cumulative gain
Red Rock to lake 290
To west side, add 40
Mitchell Lk spur, add 110
Long Lk spur, add 120
Cumulative loss 0

TIME (hours)
Red Rock to lake 1.2
To west side, add 0.2
Either spur, add 0.2

TRAIL MAP Side 1 (North)

MAP COORDINATES 51/36

PAGE-SIZE MAP No.7

USGS 7 ½' QUADRANGLES
Ward (B3)

DISTANCE (one way)
Red Rock to lake 2.1 miles
To west side, add 0.2 miles
Either spur, add 0.2 miles

ACCESS
At Red Rock Trailhead (J).

ROUTE DESCRIPTION (westbound)
The wide paved road continues west from the winter closure gate at the Red Rock Trailhead (J) to Brainard Lake at 2.1 miles. As the lake is approached, either continue straight on the old road, which now provides summer access to a campground, or jog south on the main road. Follow the Brainard Lake Loop Road (14A) around the lake in either direction to the junction with the spur road, marked with a road sign. The common spur road divides in 200 yards, with the Mitchell Lake Road Spur (14B) continuing straight while the Long Lake Road Spur (14C) turns to the left. Both continue 0.4 mile to end at summer parking lots. The Long Lake Road Spur is marked with a sign at the junction *Long Lake Ski Trail*.

ADDITIONAL CONNECTING TRAIL INFORMATION
An unmarked 100 yard bushwhacking route to the Waldrop (North) Trail (13) may be done west of the outlet creek of Red Rock Lake, crossed at 0.5 miles.

A blue diamond-blazed trail south to the CMC South Trail (15) is marked by a sign at 1.3 miles.

A blue diamond-blazed trail north to the Waldrop (North) Trail (13) is marked by a sign at 1.4 miles.

A sign post marks the junction with the CMC South (15) and Little Raven (16) Trails, at a brushy clearing at the southwest corner of the Brainard Lake Loop Road (14A).

An unmarked junction with the Long Lake Cutoff Trail (24) is near the southwest corner of the Brainard Lake Loop Road (14A). It is at the top of a roadcut across the road from the toilet in the Niwot Mountain Picnic Ground.

A sign *Waldrop Trail 1 mile* marks the junction with the Brainard Bridge Cutoff Trail (13A), at the northwest end of the bridge across the outlet creek on the northeast shore.

The Mitchell Lake Trail (20) and the Beaver Creek Trail (21) both begin at the summer parking lot at the end of the Mitchell Lake Road Spur (14B). The Pawnee Pass Trail (22) continues on from the summer parking lot at the end of the Long Lake Road Spur (14C).

Colorado Mountain Club
Brainard Lake cabin

SKILLS RECOMMENDED

Skiing ability— Novice.

Endurance— Very easy for the Brainard Lake Road. Easy for the loop and road spurs.

Routefinding skill— Novice.

SNOW CONDITIONS

Generally poor due to the wind. Some sections, especially on the spur trails are rated medium.

WIND EXPOSURE

These unprotected roads are exposed to the effects of the high winds that are common in the area. Expect hard wind packed snow, bare areas where the snow has been blown away, reduced visibility in ground blizzards, and the possibility of frostbite to exposed skin.

Nearly flat.

AMOUNT OF USE
Heavy.

VIEWS
Unobstructed views of the Indian Peaks are gained from the wide road. At the head of the South St. Vrain Valley, this section of the continental divide is bounded by Niwot Ridge on the south and Mt. Audubon on the north. The peaks are, from left to right: Navajo, Apache, Shoshoni, and Pawnee Peaks, Mt. Toll, Paiute Peak, and Mt. Audubon.

PRIVATE PROPERTY AND OTHER RESTRICTIONS
None, this is the only trail west from the Red Rock Trailhead on which dogs are permitted.

* * * * *

TRAIL NO. 15

CMC SOUTH TRAIL

SUMMARY
The easiest of the trails extending west from Red Rock Trailhead, it follows an abandoned ditch on a contouring route through dense timber much of the way to Brainard Lake. Coupled with the Waldrop (North) Trail, it makes a enjoyable loop trip with a warming stop at the CMC Brainard Cabin. The more ambitious continue on the multitude of trails west from Brainard Lake.

CLASSIFICATION Easy

ALTITUDE (feet)
Starting 10,120
Highest 10,420
Cumulative gain 360
Cumulative loss 60

TIME (hours)
Westbound 1.1
Eastbound 0.9

TRAIL MAP Side 1 (North)

MAP COORDINATES 53/36

PAGE-SIZE MAP No.8

USGS 7 ½' QUADRANGLES
Ward (B3)

DISTANCE (one way)
2.2 miles

ACCESS
At Red Rock Trailhead (J).

ROUTE DESCRIPTION (westbound)

The Left Hand Park Reservoir Road and the recently relocated beginning of this trail are both found across the Brainard Lake Road from the large roofed sign near the center of Red Rock Trailhead. After following the reservoir road 40 yards, the trail branches off to the right (west) and in about 400 yards rejoins the original trail at a sign-marked junction.

On the return trip, this section of the old trail which contains a fun little hill and is now designated one way eastbound, may be descended to the curve on the Brainard Road 50 yards west of the winter closure gate.

Continuing west, much of the trail follows the contouring route of a ditch. At 2.1 miles the bridge and the clearing at the east end of Brainard Lake are visible through the trees to the north. Also visible is an emergency telephone, 150 yards south of the bridge.

The chimney remnants of two summer cabins are passed shortly before a junction is reached with the Little Raven Trail (16). The junction is marked with a bronze monument honoring Chief Little Raven. The Brainard Loop Road (14A) is 70 yards across a brushy clearing, either by a westerly route directly to the corner of the loop or a northerly route to a trail sign.

CMC South Trail

ADDITIONAL CONNECTING TRAIL INFORMATION

A sign-marked junction with an 80 yard unblazed connecting trail to the Left Hand Park Reservoir Road (17) is in a 20 yard diameter clearing 150 yards west of the junction of the old and relocated segments of trail.

At 1.2 miles a trail sign marks a junction with a blue diamond blazed trail leading 300 yards north to the Brainard Lake Road (14).

SKILLS RECOMMENDED

Skiing ability— Novice.

Endurance— Very easy.

Routefinding skill— Novice.

SNOW CONDITIONS
Good.

WIND EXPOSURE
Generally well protected by trees, a few open meadows are exposed along the way. A brushy clearing at the west end where the trail joins the Brainard Lake Loop Road is exposed to the wind.

GRADIENT OR STEEPNESS
Nearly flat except for a short moderate sections near the start and at 1.8 miles.

AMOUNT OF USE
Heavy.

VIEWS
The rounded mass of Mt. Audubon with its glacial cirque is occasionally seen through the dense woods.

PRIVATE PROPERTY AND OTHER RESTRICTIONS
Posted Forest Service rules prohibit dogs on the trail.

* * * * *

TRAIL NO. 16

LITTLE RAVEN TRAIL

SUMMARY
This is the newest of the trails from Red Rock Trailhead to Brainard Lake. It climbs more than the other trails and is over slightly more difficult terrain, but it sees the least use and has by far the best snow. The steep eastern part of the trail can be bypassed with the Left Hand Park Reservoir Road.

CLASSIFICATION Moderate-difficult

ALTITUDE (feet)

Starting 10,040
Highest 10,580
Cumulative gain 520
Cumulative loss 200

TIME (hours)

Westbound 1.5
Eastbound 0.9

TRAIL MAP Side 1 (North)

MAP COORDINATES 53/36

PAGE-SIZE MAP No.8

USGS 7 ½' QUADRANGLES
  Ward (B3)

DISTANCE (one way)
  2.7 miles

ACCESS
From the Red Rock Trailhead (J), ski south on the South Sourdough Trail (18), 0.4 miles to a sign-marked junction.

ROUTE DESCRIPTION (westbound)
From the sign-marked junction on the South Sourdough Trail (18), climb the steep, narrow, blue diamond blazed trail through trees 0.6 miles to the Left Hand Park Reservoir Road (17) at a sign-marked junction. Follow the road on a gradual climb southwest. At 1.0 miles, leave the road at a sign and head west on a near level, unblazed but distinct trail cut through trees 300 yards to the clearing along Left Hand Creek. Blue diamond blazes mark a route through the treeless area.

A long traverse and easy descent to the CMC South Trail (15) at 2.7 miles is marked with blue diamond blazes. A stone and bronze monument at the junction honors Chief Little Raven. The Brainard Lake Loop Road (14A) is 70 yards northwest across a brushy meadow.

ADDITIONAL CONNECTING TRAIL INFORMATION
The trail is coincident with the Left Hand Park Reservoir Road (17) for 0.4 miles.

SKILLS RECOMMENDED
Skiing ability— Intermediate. Advanced for a descent of the east end.

Endurance— Easy.

Routefinding skill— Novice.

SNOW CONDITIONS
Snow quality will likely be good to excellent on the western half of the trail. The shared route with Left Hand Park Reservoir Road may be blown clear.

WIND EXPOSURE
Exposed on road and along Left Hand Creek.

GRADIENT OR STEEPNESS
The section from the beginning to the Left Hand Park Reservoir Road at 0.6 miles is a steep narrow path bordered with trees. Beyond there, the slope is slight to moderate.

AMOUNT OF USE
Light.

VIEWS
Unobstructed views of the Indian Peaks are obtained from the clearing along Left Hand Creek and from the road. The peaks are the same as listed for the Left Hand Park Reservoir Road (17).

Dogs are not allowed on the Little Raven Trail.

* * * * *

TRAIL NO. 17

LEFT HAND PARK RESERVOIR ROAD

SUMMARY

Sometimes offering wide packed slopes reminiscent of a downhill ski area and at other times only a rocky roadbed, this moderately steep road climbs from Red Rock Trailhead, 550 feet to the nearly always windy reservoir. The lower part can be used to avoid either the steep eastern part of the Little Raven Trail or the wearisome, recently relocated 400 yard section at the east end of the CMC South Trail.

CLASSIFICATION Moderate

ALTITUDE (feet)
Starting 10,070
Highest 10,620
Cumulative gain 550
Cumulative loss 0

TIME (hours)
Southwestbound 1.0
Northeastbound 0.6

TRAIL MAP Side 1 (North)

MAP COORDINATES 53/36

PAGE-SIZE MAP No.8

USGS 7 ½' QUADRANGLES
Ward (B3)

DISTANCE (one way)
1.7 miles

ACCESS

At the Red Rock Trailhead (J).

ROUTE DESCRIPTION (southwestbound)

Start from a sign *Lefthand Ski Trail* across the Brainard Lake Road from the large roofed sign near the center of Red Rock Trailhead. Follow this wide road, crossing Left Hand Creek on a vehicle bridge at 0.8 miles and pass the sign marked junction where the Little Raven Trail branches off to the right at 1.2 miles. Beyond here, tracks may deviate into the scrubby trees along the right (northwest) side of the road where skiers have sought better snow and shelter from the high winds.

The road ends in a large cleared area below the dam near a large sign. The sign can be helpful in finding the road for the return if visibility is restricted by blowing snow.

ADDITIONAL CONNECTING TRAIL INFORMATION

At 0.4 miles, where the road curves left, a trail sign marks a link to the CMC South Trail (15) which is 80 yards to the right on a distinct but unblazed trail.

Niwot Ridge, Left Hand Park Reservoir

A sign at 0.9 miles, 120 yards beyond a vehicle bridge, marks a junction with the Little Raven Trail (16) to the east. The same trail forks off to the west at a sign-marked junction at 1.2 miles. The trails are coincident between.

The Niwot Ridge Traverse Route (19A) continues west from the reservoir.

SKILLS RECOMMENDED
Skiing ability— Beginner.

Endurance— Easy.

Routefinding skill— Novice.
SNOW CONDITIONS
Poor, exposed corners on the lower part of the road may be blown clear of snow. The final 0.4 mile is frequently blown clear of snow.
WIND EXPOSURE
Exposure of this wide road to wind increases to become extreme for the final 0.4 miles to the reservoir.
GRADIENT OR STEEPNESS
The gradient from about 0.4 miles to the junction with the Little Raven Trail at 0.9 miles is moderate. Gradients above and below are less steep.

AMOUNT OF USE
Moderate.

A dramatic view of the Indian Peaks on the continental divide greets the skier at the reservoir. They are, from left to right: Kiowa and Arikaree Peaks, a straight section of Niwot Ridge, Navajo, Apache, Shoshoni and Pawnee Peaks, Mt. Toll, Paiute Peak and Mt. Audubon. Longs Peak and Mt. Meeker are visible to the north.

PRIVATE PROPERTY AND OTHER RESTRICTIONS
None.

* * * * *

TRAIL NO. 18

SOUTH SOURDOUGH TRAIL

SUMMARY
After crossing the steep forested eastern flank of Niwot Mountain on a near level traverse south from Red Rock Trailhead, the trail drops a thousand feet to the Mountain Research Station Trailhead. It can be an enjoyable trip done one way (north to south) with a car shuttle, or as part of a loop trip over Niwot Ridge.

CLASSIFICATION Moderate-difficult

ALTITUDE (feet)

Starting	10,060
Highest	10,260
Cumulative gain	450
Cumulative loss	1,260

TIME (hours)

Southbound	2.5
Northbound	3.1

TRAIL MAP Side 1 (North)

MAP COORDINATES 54/34

PAGE-SIZE MAP No.8

USGS 7 ½' QUADRANGLES
Ward (B3)

DISTANCE (one way)
5.5 miles

ACCESS
North end. At Red Rock Trailhead (J).

South end. At Mountain Research Station East Trailhead (L).

ROUTE DESCRIPTION (Southbound)
At Red Rock Trailhead (J), 125 yards east of the centrally located large roofed sign, a sign on the south side of the road marks the beginning of this blue diamond-blazed trail. The near level traverse of the forested east side of Niwot Mountain is interrupted by a switchback (to the left) before entering a gully at the head of Fourmile Creek, and again (to the right) in 100 yards to cross the Peace Memorial Footbridge at 3.0 miles.

A gradual descent leads to a trail junction at 4.0 miles where a *Trail Closed* sign is posted on the upper trail. Take the left, slightly descending fork, to cross an open gully below an abandoned sawmill at 4.2 miles. Climb slightly out of the gully and pass under a power line at 4.4 miles. The trail descends the forested slope to the east through a series of easy switchbacks. After a final view north into Fourmile Creek at 4.8 miles, a gentle run south southeast through the trees intercepts the plowed road at the Mountain Research Station East Trailhead (L) at 5.5 miles.

ADDITIONAL CONNECTING TRAIL INFORMATION
The junction at 4.0 miles mentioned in the preceding paragraph is with the east end of the Niwot Ridge Road (19). It continues beyond the *Trail Closed* sign on a near level trail to the south.

SKILLS RECOMMENDED
Skiing ability— Beginner.

Endurance— Strenuous.

Routefinding skill— Novice.
SNOW CONDITIONS
Poor.

WIND EXPOSURE
Very little.

GRADIENT OR STEEPNESS
Only slight gradients are encountered north of the moderate slope near the switchbacks at the head of Fourmile Creek at 3.0 miles. Additional moderate slopes occur near the south end of the trail.

AMOUNT OF USE
Light.

VIEWS
A saddle at 0.6 miles provides views of Ward, Green Mountain, Bear Peak, Mt. Thorodin, and the plains to the east. The overlook at 4.8 miles furnishes a view of the head of Fourmile Creek and the Peak to Peak highway.

PRIVATE PROPERTY AND OTHER RESTRICTIONS
Skiers should stay on the established Sourdough Trail in the vicinity of Niwot Ridge Road. Other ski and snowmobile trails provide access to experiments within the Niwot Ridge Biosphere Reserve of the University of Colorado.

TRAIL NO. 19

NIWOT RIDGE ROAD

SUMMARY

Extending west from near the southern end of the South Sourdough Trail above the University of Colorado Mountain Research Station, this pleasant forested trail can be continued to the wind swept slopes of Niwot Ridge and beyond. It may be part of a loop tour around Niwot Mountain.

CLASSIFICATION Moderate-difficult

ALTITUDE (feet)
Starting 9,800
Highest 11,000
Cumulative gain 1,140
Cumulative loss 0

TIME (hours)
Westbound 1.9
Eastbound 1.0

TRAIL MAP Side 1 (North)

MAP COORDINATES 52/32

PAGE-SIZE MAP No.11

USGS 7 ½' QUADRANGLES
Ward (B3)

DISTANCE (one way)
2.7 miles

ACCESS

From the Mountain Research Station East Trailhead (L), ski 1.5 miles north and west on the South Sourdough Trail (18), gaining 650 feet to a trail sign and where an upper trail to the south is posted *Trail Closed*. Switchback onto this near level trail.

ROUTE DESCRIPTION (westbound)

From the *Trail Closed* sign, the near level route passes between two abandoned buildings and crosses 100 yards of meadow to the road at 0.2 miles.

Continue west up the road, past a weather station and trailer at 0.4 miles and 9,960 feet altitude. The road climbs steadily to timberline at 2.7 miles and 11,000 feet altitude. Trails paralleling parts of the road may offer alternative routes with better snow.

ADDITIONAL CONNECTING TRAIL INFORMATION

The summer Niwot Ridge Road continues east from the meadow at 0.2 miles to descend to the University of Colorado Mountain Research Station.

The Niwot Ridge Traverse Route (19A) continues over Niwot Ridge from the west end of this road/trail.

SKILLS RECOMMENDED

Skiing ability— Beginner.

Endurance— Moderate.

Routefinding skill— Beginner.

SNOW CONDITIONS
Medium overall, good in the protection of trees, but poor where exposed.

WIND EXPOSURE
A significant part of the road is exposed to wind.

GRADIENT OR STEEPNESS
The gradient is never more than moderate, but is unrelenting.

AMOUNT OF USE
Light.

VIEWS
North and South Arapaho Peaks, the forbidden peaks of the City of Boulder's watershed (Mt. Albion, Kiowa and Arikaree Peaks) and Navajo Peak are visible to the west on the continental divide.

PRIVATE PROPERTY AND OTHER RESTRICTIONS
The City of Boulder watershed is to the south. Heavy fines have been imposed for trespassing.

* * * * *

TRAIL NO. 19A

NIWOT RIDGE TRAVERSE ROUTE

SUMMARY
Crossing over wind swept Niwot Ridge, this untracked route connects the Niwot Ridge Road, from the Mountain Research Station Trailhead to the south, with the Left Hand Park Reservoir Road, from Red Rock Trailhead. An eleven mile loop trip around Niwot Mountain uses this as the high link.

CLASSIFICATION Difficult   **TRAIL MAP** Side 1 (North)

ALTITUDE (feet)

Starting 11,000
Highest 11,440
Cumulative gain 440
Cumulative loss 840

TIME (hours)

Northbound 1.7
Southbound 2.0

MAP COORDINATES 51/36

PAGE-SIZE MAP No.10

USGS 7 ½' QUADRANGLES
Ward (B3)

DISTANCE (one way)
2.4 miles

ACCESS

South end. From the Mountain Research Station Trailhead (L), ski 1.5 miles on the South Sourdough Trail (18) to a junction with the Niwot Ridge Road (19). This is then skied 2.7 miles to its end. A total distance of 4.2 miles.

North end. From the Red Rock Trailhead (J), ski the Left Hand Park Reservoir Road (17), 1.7 miles to its end at the reservoir.

ROUTE DESCRIPTION (northbound)

From the end of the identifiable Niwot Ridge Road (19), continue northwest on an easy climb through scattered trees past a weather station trailer. Turn north and climb the wind packed slope 0.5 miles to cross Niwot Ridge at a saddle near Point 11,442. This is about 400 yards east of a small research station building on the ridgeline which is visible from below.

Niwot Ridge traverse

Left Hand Park Reservoir is visible from the ridge, 800 feet below. In poor visibility, following the fall line will lead to the west end of the lake. Cross to the east end and dam at 2.4 miles, going either across the ice if snow covered, or along the south shoreline. A large sign below the dam marks the west end of the Left Hand Park Reservoir Road (17), which leads to Red Rock Trailhead (J).

ADDITIONAL CONNECTING TRAIL INFORMATION

A 10.8 mile loop trip around Niwot Mountain from Red Rock Trailhead (J) utilizes the South Sourdough Trail (18), Niwot Ridge Road (19), and Left Hand Park Reservoir Road (17), along with this route.

SKILLS RECOMMENDED

Skiing ability— Intermediate skill is recommended to be able to ski difficult snow conditions.

Endurance—Strenuous.

Routefinding skill—Advanced, visibility is often reduced by blowing snow.

SNOW CONDITIONS

Poor, the ridge crest is frequently blown clear of snow and the above timberline snowpack may be sastrugi or hard wind slab. Left Hand Park Reservoir is often blown clear of snow. As it is difficult to maintain ones balance on the ice, the south bank is probably the better route.

WIND EXPOSURE

The entire route is very exposed to wind. The most sheltered site is among the scattered clumps of trees at the west end of the lake.

GRADIENT OR STEEPNESS

Uniformly moderate to steep. Long traverses are possible on the descent of the broad slopes above Left Hand Park Reservoir.

AMOUNT OF USE

Nearly unused.

VIEWS

An outstanding view extends to the south as far as James Peak and Pikes Peak. Closer in are the Indian Peaks; South and North Arapaho, Mt. Albion, Kiowa, Arikaree, and Navajo Peaks. Close to the north are Mt. Toll, Paiute Peak, and Mt. Audubon. Mt. Meeker and Longs Peak dominate the peaks in Rocky Mountain National Park further north.

PRIVATE PROPERTY AND OTHER RESTRICTIONS

None.

Wind swept Niwot Ridge

* * * * *

TRAIL NO. 20

MITCHELL LAKE TRAIL

SUMMARY
At the heart of the Indian Peaks Wilderness, summer or winter, and of this guidebook, this trail characterizes skiing the eastern slope of the Front Range better than any other. Crowded on week ends, the Red Rock Trailhead can be reached from Boulder in 45 minutes and Brainard Lake and the start of this trail in little more than an another hour. After a possible warming stop at the CMC Brainard Lake Cabin, other skiers are largely left behind as the trail climbs in deep powder snow through stands of towering Englemann spruce. These yield to more open slopes, playgrounds for telemarking, and then to the harsh wind swept slopes of incredible beauty among the cirques at the base of the high peaks.

CLASSIFICATION Difficult

ALTITUDE (feet)

Starting 10,480
Highest 11,320
Cumulative gain 840
Cumulative loss 0

TRAIL MAP Side 1 (North)

MAP COORDINATES 50/37

PAGE-SIZE MAP No.7

TIME (hours)

Westbound 1.7

Eastbound .... 1.0   **DISTANCE** (one way)

2.3 miles

ACCESS

From the Brainard Lake Trailhead (K), ski the Mitchell Lake Road Spur (14B), 0.4 miles to its end at the summer parking lot. A total skiing distance of 3.0 miles from the car at Red Rock Trailhead (J). This trail begins at the southwest corner of the parking lot. Do not confuse with the Beaver Creek Trail (21) which begins at the northwest corner of this parking lot.

ROUTE DESCRIPTION (westbound)

From the sign-marked trailhead near the summer information booth at the Mitchell Lake trail summer parking lot, follow the blue diamond-blazed trail to where it turns left near a distinctive brown stained eight foot stump at 0.3 miles. Continue straight, picking a route through clearings up the valley to Little Mitchell Lake and over a wind swept knoll to Mitchell Lake at 0.8 miles. Cross the outlet and ski westward in the shelter of trees along the south side of the lake to the inlet of Mitchell Creek at 1.0 miles.

Climb the moderately steep treeless gorge to the wide gentle valley above. Select a route over the open slopes and through scattered clumps of trees up the valley to Blue Lake at 2.3 miles. Stay away from avalanche danger at the base of the steep slopes to the south.

ADDITIONAL CONNECTING TRAIL INFORMATION

An alternative route as far as Mitchell Lake follows the unblazed summer trail and is less exposed to wind. It is however, difficult to follow unless tracked and trailbreaking in the loose powder among the trees is strenuous. From the left turn at 0.3 miles, cross Mitchell Creek on a footbridge in 120 yards. The blue diamond blazes end at the sign-marked wilderness boundary 50 yards beyond here. The trail switchbacks in 150 yards more to climb to Mitchell Lake.

Long undulating slopes with scattered lofty trees and legendary powder snow characterize the choice telemarking area known as *Hero Hill* at the northwest end of Mitchell Lake. An alternate route can be followed from here to join the gully route a half mile further up.

SKILLS RECOMMENDED

Skiing ability— Intermediate.

Endurance— Strenuous.

Routefinding skill— Intermediate.

Above Mitchell Lake

SNOW CONDITIONS
Excellent.

WIND EXPOSURE
Exposure to wind is significant in the treeless area east of Mitchell and Little Mitchell Lakes and also above timberline as Blue Lake is approached.

GRADIENT OR STEEPNESS
Moderate, the steepest is in the gully above Mitchell Lake.

AMOUNT OF USE
Light.

VIEWS
Little Pawnee and Pawnee Peaks, Mt. Toll, Paiute Peak, and Mt. Audubon tower over Blue Lake.

PRIVATE PROPERTY AND OTHER RESTRICTIONS
All but the eastern 0.3 mile of the route is within the Indian Peaks Wilderness.

* * * * *

TRAIL NO. 21

BEAVER CREEK TRAIL

SUMMARY

One of the premier routes of the area— remote, challenging, arduous, and adventurous. It combines travel on established forest trails with bushwhacking through thick timber, the freedom of above timberline wandering and skiing untouched silent trails through towering trees. This is a high level route from Brainard Lake to Coney Flats. Combined with one of the trails providing access to Brainard Lake and with the Coney Flats Trail at the north end, it affords a ten mile link on the fringe of timberline from Red Rock Trailhead to Beaver Reservoir.

CLASSIFICATION Very difficult

ALTITUDE (feet)

Starting	10,500
Highest	11,320
Cumulative gain	820
Cumulative loss	1,540

TIME (hours)

Northbound	4.4
Southbound	4.4

TRAIL MAP Side 1 (North)

MAP COORDINATES 50/39

PAGE-SIZE MAP No.7

USGS 7 ½' QUADRANGLES
Allens Park (A3)
Ward (B3)

DISTANCE (one way)
4.4 miles

ACCESS

South end. From the Brainard Lake Trailhead (K), ski the Mitchell Lake Road Spur (14B), 0.4 miles to its end at the summer parking lot. A total skiing distance of 3.0 miles from the car at Red Rock Trailhead (J). This trail begins at the northwest corner of the parking lot. Do not confuse with the Mitchell Lake Trail (20) which begins at the southwest corner of the parking lot.

North end. From Beaver Reservoir North Trailhead (F), ski the Coney Flats Trail (10) west 2.6 miles to where the open slopes south of Coney Flats are accessible.

ROUTE DESCRIPTION (northbound)

The trailhead at the northwest corner of the summer Mitchell Lake parking lot is marked with signs *Mt. Audubon Ski Trail* and 15 yards further *Beaver Creek Trail*. The unblazed trail climbs to the northwest through large Englemann Spruce with two switchbacks not shown on the topographic map. This leads to a clearing at the base of a steep slope at 0.7 miles and 10,840 feet. The slope to the west is a boulder field, to the north is a swath of trees up the slope, and to the east the slope is tree covered. (If you are southbound, on arrival here go west to the center of the 70 yard wide bowl, then south into a small gully which leads to the trail in the trees.)

103

Above timberline routefinding

Continue northbound by heading east on a climbing traverse into the switchbacks. The steep side slope here may be icy and the snow cover windslab. It may be easier to detour to the east of the summer trail where the slope lessens up higher. Climb north through the low brush above timberline to the low saddle, marked with a cairn and signpost at 1.6 miles, the junction with the summer Mt. Audubon trail. This saddle is approximately 100 yards west of a small knoll.

Continue north from the saddle down into the low trees and brush of the Beaver Creek drainage. Pass through a large (200 by 600 yard) clearing in the drainage bottom at 2.7 miles and on through a series of small clearings and dense trees to reach the top of a second large clearing 200 yards in diameter at 10,440 feet. Point 10,964 on the Audubon Cutoff Route (21A) is visible on the skyline to the south from here as is the previously mentioned 200 by 600 yard clearing to the southwest.

At the base of the clearing (10,390 feet), contour out to the northwest, following a tongue of the clearing and continue another 100 yards to intercept the summer trail in the sparse to moderately dense trees here. An alternate easier and higher route to the summer trail contours out at the base of the 200 yard by 600 yard clearing. The summer trail here however, is in an area of thinner trees and more difficult to recognize. Continue north on the now easy to follow trail through large trees to cross a drainage tributary to Beaver Creek at 3.3 miles.

Continue north on the Beaver Creek Trail to arrive at the top of open telemark slopes at 3.9 miles. The summer trail is difficult to follow north to Coney Flats from here through the widely scattered trees. A better alternative is to descend the open slopes and follow the minor drainage northeast to intercept the Coney Flats Trail (10) at 4.4 miles. It is 2.6 miles east to Beaver Reservoir North Trailhead (F).

ADDITIONAL CONNECTING TRAIL INFORMATION
The unmarked junction with the Audubon Cutoff Trail (21A) is at the midpoint of the 200 by 600 yard clearing at 2.7 miles and 10,760 feet altitude.

The unmarked junction with the Firebreak Cutoff Trail (21B) is at the crossing of a drainage at 3.3 miles. The west end of the 20 yard wide firebreak is 200 yards east down the drainage. An emergency exit to Beaver Reservoir could be made here by going down the wide swath of the firebreak and continuing east on easy terrain through the private property at Stapp Lakes.

SKILLS RECOMMENDED
Skiing ability— Expert. The switchbacks at 0.7 miles and the above timberline section require good technique and equipment. Climbing skins, metal edges, and ski mountaineering boots are recommended. The switchbacks are more difficult southbound (downhill).

Endurance— Very strenuous. The total distance including the connecting trails is 10.0 miles with 1330 feet altitude gained and 2240 lost on a south to north passage. Probably all of the 4.4 miles of the Beaver Creek Trail will be untracked, with deep powder in the trees, hard wind packed snow above timberline, and ice likely on the switchbacks.

Routefinding skill— Expert. Maps, compass, and altimeter are recommended along with an early start, good weather and capable companions. The routefinding is more difficult southbound due to the difficulty in recognizing the untracked trail in the area of sparse trees and open slopes above the junction with the Coney Flats Trail (10).

SNOW CONDITIONS
Snow conditions can be expected to range from poor to excellent. Above timberline slopes may have bare tundra, rocks, sastrugi, and wind slab. The switchbacks at 0.8 miles are on a steep south facing side slope and may be icy. Snow on the trail through the large trees north of Beaver Creek will likely be deep powder and untracked.

WIND EXPOSURE
The 1.9 mile section from the switchbacks at 0.8 miles to where the shelter of trees is regained on the north side of Beaver Creek is exposed to frequent high winds. Open slopes near the junction with the Coney Flats Trail (10) are likewise exposed.

GRADIENT OR STEEPNESS
Moderate but with a very steep section on the switchbacks at 0.7 miles, steep slopes on the descent into Beaver Creek drainage and steep open slopes at the junction with the Coney Flats Trail (10) at 4.4 miles.

Nearly unused.

VIEWS

From the top of the switchbacks at 0.7 miles the view to the south includes Niwot Mountain, the slopes above Left Hand Park Reservoir crossed by the Niwot Ridge Traverse Route (19A), Mt. Albion, Kiowa and Arikaree Peaks.

At the saddle near the junction of the Mt. Audubon trail (1.6 miles), views to the north and east are similar to those listed for the Audubon Cutoff Route (21A). The nearly flat terrain with scattered clumps of trees traversed by the Audubon Cutoff Route is visible below and 700 yards to the southeast. The view to the west on a windless day is of the above timberline slopes of Mt. Audubon.

PRIVATE PROPERTY AND OTHER RESTRICTIONS

Exit by the Firebreak Cutoff (21B) to Beaver Reservoir via Stapp Lakes is suggested only as an emergency route. Property at Stapp Lakes is privately owned and trespass is prohibited.

Dogs are not allowed on the Waldrop (North) (13), CMC South (15), nor Little Raven (16) Trails which provide access to the south end of the route.

South of Beaver Creek the route is within the Indian Peaks Wilderness, to the north the trail is the eastern boundary.

* * * * *

TRAIL NO. 21A

AUDUBON CUTOFF ROUTE

SUMMARY

An alternative to the southern 2.7 miles of the Beaver Creek Trail (21), it avoids the climb and descent of 370 feet of altitude as well as avoiding the steep icy switchbacks and the extended exposure above timberline of that trail. From near the west end of the South St. Vrain or Waldrop (North) Trails, a compass course north through large trees with good snow leads to a bushwhack up a steep slope and finally a climbing traverse and descent through scattered clumps of trees near timberline to a junction with the Beaver Creek Trail.

CLASSIFICATION Very difficult

TRAIL MAP Side 1 (North)

ALTITUDE (feet)
Starting 10,450
Highest 10,970

MAP COORDINATES 50/38

PAGE-SIZE MAP No.7

Cumulative gain 540
Cumulative loss 590   **USGS 7 ½' QUADRANGLES**
                                              Ward (B3)
TIME (hours)
Northbound . . . . 2.1   **DISTANCE** (one way)
                                              2.0 miles

ACCESS (south end)

From Red Rock Trailhead (J), ski the Waldrop (North) Trail (13) 2.7 miles to the
east end of a wind swept clearing.

Alternatively, from Brainard Lake Trailhead (K), ski 0.3 miles northwest on the
Mitchell Lake Road Spur (14B) to the junction with the South St. Vrain Trail (11).
Go east on this 300 yards to the end of the clearing and turn north into the trees.
A total skiing distance of 3.0 miles from Red Rock Trailhead (J).

ROUTE DESCRIPTION (northbound)

From the east end of the 300 yard long clearing near the western end of the South
St. Vrain Trail (11), ski a compass course north northwest through large widely
spaced trees 900 yards, to intersect an elongated clearing along the northern fork of
South St. Vrain Creek (0.4 miles). Follow this clearing to its western end, and then
follow a 20 yard wide tongue about
250 yards to the northwest on a gentle
climb directly away from Niwot Mountain. The steep side of the glacial
valley which must be climbed is visible
ahead. Enter the trees and climb
moderately steeply to a long, east-west
boulder field across the slope where
the slope steepens markedly. Move to
the right (east) of the boulder field and
climb the short steep section to the top
of the ridge (0.8) miles. Keep as far
west as possible to avoid the closely
spaced trees and large boulders further
east.

Once the top is gained, head west
along the ridge to the open meadow at
10,880 feet where there is a pronounced steepening of the ridge to the
west and only scattered clumps of
stunted trees above. The rocky, above
timberline knoll just northeast of the
junction of the Mt. Audubon trail with
the Beaver Creek Trail (21) is visible

Mt. Toll

on the skyline a half mile to the north. To the east of this knob is the rocky Point 10,964, lower and with low stunted trees. Contour north, along the base of the steeper slope to the west and at the edge of the trees, toward Point 10,964. Force a passage through the low trees at the top of the ridge into a 100 yard diameter clearing and the rock outcrop of Point 10,964 at 1.6 miles.

Descend the fall line north northwest through a series of four nearly linked clearings in low trees to reach the mid-point at 10,760 feet of a 200 by 600 yard clearing on the main drainage of Beaver Creek. A narrow passage into the clearing through the thick low trees exists here at a minor step 90 yards above and southwest of a more prominent step near the lower end of the clearing. This is the 200 by 600 yard clearing at 2.7 miles on the Beaver Creek Trail (20). The Audubon Cutoff Route ends here.

ADDITIONAL CONNECTING TRAIL INFORMATION

None.

SKILLS RECOMMENDED

Skiing ability— Advanced. The steep climb through thick trees on untracked snow to the ridge at 0.8 miles and the above timberline conditions require expert technique and equipment. The initial 0.6 miles are intermediate.

Endurance— Very strenuous. The requirements are nearly identical with those for the main Beaver Creek Trail (21).

Routefinding skill— Expert. The requirements are also nearly identical with those for the main Beaver Creek Trail.

SNOW CONDITIONS

Expect excellent snow conditions for the first part where the snow is protected by large trees, medium conditions for the steep bushwhack, and poor to medium conditions for the mixed clearings and trees near timberline.

WIND EXPOSURE

Once the ridge is reached at 0.8 miles there is considerable wind exposure. Scattered clumps of trees provide some protection.

GRADIENT OR STEEPNESS

Generally moderate, but with a short very steep climb from the boulder field up to the ridge at 0.8 miles, and a steep descent from Point 10,894 into Beaver Creek.

AMOUNT OF USE

Nearly unused.

VIEWS

Good views are to be had in all directions from Point 10,984. To the west is the summit of Mt. Audubon. To the north are Ogallala Peak, Elk Tooth, Mt. Copeland, the tips of Chiefs Head and Pagoda, Longs Peak, St. Vrain Mountain, Meadow Mountain, and the saddle on the Rock Creek Saddle Route (8B). To the east, the plains, Green Mountain, Nebelhorn, Sugarloaf, Bear Peak, and South Boulder Peak are discernible. To the south, Niwot Mountain, the slopes above Left Hand Park Reservoir on the Niwot Ridge Traverse Route (19A), Mt. Albion, Kiowa and Arikaree Peaks.

PRIVATE PROPERTY AND OTHER RESTRICTIONS
The route is within the Indian Peaks Wilderness.

*****

TRAIL NO. 21B

FIREBREAK CUTOFF TRAIL

SUMMARY
This trail, when used along with the Four Wheel Drive Trail (10A), serves as an a link between the Coney Flats Trail (10) and the Beaver Creek Trail (21). The north end of the Beaver Creek Trail, difficult to recognize with snow cover as it has only scattered trees, is thereby bypassed. The wide swatch of the firebreak can also serve as an emergency exit from the Beaver Creek Trail to Beaver Reservoir by continuing eastward on the easy terrain past Stapp Lakes. This should be used only in an emergency as the land is private and trespass is prohibited.

CLASSIFICATION Difficult

ALTITUDE (feet)
Starting	9,360
Highest	10,160
Cumulative gain	670
Cumulative loss	170

TIME (hours)
Westbound	1.4
Eastbound	1.0

TRAIL MAP Side 1 (North)

MAP COORDINATES 52/41

PAGE-SIZE MAP No.8

USGS 7 ½' QUADRANGLES
Allens Park (A3)
Ward (B3)

DISTANCE (one way)
1.6 miles

ACCESS
East end. From the Beaver Reservoir North Trailhead (F), ski 1.3 miles west on the Coney Flats Trail (10) to the junction with the Four Wheel Drive Trail (10A). Turn left and ski southwest on it 0.4 miles to a switchback.

West end. From the crossing of the tributary drainage to Beaver Creek at 3.3 miles on the Beaver Creek Trail (21) ski 200 yards downhill (east) to find the 20 yard wide firebreak.

ROUTE DESCRIPTION (westbound)

From the switchback at 0.4 miles on the Four Wheel Drive Trail (10A), continue south on a compass course without climbing. Intersect a rough bulldozed road which is followed southeast about 150 yards before leaving it to descend a short steep hillside to a large meadow at 0.6 miles. Cross to the west side of the clearing and pass two large concrete posts to enter the 20 yard wide firebreak cut through the dense forest on a straight line west.

The firebreak ends at 1.5 miles and 10,040 feet altitude in the bottom of a small tributary to Beaver Creek from the north. It is 200 yards west and 120 feet up to the Beaver Creek Trail. Careful attention to find the untracked trail is required. Once on it, it is generally easy to follow.

ADDITIONAL CONNECTING TRAIL INFORMATION

None.

SKILLS RECOMMENDED

Skiing ability— Intermediate.

Endurance— Strenuous. The route will likely be untracked.

Routefinding skill— Advanced skill is necessary for finding the route from the switchback at the start of the route to where the actual firebreak begins.

SNOW CONDITIONS

Medium.

WIND EXPOSURE

The 20 yard wide straight swath cut through the trees is exposed to the wind.

GRADIENT OR STEEPNESS

The moderate to steep gradient of this straight swath up the lower slopes of Mt. Audubon steepens somewhat with altitude.

AMOUNT OF USE

Nearly unused.

VIEWS

Stapp Lake and Beaver Reservoir are visible to the east, Mt. Audubon to the west.

PRIVATE PROPERTY AND OTHER RESTRICTIONS

Stapp Lake is privately owned and trespass is prohibited.

PAWNEE PASS TRAIL
(LONG LAKE TRAIL)
SUMMARY

A near twin to the Mitchell Lake Trail, access is by the same easy but well used route that offers the comfort of a warming stop at the CMC Brainard Lake cabin. The routes diverge there, with the Pawnee Pass Trail continuing up the South St. Vrain valley, past Long Lake to Isabelle Lake. Here, nestled in the deep valley at the base of Shoshoni Peak, the route ends. Of the two trails, it is shorter, climbs less and stays on an easily followed path through sheltering giant Englemann spruce.

CLASSIFICATION Moderate-difficult

ALTITUDE (feet)

Starting	10,500
Highest	10,800
Cumulative gain	380
Cumulative loss	0

TIME (hours)

Westbound	1.2
Eastbound	0.9

TRAIL MAP Side 1 (North)

MAP COORDINATES 49/36

PAGE-SIZE MAP No.7

USGS 7 ½' QUADRANGLES
Ward (B3)
Monarch Lake (B2)

DISTANCE (one way)
1.9 miles

ACCESS
From the Brainard Lake Trailhead (K), ski the Long Lake Road Spur (14C), 0.4 miles to the end at the summer parking lot. A total skiing distance of 3.0 miles from the Red Rock Trailhead (J).

ROUTE DESCRIPTION (westbound)
From the sign-marked trailhead at the Long Lake summer parking lot, ski west on the level blue diamond-blazed trail 400 yards through dense trees to the east end of Long Lake. Here at a sign-marked junction, the Jean Lunning Trail (23) branches off to cross the dam. Here also is the wilderness boundary and the end of the blue diamond blazes.

Continue up the valley on the distinct trail through the large trees on the north side of first Long Lake and then of the meadow in the valley bottom. A sign marking a junction with the west end of the Jean Lunning Trail (23) is passed at 1.3 miles. Occasional wind swept stretches, where the edge of the meadow is skirted, are encountered above here. The final 150 foot climb to Lake Isabelle and the end of the described trail at 1.9 miles is surmounted by a pair of switchbacks in the trees and a short climb onto an open slope.

Pawnee Pass Trail

ADDITIONAL CONNECTING TRAIL INFORMATION
From the east end of Long Lake, the west end of the Long Lake Cutoff Trail (24), is 100 yards to the south, across the dam.

SKILLS RECOMMENDED
Skiing ability— Intermediate.

Endurance— Strenuous.

Routefinding skill— Beginner.

SNOW CONDITIONS
Excellent except in a few places that are exposed to the wind.

WIND EXPOSURE
The trail generally stays in the protection of large trees but traverses a windy treeless slope as Lake Isabelle is approached.

GRADIENT OR STEEPNESS
The gradient is nearly flat except for a steep 150 feet climb near the end, up the glacial step to Lake Isabelle.

AMOUNT OF USE
Light.

Long Lake outlet

VIEWS
Open slopes near the shoreline of Isabelle Lake offer dramatic views of the fine pyramid of Navajo Peak, Apache Peak, and the sheer east face of Shoshoni Peak.

PRIVATE PROPERTY AND OTHER RESTRICTIONS
The entire trail except the initial 0.2 miles is in the Indian Peaks Wilderness.

* * * * *

TRAIL NO. 23

JEAN LUNNING TRAIL

SUMMARY

This is a near level, little used trail with excellent and usually untracked snow. It parallels the Pawnee Pass Trail for over a mile, then crosses the open valley bottom with an unobstructed view of the east face of Shoshoni Peak to rejoin it. Combined with the Pawnee Pass Trail, it makes a fine intermediate loop trip above Brainard Lake.

CLASSIFICATION Moderate-difficult   **TRAIL MAP** Side 1 (North)

ALTITUDE (feet)

Starting 10,520

Highest 10,650

Cumulative gain 130

Cumulative loss 40

TIME (hours)

Westbound 0.9

Eastbound 0.9

MAP COORDINATES 49/35

PAGE-SIZE MAP No.7

USGS 7 ½' QUADRANGLES
Ward (B3)
Monarch Lake (B2)

DISTANCE (one way)
1.5 miles

ACCESS (east end)

From the Brainard Lake Trailhead (K), ski west on the Long Lake Road Spur (14C) 0.4 miles to its end at the summer parking lot. From here, ski west on the Pawnee Pass Trail (22), 0.4 miles to the sign-marked junction at the north end of the dam on the eastern shore of Long Lake. A total skiing distance from Red Rock Trailhead (J), of 3.4 miles.

An alternate access route from Brainard Lake is the Long Lake Cutoff Trail (24) which ends at the south end of the dam.

ROUTE DESCRIPTION (westbound)

Cross to the south side of the dam and the sign-marked junction with the Long Lake Cutoff Trail (24). Ski southwest into the large trees to find the trail which parallels the lake shore at a distance of about 100 yards. The unblazed trail can be difficult to follow exactly if untracked. Watch for the footbridge railings at gully crossings.

Ski up valley in the trees about a half mile past the end of the lake before crossing the open valley bottom to a footbridge on the creek at 1.4 miles. Continue north to the junction in the trees on the north side of the valley with the Pawnee Pass Trail (22) at 1.5 miles.

ADDITIONAL CONNECTING TRAIL INFORMATION

This trail branches from the Pawnee Pass Trail (22) at mile 0.4 and rejoins it at mile 1.3.

Isabelle Glacier from Long Lake

SKILLS RECOMMENDED

Skiing ability— Novice.
Endurance— Moderate.
Routefinding skill— Intermediate.

SNOW CONDITIONS

Excellent, probably untracked. The area near the dam may be poor due to wind.

WIND EXPOSURE

Although very exposed to wind at the dam, and exposed to a lesser degree at the meadow crossing at the upper end, the trail is in trees and well protected for most of the route.

GRADIENT OR STEEPNESS

Nearly flat.

AMOUNT OF USE

Very light.

VIEWS

Apache and Shoshoni Peaks are visible at the head of the valley from the footbridge crossed at 1.4 miles.

PRIVATE PROPERTY AND OTHER RESTRICTIONS

The entire trail is within the Indian Peaks Wilderness.

* * * * *

TRAIL NO. 24

LONG LAKE CUTOFF TRAIL

SUMMARY

A shortcut from Brainard Lake to Long Lake and the Jean Lunning and Pawnee Pass Trails, it generally offers excellent snow, frequently untracked, for the first half of its course. Passage into the second half, an open area more subject to wind, is marked by a roadcut where one usually has to decide between a rocky roadbed or the dense thicket. In addition to being shorter, it is more challenging than the bland alternative Long Lake Road Spur.

CLASSIFICATION Moderate

ALTITUDE (feet)

Starting	10,360
Highest	10,530
Cumulative gain	170
Cumulative loss	30

TRAIL MAP Side 1 (North)

MAP COORDINATES 50/36

PAGE-SIZE MAP No.7

USGS 7 ½' QUADRANGLES
Ward (B)

TIME (hours)

Westbound . . . . 0.4   **DISTANCE** (one way)

Eastbound . . . . 0.3   0.5 miles

ACCESS (east end)

At the Brainard Lake Trailhead (K) go to the southwest corner of the Brainard Lake Loop Road (14A). The unmarked trail begins at the top of a road cut opposite an outdoor toilet at the Niwot Mountain Picnic area. A total skiing distance from Red Rock Trailhead (J), of 2.4 miles.

ROUTE DESCRIPTION
(westbound)

From a signpost *FS Trail 907.2* at the south end of the above road cut, ski 30 yards to the top of the road cut and a short log rail fence. Ski west on the unblazed trail, through moderately spaced large trees, as it climbs 120 feet through four switchbacks, at intervals of 60 to 120 yards. After passing through a dense thicket of stunted trees to avoid the rocky course of a jeep road, continue west through mixed trees and clearings, without climbing appreciably. The sign-marked junction with the Jean Lunning Trail (23) is in an open meadow at the east end of Long Lake at 0.5 miles.

Shoshoni Peak from Jean Lunning Trail

To further clarify the beginning of the trail, the initial heading is 292°. Do not confuse with another faint trail more to the southwest.

ADDITIONAL CONNECTING TRAIL INFORMATION

The Pawnee Pass Trail (22) is across the dam, 100 yards north of the western end of the trail.

SKILLS RECOMMENDED

Skiing ability— Beginner.

Endurance— Moderate.

Routefinding skill— Intermediate.

SNOW CONDITIONS
Excellent in the protection of large trees for the eastern half, but poor in the wind swept open areas to the west.

WIND EXPOSURE
Protected by large trees in the east, more exposed in the west where the force of the wind is broken only by scattered clumps of trees.

GRADIENT OR STEEPNESS
Moderate in the east, slight to moderate in the west.

AMOUNT OF USE
Very light.

VIEWS
Apache and Shoshoni Peaks are visible from the open areas near the western end.

PRIVATE PROPERTY AND OTHER RESTRICTIONS
None.

* * * * *

TRAIL NO. 25

RAINBOW LAKES ROAD

SUMMARY
Memories of the bustle of summer activity contrast with the quiet serenity of snowdrifts on picnic tables at the Rainbow Lakes Campground. It is reached by skiing the four miles of unplowed road from the Mountain Research Station West Trailhead that may at places be blown clear. It may serve as a destination itself or be the starting point for the more challenging Glacier Rim Route.

CLASSIFICATION Moderate

ALTITUDE (feet)
Starting 9,290
Highest 9,960
Cumulative gain 740
Cumulative loss 70

TIME (hours)
Westbound 2.0
Eastbound 1.5

TRAIL MAP Side 2 (South)

MAP COORDINATES 54/29

PAGE-SIZE MAP No.11

USGS 7 ½' QUADRANGLES
Ward (B3)

DISTANCE (one way)
4.0 miles

ACCESS
At the Mountain Research Station West Trailhead (M).

117

ROUTE DESCRIPTION (westbound)

From the roadside parking at the Mountain Research Station West Trailhead (M), the obvious wide road follows a curving, generally climbing course to the southwest. Pass a log arch at 1.0 miles, the locked gate to the City of Boulder watershed at 2.5 miles, and continue past the picnic tables, outhouses, and signs of the Rainbow Lakes Campground to the summer trailhead signs for the Glacier Rim and Rainbow Lakes trails at 4.0 miles.

ADDITIONAL CONNECTING TRAIL INFORMATION

The Caribou Creek Trail (27) branches off to the left (south) at 3.3 miles onto a jeep road marked with a sign *Forest Service Road 505.*

The Glacier Rim Trail (26) continues to the north from a summer trailhead sign at the end of this trail.

The Rainbow Lakes Bowl Route (26A) continues west from the end of this trail.

SKILLS RECOMMENDED

Skiing ability— Only novice skills are required to ski this wide road of slight gradient.

Endurance— Moderate to ski the entire distance.

Routefinding skill— Novice skills are adequate to follow this wide road. It can readily be followed in darkness or reduced visibility from blowing snow.

SNOW CONDITIONS

Very poor unless skied after a snowfall. Road corners exposed to sun and wind can be rocky.

WIND EXPOSURE

Exposure to wind is significant, especially for westward travel.

GRADIENT OR STEEPNESS

The gradient ranges from nearly flat to slight. Some sections of only slight gradient however, are long, and with a hard packed surface can make for a rapid return.

AMOUNT OF USE

Very light.

VIEWS

At 2.2 miles the road rounds a small knoll where views of the east shoulder of Arapaho Ridge, Arapaho Peak, Mt. Albion, Kiowa Peak, and Niwot Ridge are revealed.

PRIVATE PROPERTY AND OTHER RESTRICTIONS

The prohibited area of the City of Boulder watershed is well marked at a locked gate at 2.5 miles.

TRAIL NO. 26

GLACIER RIM TRAIL

SUMMARY

A seldom traveled forest trail from Rainbow Lakes Campground, it leads to a timberline overlook of the headwaters of North Boulder Creek, with views up valley to North Arapaho Peak and Arapaho Glacier. The price of admission is the long ski-in on the Rainbow Lakes Road. An attractive alternative return to the campground descends the open slopes of the Rainbow Lakes Bowl Route.

CLASSIFICATION Difficult

ALTITUDE (feet)
Starting 9,960
Highest 11,030
Cumulative gain 1,070
Cumulative loss 0

TIME (hours)
Westbound, up 1.8
Eastbound, down 1.0

TRAIL MAP Side 2 (South)

MAP COORDINATES 51/30

PAGE-SIZE MAP No.10

USGS 7 ½' QUADRANGLES
Ward (B3)

DISTANCE (one way)
1.9 miles

ACCESS

From Mountain Research Station West Trailhead (M), ski the Rainbow Lakes Road (25) 4.0 miles to the end at Rainbow Lakes Campground.

ROUTE DESCRIPTION (westbound, up)

From the sign-marked trailhead at the west end of the Rainbow Lakes Campground area, the unblazed but easy to follow trail climbs to the north. It soon encounters and follows the City of Boulder watershed barbed wire fence and signs to 10,530 feet, where it switchbacks to the left at a larger *No Trespassing* sign. The trail then stays on the south side of the distinct ridge. A group of four switchbacks at 10,660 and a pair at 10,860 are not shown on the USGS topographic map. The last section of trail becomes difficult to follow and is lost as it emerges from the trees near the ridge crest at 11,000 feet.

ADDITIONAL CONNECTING TRAIL INFORMATION

The west or upper end of the trail connects with the Rainbow Lakes Bowl Route (26A), an alternate return route to Rainbow Lakes Campground.

SKILLS RECOMMENDED

Skiing ability— Intermediate, a return by this route is less difficult than the optional return by the Rainbow Lakes Bowl Route.

Endurance— Very strenuous, this trail has to be combined with the long access road.

Routefinding skill— Intermediate, routefinding on this generally untracked trail becomes increasingly difficult with distance and altitude.

SNOW CONDITIONS
Excellent

WIND EXPOSURE
The trail is well protected until it emerges from the trees at a timberline overlook near the end of the trail.

GRADIENT OR STEEPNESS
Moderate, the last 500 vertical feet are steepest.

AMOUNT OF USE
Nearly unused.

VIEWS
There is little to see until the trail emerges from the trees near the end. Mt. Albion, Arikaree and Kiowa Peaks come into view across the southern fork of North Boulder Creek. The lakes of the City of Boulder's forbidden watershed: Triple Lakes, Goose, Island, and Silver Lakes are immediately below. North Arapaho Peak and Arapaho Glacier make a splendid view at the head of the valley to the west.

The permanent snowfield on the eastern end of Arapaho Ridge, so prominent as to be readily visible from Boulder, is visible to the southwest and the pediment surface of the eastern slope of the Front Range is to the south and east.

PRIVATE PROPERTY AND OTHER RESTRICTIONS
Trespass into the City of Boulder watershed immediately to the north is prohibited.

* * * * *

TRAIL NO. 26A

RAINBOW LAKES BOWL ROUTE

SUMMARY
An alternate return route from the Glacier Rim Trail, this off trail route descends open slopes 650 feet to more gentle wooded terrain. Bushwhacking down the drainage then provides a return to the Rainbow Lakes Campground.

CLASSIFICATION Difficult   **TRAIL MAP** Side 2 (South)

ALTITUDE (feet)		MAP COORDINATES 50/29

ALTITUDE (feet)
Starting 11,030
Highest 11,030
Cumulative gain 0
Cumulative loss 1,070

TIME (hours)
Eastbound, down 1.7
Westbound, up 2.0

MAP COORDINATES 50/29

PAGE-SIZE MAP No.10

USGS 7 ½' QUADRANGLES
Ward (B3)

DISTANCE (one way)
1.9 miles

ACCESS
Access the upper end by skiing from the Mountain Research Station Trailhead (M) 4.0 miles on the Rainbow Lakes Road (25), to its end at Rainbow Lakes Campground. From here, ski 1.9 miles on the Glacier Rim Trail (26), 1.9 miles to its end. A total distance of 5.9 miles.

Access to the lower end is at the Rainbow Lakes Campground.

ROUTE DESCRIPTION (eastbound, down)
From the high point of the Glacier Rim Trail, descend south to the bowl, and then east southeast down the treeless slopes to the flat clearing. Head south through dense forest a quarter mile down the drainage to intercept the summer trail, or continue down the drainage as it turns east and bushwhack to Rainbow Lakes Campground.

ADDITIONAL CONNECTING TRAIL INFORMATION
None.

SKILLS RECOMMENDED
Skiing ability— Expert, hard windslab can be encountered in the bowl.

Endurance— Very strenuous when combined with the access trails.

Routefinding skill— Advanced skills are required as most of the route follows no recognizable feature other than drainage.

SNOW CONDITIONS
Good in the shelter of the trees, medium on the open slopes of the bowl where it can be hard wind slab, and also only medium where exposed along the Rainbow Lakes.

WIND EXPOSURE
Very exposed on the descent of the open bowl and again along the lakes.

GRADIENT OR STEEPNESS
The gradient of the bowl is steep, 650 feet in a half mile.

Nearly unused.

VIEWS
Those at the high end are the same as listed for the Glacier Rim Trail (26).

PRIVATE PROPERTY AND OTHER RESTRICTIONS
None.

* * * * *

TRAIL NO. 27

CARIBOU CREEK TRAIL

SUMMARY
Despite its high altitude, this remote trail doesn't have the tree cover to give adequate protection for predictably good snow. This, along with uncertainty of the winter maintenance of the access road to Caribou trailhead results in limited use.

CLASSIFICATION Moderate

ALTITUDE (feet)
Starting 9,820
Highest 9,990
Cumulative gain 280
Cumulative loss 110

TIME (hours)
Southbound 1.1
Northbound 1.1

TRAIL MAP Side 2 (South)

MAP COORDINATES 51/27

PAGE-SIZE MAP No.11

USGS 7 ½' QUADRANGLES
Ward (B3)
Nederland (C3)

DISTANCE (one way)
2.3 miles

ACCESS
North end. From the Mountain Research Station West Trailhead (M), ski the Rainbow Lakes Road (25) 3.3 miles to where a jeep road, marked with a sign *Forest Service Road 505*, branches to the left.

South end. At Caribou Trailhead (N).

ROUTE DESCRIPTION (southbound)
Ski south on Forest Service Road 505 as it descends toward Caribou Creek. At 130 yards, take the less prominent fork to the right and descend to the creek on an easy route.

Ski up the broad gradual valley and cross to the east side at Pomeroy Mountain, then follow a jeep road which generally stays in the shelter of trees and is better protected than the open brushy bottom of Caribou Park. The road climbs on a gentle grade past a winter closure gate, and in 170 yards more to the saddle and the Caribou Trailhead (N) at 2.3 miles.

ADDITIONAL CONNECTING TRAIL INFORMATION
The left fork at 130 yards continues 700 yards more to dead end at an overlook of Caribou Creek.

The south end joins the Caribou Flat Route (28) at the Caribou Trailhead (N).

SKILLS RECOMMENDED
Skiing ability— Novice.

Endurance— Easy.

Routefinding skill— Beginner.

SNOW CONDITIONS
Very poor, the southern part, where the jeep road is more sheltered by trees, is better.

WIND EXPOSURE
Moderate, sheltering trees are sparse.

GRADIENT OR STEEPNESS
Nearly flat.

AMOUNT OF USE
Nearly unused.

VIEWS
The hulking mass of the Arapaho Peaks dominates the skyline to the northwest.

PRIVATE PROPERTY AND OTHER RESTRICTIONS
Private mining operations are in the area. The road to the Caribou Trailhead may not always be plowed.

* * * * *

TRAIL NO. 28

CARIBOU FLAT ROUTE

SUMMARY
Along with the Caribou Creek Trail, Rainbow Lakes Road, and Sourdough South Trail, it is a link through hostile ski terrain tying the popular ski trails in the south, centered around Eldora town and ski area, to the even more popular trails of the Brainard area. From the Fourth of July Road in the valley bottom of the North Fork

of Middle Boulder Creek, this route climbs a steep grueling thousand feet through dense small trees onto Caribou Flat. The remainder of the route follows a jeep road over easy terrain but generally poor snow, to a trailhead at the ghost town of Caribou.

CLASSIFICATION Difficult	**TRAIL MAP** Side 2 (South)

ALTITUDE (feet)

Starting	9,320
Highest	10,330
Cumulative gain	1,010
Cumulative loss	330

MAP COORDINATES 50/24

PAGE-SIZE MAP No.13

USGS 7 ½' QUADRANGLES
Nederland (C3)

TIME (hours)

Northbound	2.2
Southbound	1.7

DISTANCE (one way)
2.6 miles

ACCESS
South end. From the Eldora Trailhead (P), ski west on the King Lake Trail (29) 0.8 miles, then 0.9 miles north up the Fourth of July Road (32) to an unmarked turn off at 9,370 feet altitude. The road makes a slight turn to the left here at the crest of a long moderate climb through an aspen bordered clearing. Total distance 1.7 miles.

North end. At Caribou Trailhead (N).

ROUTE DESCRIPTION (northbound)
Climb moderately steeply from the Fourth of July Road east through large, well separated trees to 9,500 feet. Switchback right and climb steeply through dense small trees, passing below a boulder field, and up a natural ramp to the ridge at 0.7 miles and 10,040 feet. Climb a steep treeless section up the ridge and continue through scattered trees to the summit of Point 10,335 at 1.1 miles.

Descend slightly through low trees to the jeep road and follow it north across the nearly level Caribou Flat where signs warning of the dangers of abandoned mines in the area help mark the path of the road. The road descends northeast across the east side of Caribou Hill, past an abandoned cabin to the saddle and the Caribou Trailhead (N) at 2.6 miles.

ADDITIONAL CONNECTING TRAIL INFORMATION
None
SKILLS RECOMMENDED
Skiing ability— Advanced level skill is recommended for the ridge south of Point 10,335.

Endurance— Very strenuous because of the steep, thousand foot ascent or descent through dense small trees on an untracked route.

Routefinding skill— Advanced. Extra attention is necessary on the featureless terrain of Caribou Flat if visibility is limited by weather.

SNOW CONDITIONS

Poor overall. A variety of snow conditions will probably be encountered, with deep unconsolidated snow in the small dense trees on the climb out of the valley, wind slab at the ridge, and thin snow on Caribou Flat due to the lack of tree cover.

WIND EXPOSURE

A major portion of the route, on Caribou Flat and on the ridge south of Point 10,335, lacks adequate tree cover to provide wind protection.

GRADIENT OR STEEPNESS

The southern part of the route, on the climb out of the valley and up the ridge up to Point 10,334 is very steep. Thereafter, as implied, Caribou Flat is nearly flat.

AMOUNT OF USE

Nearly unused.

VIEWS

From the ridge south from Point 10,335, a panorama of peaks and valleys can be seen in all directions. To the north, from left to right, are Arapaho Peak, Klondike Mountain, Bald Mountain, Arapaho Ridge with the snow bowl above Rainbow Lakes, Caribou Hill, and the saddle at Caribou townsite at the north end of this trail.

To the south, James Peak rises above Bryan Mountain and the Eldora ski runs. The North Gully of Bryan Mountain Route (34), the wind swept slopes of Bryan Mountain, and the mine cabin above Lost Lake are visible. Beyond are Mt. Thorodin, the north facing slopes of the bowl above the Jenny Lind Gulch Trail (38), and Mt. Evans.

To the west is Guinn Mountain, Rollins Pass, the trestles of the Moffat Railroad high above the valley of the South Fork of Middle Boulder Creek, and the King Lake Trail (29) in the valley bottom.

PRIVATE PROPERTY AND OTHER RESTRICTIONS

Stay on the jeep road on Caribou Flat to avoid mine workings.

* * * * *

TRAIL NO. 29

KING LAKE TRAIL

SUMMARY

Starting at the town of Eldora, the trail follows the valley bottom of the South Fork of Boulder Creek upstream to its head beneath Rollins Pass at the continental divide.

The ski trail is initially a well used unplowed road, but as trails branch off to go up tributary valleys, it changes to a trail and eventually an untracked route as it becomes impossible to recognize the summer trail.

CLASSIFICATION Difficult

ALTITUDE (feet)
Starting 8,810
Highest 10,900
Cumulative gain 2,090
Cumulative loss 0

TIME (hours)
Westbound 3.8
Eastbound 2.3

TRAIL MAP Side 2 (South)

MAP COORDINATES 45/22

PAGE-SIZE MAP No.13

USGS 7 ½' QUADRANGLES
Nederland (C3)
East Portal (C2)

DISTANCE (one way)
6.1 miles

ACCESS
At Eldora Trailhead (P).

ROUTE DESCRIPTION (westbound)
Ski the unplowed road west from Eldora past the turn off of the Fourth of July Road (32) at 0.8 miles. Follow the left fork with the *Hessie Road* sign, passing cabins at Hessie at 1.1 miles. Continue to the summer trailhead at a crossing of the North Fork of Middle Boulder Creek at 1.3 miles.

After switchbacking to climb a steep treeless slope, the road levels out before reaching a vehicle bridge over the South Fork of Middle Boulder Creek at 2.3 miles. A sign here shows the Devils Thumb Trail to branch off to the right onto a steep narrow summer hiking trail. The road is the better choice even if Devils Thumb Trail is one's goal. A junction with it is reached later at 2.8 miles.

From the bridge, continue up the wind scoured road to the crest of a moderate climb and a sign-marked junction with the Lost Lake Trail (33) at 2.6 miles. Proceed another 400 yards along the flat valley bottom to a sign-marked junction with the Devils Thumb Trail (30) at 2.8 miles, in a level open area at the confluence of Jasper Creek, on the right, and South Fork of Middle Boulder Creek, straight ahead.

The distinct trail climbs through trees up a moderate slope, past the last two blue diamond blazes and enters the Indian Peaks Wilderness. The now unblazed trail can be followed only for about a mile, up the north side of the valley of the South Fork, until it becomes too indistinct to follow.

The route goes well either on the north side or in the creek bed. As you pass below the railroad trestles the valley floor widens and it is possible to ski either side. End the tour at a clearing at 10,900 feet and 6.1 miles. The steep slopes at the end of the valley present a possible avalanche hazard for travel beyond here.

Moffat Road trestles above King Lake Trail

ADDITIONAL CONNECTING TRAIL INFORMATION
An unmarked junction with the Lower Gully Bryan Mountain Route (34A) is at 1.5 miles.

SKILLS RECOMMENDED
Skiing ability— Beginner.

Endurance— Very strenuous.

Routefinding skill— Intermediate.

SNOW CONDITIONS
Excellent at the upper end and overall, but poor at the beginning.

WIND EXPOSURE
Generally well protected by trees, there are a few exposed areas at the east end.

GRADIENT OR STEEPNESS
The gradient is nearly flat for 1.5 miles. The remainder is slight to moderate.

AMOUNT OF USE
Very light, although this grades from heavy at the east end to nearly unused at the upper end.

VIEWS
Devils Thumb on the continental divide may be seen up the valley of Jasper Creek from near the junction with the Lost Lake Trail at 2.6 miles.

The railroad trestles, high above on the south valley wall, are visible from the upper part of the trail, as is the corniced ridge on the divide at the head of the valley.

PRIVATE PROPERTY AND OTHER RESTRICTIONS
Posted private property is along the roadway at the lower end and cabins and property at Hessie are privately owned. The trail beyond the junction with the Devils Thumb Trail at 2.8 miles is within the Indian Peaks Wilderness.

* * * * *

TRAIL NO. 30

DEVILS THUMB ROUTE

SUMMARY
One of the most spectacular and exhilarating powder ski runs described in this book, it follows a tributary valley to Middle Boulder Creek above Eldora. Starting as a jeep road in the wide gentle valley, it becomes a trail which is soon unrecognizable and one must pick a route through widely spaced trees to climb to the bench of Jasper Lake and then over open rolling terrain to Devils Thumb Lake.

CLASSIFICATION Very difficult

ALTITUDE (feet)
Starting 9,620
Highest 11,280
Cumulative gain 1,660
Cumulative loss 0

TIME (hours)
Westbound 3.6
Eastbound 2.0

TRAIL MAP Side 2 (South)

MAP COORDINATES 45/25

PAGE-SIZE MAP No.13

USGS 7 ½' QUADRANGLES
Nederland (C3)
East Portal (C2)

DISTANCE (one way)
4.2 miles

ACCESS
From the Eldora Trailhead (P), ski west on the King Lake Trail (29), 2.8 miles to a sign-marked junction.

ROUTE DESCRIPTION
(westbound)
From the sign-marked junction on the King Lake Trail (29), follow the jeep road along the west side of the broad flat valley past a wilderness boundary sign in 300 yards and a sign-marked junction with the Woodland Lake Trail (31) at 0.9 miles.

Beyond this junction, the jeep road crosses the creek and as the trees thin out, climbs more steeply along the north valley wall and onto the crest of a small medial ridge in the valley bottom. It then descends slightly to the right and becomes unidentifiable. Climb to the west along the north side of the valley, switchbacking where necessary to gain the bench containing Jasper Lake at 10,814 feet and 3.1 miles. Continue west without climbing significantly to the open slopes east of Devils Thumb Lake, then climb 500 feet past the lake to the top of the 11,290 foot knoll, 200 yards south of the lake and the end of the tour at 4.2 miles.

ADDITIONAL CONNECTING TRAIL INFORMATION

The upper end of the route joins the Jasper Creek Route (30A), an alternate descent route.

Toward Devils Thumb

SKILLS RECOMMENDED

Skiing ability— Expert.

Endurance— Very strenuous.

Routefinding skill— Advanced.

SNOW CONDITIONS

Excellent.

WIND EXPOSURE

Only moderate, much of the route is not protected by dense forest, but the snow pack does not exhibit much effect from the wind.

GRADIENT OR STEEPNESS

Moderate with locally steep sections.

AMOUNT OF USE

Very light.

VIEWS

The knoll at the end of the tour gives unobstructed views of the corniced ridge of the continental divide and the rock spire of Devils Thumb, both a half mile distant.

PRIVATE PROPERTY AND OTHER RESTRICTIONS
Almost all of the route is within the Indian Peaks Wilderness.

* * * * *

TRAIL NO. 30A

JASPER CREEK ROUTE

SUMMARY
An alternate to the upper part of the Devils Thumb Route, the moderate treeless slopes at the upper end provide superb telemarking for the descent to the valley bottom. Here a gentle route through tall trees can be followed a mile before contouring out to rejoin the Devils Thumb Route.

CLASSIFICATION Very difficult

ALTITUDE (feet)
Starting 11,280
Highest 11,280
Cumulative gain 0
Cumulative loss 990

TIME (hours)
Eastbound, down 0.8
Westbound, up 1.7

TRAIL MAP Side 2 (South)

MAP COORDINATES 45/24

PAGE-SIZE MAP No.12

USGS 7 ½' QUADRANGLES
East Portal (C2)

DISTANCE (one way)
2.2 miles

ACCESS
West end. From the Eldora Trailhead (P), ski west on the King Lake Trail (29), 2.8 miles to the Devils Thumb Route (30). Ski 4.2 miles to its end on the 11,290 foot knoll south of Devils Thumb. A total distance of 7.0 miles from the Eldora Trailhead.

East end. At mile 2.8 on the Devils Thumb Route. This is on a small medial ridge at 10,300 feet and 4.9 miles from Eldora Trailhead.

ROUTE DESCRIPTION
(eastbound, down)
Descend the steep treeless slopes south from the 11,290 foot knoll south of Devils Thumb Lake, into the tall trees of the Jasper Creek drainage. Continue east along the bottom as the slope lessens and contour out to the north at 10,300 feet, to join the Devils Thumb Route (30). Avoid the steep section lower on the creek.

ADDITIONAL CONNECTING TRAIL INFORMATION
Both ends of this alternate route connect with the Devils Thumb Route (30).

SKILLS RECOMMENDED
Skiing ability— Expert.

Endurance— Very strenuous.

Routefinding skill— Advanced.

SNOW CONDITIONS
Excellent.

WIND EXPOSURE
Moderate, the west end is unprotected by trees but the snow shows little effect from the wind.

GRADIENT OR STEEPNESS
Steep at the west end, nearly flat in the valley bottom.

AMOUNT OF USE
Very light.

VIEWS

Jasper Creek

The best views of the corniced ridge of the continental divide and Devils Thumb are from the knoll at the west end. These are identical with those described for the Devils Thumb Route.

PRIVATE PROPERTY AND OTHER RESTRICTIONS
The entire route is within the Indian Peaks Wilderness.

* * * * *

TRAIL NO. 31

WOODLAND LAKE TRAIL

SUMMARY
A steep climb up a tributary valley to Middle Boulder Creek above Eldora leads to a timberline lake set in a glacial cirque. Much of the way is not on a recognizable trail. The deep powder snow among the large trees on the steep lower section gives way to wind sculptured snow and stunted trees as the lake is approached.

CLASSIFICATION Very difficult   **TRAIL MAP** Side 2 (South)

ALTITUDE (feet)

Starting	9,710
Highest	10,980
Cumulative gain	1,270
Cumulative loss	0

TIME (hours)

Westbound	1.7
Eastbound	1.2

MAP COORDINATES 45/23

PAGE-SIZE MAP No.12

USGS 7 ½' QUADRANGLES
East Portal (C2)

DISTANCE (one way)
1.9 miles

Woodland Lake

ACCESS

From the Eldora Trailhead (P), ski west on the King Lake Trail (29), 2.8 miles to the Devils Thumb Route (30), and 0.9 miles up it to a sign-marked junction. A total distance of 3.7 miles.

ROUTE DESCRIPTION (westbound)

From the sign-marked junction on the Devils Thumb Route (30), ski west up a jeep road as it climbs high on the south side of Woodland Creek. At 0.4 miles the road crosses the creek where two old cabins are visible 200 yards ahead. Beyond here, the road is no longer identifiable. Climb about 300 feet up the steep open slopes beyond the cabins and move left into the trees and a minor gully, where the opportunity is offered. As the slope lessens, move left toward the streambed in the relatively widely spaced groups of trees and open wind swept areas, until the lake is reached at 1.9 miles.

ADDITIONAL CONNECTING TRAIL INFORMATION

The route may be continued beyond Woodland Lake on the Woodland Mountain Overlook Route (31A).

SKILLS RECOMMENDED

Skiing ability— Expert.

Endurance— Strenuous.

Routefinding skill— Advanced.

SNOW CONDITIONS

Good overall. Excellent in the trees but only medium on the open slope encountered when entering the drainage. Medium in the wind swept area near the lake.

WIND EXPOSURE

Exposed to high winds east of the lake.

GRADIENT OR STEEPNESS

Moderate to steep overall with a very steep section above the cabins at 0.5 miles.

AMOUNT OF USE

Nearly unused.

VIEWS

The spectacular glacial cirque setting of Woodland Lake and Skyscraper Reservoir is visible ahead through the stunted trees as the lake is approached.

PRIVATE PROPERTY AND OTHER RESTRICTIONS

The entire trail is within the Indian Peaks Wilderness.

* * * * *

TRAIL NO. 31A

WOODLAND MOUNTAIN OVERLOOK ROUTE

SUMMARY

A short bushwhacking climb through tall trees south from Woodland Lake leads to the ridgetop. Here, a unique view of Rollins Pass and the railroad trestles high above the valley of the South Fork of Middle Boulder Creek is revealed.

CLASSIFICATION Very difficult   **TRAIL MAP** Side 2 (South)

ALTITUDE (feet)
Starting 10,980
Highest 11,260
Cumulative gain 280
Cumulative loss 0

TIME (hours)
Up, southwestbound 0.5
Down, northeastbound 0.3

MAP COORDINATES 43/23

PAGE-SIZE MAP No.12

USGS 7 ½' QUADRANGLES
East Portal (C2)

DISTANCE (one way)
0.3 miles

Moffat Road trestles from Woodland Mountain

ACCESS
From the Eldora Trailhead (P), ski west on the King Lake Trail (29) 2.8 miles to the Devils Thumb Route (30), 0.9 miles on it to the Woodland Lake Trail (31), and 1.9 miles up it to its end at Woodland Lake. A total distance of 5.6 miles.

ROUTE DESCRIPTION (up, southwestbound)
Pick a route south from the lake, 300 feet up through deep untracked powder snow between the widely spaced tall trees, to the ridgetop at 0.3 miles.

ADDITIONAL CONNECTING TRAIL INFORMATION
A descent south from the ridgetop into the South Fork of Middle Boulder Creek to the King Lake Trail (29) should not be attempted if unstable snow conditions exist.

Skiing ability—Expert.

Endurance—Strenuous.

Routefinding skill—Advanced.

SNOW CONDITIONS
Excellent.

WIND EXPOSURE
Very little.

GRADIENT OR STEEPNESS
Very steep.

AMOUNT OF USE
Nearly unused.

VIEWS
The view across the South Fork of Middle Boulder Creek to the railroad trestles and Rollins Pass is spectacular.

PRIVATE PROPERTY AND OTHER RESTRICTIONS
The entire route is within the Indian Peaks Wilderness.

* * * * *

TRAIL NO. 32

FOURTH OF JULY ROAD

SUMMARY
A long but easy tour follows the road up the straight glacial trough of the valley of the North Fork of Middle Boulder Creek above Eldora. The road ends at the City of Boulder's Buckingham Campground at the base of Arapaho Pass.

CLASSIFICATION Moderate-difficult

ALTITUDE (feet)

Starting	8,990
Highest	10,160
Cumulative gain	1,170
Cumulative loss	0

TIME (hours)

Northbound	2.5
Southbound	1.7

TRAIL MAP Side 2 (South)

MAP COORDINATES 47/26

PAGE-SIZE MAP No.13

USGS 7 ½' QUADRANGLES
East Portal (C2)
Nederland (C3)
Monarch Lake (B2)

DISTANCE (one way)
4.3 miles

ACCESS

From the Eldora Trailhead (P), ski west on the King Lake Trail (29), 0.5 miles to a sign-marked junction.

ROUTE DESCRIPTION (northbound)

The unplowed passenger car road is followed up the bottom of the valley to Buckingham Campground. It continues 200 yards more in the shelter of trees to a gate and a sign marking the boundary of private property at 4.2 miles.

ADDITIONAL CONNECTING TRAIL INFORMATION

A junction with the unmarked Caribou Flat Route (28) is at 0.9 miles, where the road makes a slight turn to the left at the crest of a long easy climb through an aspen bordered clearing.

SKILLS RECOMMENDED

Skiing ability— Beginner.

Endurance— Moderate.

Routefinding skill— Novice.

SNOW CONDITIONS

Medium overall. Poor and frequently icy for the first 0.7 mile on a south facing slope which has the steepest gradient of the trip. Snow conditions improve to medium to good thereafter, but are affected by wind near the end.

WIND EXPOSURE

The road becomes increasingly exposed to the wind in the final mile.

GRADIENT OR STEEPNESS

Moderate for the first 0.7 mile, slight thereafter.

AMOUNT OF USE

Moderate at the bottom, decreasing to light at the top.

VIEWS

Arapaho Pass and South Arapaho Peak tower ahead for most of the trip. Mt. Neva and unnamed glaciated peaks are visible to the left from near Buckingham Campground.

PRIVATE PROPERTY AND OTHER RESTRICTIONS

Numerous private cabins crowd the roadway for most of its length. Passage up the bottom of the valley beyond Buckingham Campground is blocked by private land.

TRAIL NO. 33

LOST LAKE TRAIL

SUMMARY

A short, easy climb from the King Lake Trail west of Eldora leads to this secluded lake nestled on a bench on the steep north slopes of Bryan Mountain.

CLASSIFICATION Moderate

ALTITUDE (feet)

Starting 9,620
Highest 9,780
Cumulative gain 160
Cumulative loss 0

TIME (hours)

Up, southbound 0.5
Down, northbound 0.3

TRAIL MAP Side 2 (South)

MAP COORDINATES 47/22

PAGE-SIZE MAP No.13

USGS 7 ½' QUADRANGLES
Nederland (C3)

DISTANCE (one way)
0.5 miles

Mining cabin above Lost Lake

ACCESS

From the Eldora Trailhead (P), ski west on the King Lake Trail (29), 2.6 miles to a sign-marked junction at the top of a moderate climb.

ROUTE DESCRIPTION (up, southbound)

From the sign-marked junction with the King Lake Trail (29), follow the easy, well defined but unblazed trail, as it climbs through trees up the drainage below Lost Lake. Take the right fork where the left can be seen to cross the drainage on a footbridge with a handrail. The trail becomes difficult to recognize as it curves to the west through a brushy meadow but reappears in the trees at the west end. Here it curves back east and climbs to Lost Lake at 0.5 miles.

ADDITIONAL CONNECTING TRAIL INFORMATION

The North Gully of Bryan Mountain Route (34), and Lower Gully Route (34A) both connect with the end of the trail at Lost Lake.

SKILLS RECOMMENDED

Skiing ability— Beginner.

Endurance— Easy.

Routefinding skill— Beginner.

SNOW CONDITIONS

Medium.

WIND EXPOSURE

Exposed to wind at a brushy meadow about midway along the trail.

GRADIENT OR STEEPNESS

Slight.

AMOUNT OF USE

Very light.

VIEWS

An abandoned mine building is visible above the lake on the precipitous scree slopes of Bryan Mountain. Chittenden Mountain is north, across Middle Boulder Creek.

PRIVATE PROPERTY AND OTHER RESTRICTIONS

None.

* * * * *

TRAIL NO. 34

NORTH GULLY BRYAN MOUNTAIN ROUTE

SUMMARY

The trails of Middle Boulder Creek west of Eldora are joined with those above Eldora Ski Area and Jenny Creek by this connecting route. It ascends a very steep gully and then follows the natural gas pipeline swath along the ridge top to Arestua Hut.

CLASSIFICATION Very difficult   **TRAIL MAP** Side 2 (South)

ALTITUDE (feet)

Starting 9,780

Highest 10,960

Cumulative gain 1,240

Cumulative loss 60

TIME (hours)

Up, southwestbound 2.0

Down, northeastbound 1.4

MAP COORDINATES 46/21

PAGE-SIZE MAP No.13

USGS 7 ½' QUADRANGLES
Nederland (C3)
East Portal (C2)

DISTANCE (one way)
2.1 miles

ACCESS

North end. From the Eldora Trailhead (P), ski west on the King Lake Trail (29), 2.6 miles to the Lost Lake Trail (33), and follow it 0.5 miles to its end at Lost Lake. A total distance of 3.1 miles.

South end. From the Eldora Ski Area Trailhead (R), ski the Jenny Creek Trail (35), 1.9 miles to the Guinn Mountain Trail (36). Follow this trail 2.1 miles to its end at the Arestua Hut. A total distance of 4.0 miles.

ROUTE DESCRIPTION (up, southwestbound)

From the north end of Lost Lake, follow an unblazed trail east of the lake, along the low ridge to the saddle east of the south end of the lake. Climb southwest to find a road climbing steeply to the left. Follow this road to enter the gully at the level of a prominent mine dump at 0.4 miles.

Climb 600 feet up the steep gully, curving to the west as the slope levels out, to the wind swept flat treeless area south of Peak 10,918. Continue west on a climbing traverse to find the natural gas pipeline, a 20 yard wide swath that follows the crest of the ridge.

Ski the pipeline to the west end of a wide saddle from where the ridge can be seen to climb continuously westward to the summit of Guinn Mountain. The ruins of a small log cabin on the north side of the pipeline swath here may be buried in snow.

The Arestua Hut, which marks the end of this route at 2.1 miles, is visible to the keen eyed from here, about 100 yards to the south in the second clearing. Only the front peak of the roof is visible.

The hut is operated by the Boulder Group of the Colorado Mountain Club, is open to all, and is not locked. It can comfortably accommodate about eight persons and has a wood stove. The operation of other cooking stoves is not permitted because of the fire hazard they pose.

ADDITIONAL CONNECTING
TRAIL INFORMATION

The west end connects with the Guinn Mountain Trail (36) and the Rollins Pass Route (45) at the Arestua Hut.

SKILLS RECOMMENDED
Skiing ability— Expert.

Endurance— Strenuous.

Routefinding skill— Advanced.

SNOW CONDITIONS
Poor, the snow in the gully can be hard windslab and subject to avalanche. On top some areas may be blown clear but where protected by trees, even the broad swath of the pipeline can hold good snow.

WIND EXPOSURE
The route is very exposed to wind along the ridgetop.

GRADIENT OR STEEPNESS
Very steep in the gully, moderate thereafter.

AMOUNT OF USE
Nearly unused.

South Arapaho Peak from Guinn Mountain

VIEWS
From the ridge top, distant vistas to the south include James Peak and Pikes Peak. To the north are South Arapaho Peak, the Indian Peaks, Mt. Meeker and Longs Peak.

PRIVATE PROPERTY AND OTHER RESTRICTIONS
If the Arestua Hut is used overnight or for a rest stop, read and abide by the posted rules so as to not endanger it by fire and to insure that it will be clean and usable for the next group.

* * * * *

TRAIL NO. 34A

LOWER GULLY BRYAN MOUNTAIN ROUTE

SUMMARY
Descent of the North Gully of Bryan Mountain (34) can be continued down the same steep gully to the valley floor near Hessie. Direct and quicker, it is more difficult than the alternative Lost Lake-King Lake Trails combination. It offers little advantage for the ascent.

CLASSIFICATION Difficult

TRAIL MAP Side 2 (South)

ALTITUDE (feet)

Starting 9,940
Highest 9,940
Cumulative gain 0
Cumulative loss 820

MAP COORDINATES 48/22

PAGE-SIZE MAP No.13

USGS 7 ½' QUADRANGLES
Nederland (C3)

TIME (hours)

Down, northeastbound 0.5
Up, souuthwestbound 1.0

DISTANCE (one way)
0.8 miles

ACCESS

South (upper) end. Most commonly, one would reach this end by descending the North Gully Bryan Mountain Route (34), 1.7 miles from Arestua Hut to where it turns out of the gully at a prominent mine dump. A total distance of 5.7 miles from the Eldora Ski Area Trailhead (R).

South (upper) end. A shorter but less used route from the Eldora Trailhead (P) goes 2.6 miles west on the King Lake Trail (29), 0.5 miles to the end of the Lost Lake Trail (33), and 0.4 miles on the North Gully Bryan Mountain Route to the prominent mine dump. A total distance of 3.5 miles.

North (lower) end. From the Eldora Trailhead (P), ski 1.5 miles west on the King Lake Trail (29) to an unmarked junction where the road switchbacks right.

ROUTE DESCRIPTION (down, northeastbound)

From the prominent mine dump, descend the gully to the valley bottom, then continue north to intercept the King Lake Trail at 0.8 miles.

ADDITIONAL CONNECTING TRAIL INFORMATION

None.

SKILLS RECOMMENDED

Skiing ability— Expert.

Endurance— Moderate.

Routefinding skill— Intermediate.

SNOW CONDITIONS

Excellent once the shelter of the trees on this untracked north facing slope is reached. The upper part can be hard windslab and subject to avalanche.

WIND EXPOSURE

While the upper part is exposed to the effect of wind, most of the route is protected by trees.

GRADIENT OR STEEPNESS
Very steep in the upper part, decreasing to moderate in the lower.

AMOUNT OF USE
Nearly unused.

VIEWS
Hessie townsite is visible in the valley of Middle Boulder Creek below.

PRIVATE PROPERTY AND OTHER RESTRICTIONS
Cabins on private property are passed in the valley bottom.

* * * * *

TRAIL NO. 35
JENNY CREEK TRAIL

SUMMARY
Starting at Eldora Ski Area, this popular trail climbs a beginners downhill slope, skirts the edge of others, and drops into Jenny Creek on a long traverse across a tree covered but south facing slope. The jeep road/trail continues up the valley bottom of Jenny Creek on an easy gradient and then climbs moderately, on a less obvious trail, to Yankee Doodle Lake nestled in a glacial cirque at timberline.

Jenny Creek cabin

CLASSIFICATION Moderate-difficult	**TRAIL MAP** Side 2 (South)

ALTITUDE (feet)

Starting 9,360
Highest 10,720
Cumulative gain 1,620
Cumulative loss 240

TIME (hours)

Westbound 2.5
Eastbound 1.3

ACCESS

At the Eldora Ski Area Trailhead (R).

MAP COORDINATES 47/20

PAGE-SIZE MAP No.17

USGS 7 ½' QUADRANGLES
Nederland (C3)
East Portal (C2)

DISTANCE (one way)
4.6 miles

ROUTE DESCRIPTION (westbound)

From the easternmost parking lot, climb the left side of the wide beginner *Ho-hum* downhill slope and cross behind the top of the chair lift. Follow the blue diamond blazes, arrows, and *Jenny Creek Ski Trail* signs to climb past the ski area. The trail here was relocated in 1994-95, further south, away from the downhill slopes. Cross a ridge near the top of a downhill slope and descend slightly on a blue diamond-blazed trail that then climbs to an unplowed road. From this high point the trail makes an traversing descent to Jenny Creek. A sign-marked junction with the Deadman Gulch Trail (35A) is in a clearing at 1.6 miles.

Follow the jeep road/trail west up the valley bottom. Shortly past a third clearing, a sign at 1.9 miles marks a junction with the Guinn Mountain Trail (36). Continue up the valley bottom on the unblazed left fork, passing the roofless remnant of a cabin at 3.2 miles. A treeless knoll, traversed by the railroad grade, lies ahead, between the two forks of the valley.

At 3.5 miles the trail, here indistinct if untracked, turns right and climbs more steeply through widely spaced large trees, following the right or north fork of the valley. The trail becomes less distinct as the trees thin and diminish in size with the effect of the wind becoming more pronounced as the valley route curves northward. The trail through here generally stays within 20 yards of the drainage. As the slopes become more open, the location of the lake in the glacial cirque at 4.6 miles is apparent.

ADDITIONAL CONNECTING TRAIL INFORMATION

An unmarked and probably untracked junction with the East Antelope Ridge Trail (37C) to the south is at 1.8 miles, 220 yards to the west of the second clearing along Jenny Creek. A sign *Dead End*, visible to eastbound traffic, identifies the turn off point. From here, it is 100 yards west to the sign-marked junction with the Guinn Mountain Trail (36).

A sign-marked junction with the Guinn Mountain-Jenny Creek Cutoff Trail (36B) is at a corner where the westbound trail turns south to follow the creek at 2.6 miles. This is 300 yards west of the west end of a long meadow notorious for ice and a rocky roadbed.

One hundred fifty yards west of the above junction, the West Antelope Ridge Trail (37B) crosses a bridge over Jenny Creek which may not be recognizable because of snow bridging the creek. A disfigured Forest Service trail post *502* is a few yards to the east of the junction, two metal posts are 20 yards to the west.

An indefinite junction with the South Fork Jenny Creek Route (43C) to the south is at 3.5 miles near where the trail turns right to climb more steeply.

An indefinite junction with the Jenny Creek-Forest Lakes Route (43B) is at about 4.2 miles, before the final climb to Yankee Doodle Lake.

SKILLS RECOMMENDED
Skiing ability— Intermediate. A good snowplow is helpful for the descent into Jenny Creek of the narrow trail with likely poor snow.

Endurance— Strenuous.

Routefinding skill— Beginner.

SNOW CONDITIONS
Medium to good overall but varies widely along the length of the trail. The beginners downhill slope has packed artificial snow. Although protected by trees, the descent into Jenny Creek is on a south facing slope that can become icy from heavy use and sun. Meadows in the bottom of Jenny Creek can be bare, icy, and show exposed rocks. Beyond a 300 yard meadow at 2.4 miles, the snowpack is usually good to excellent until the open slopes below Yankee Doodle Lake are reached. Conditions here are variable.

WIND EXPOSURE
The trail is generally well protected from wind by large trees except in a few clearings. The open slopes near Yankee Doodle Lake are very exposed.

GRADIENT OR STEEPNESS
Moderate slopes are climbed past the ski area. The descent into Jenny Creek has a short moderately steep section. The valley bottom gradient is slight to 3.5 miles where the trail turns more northerly and climbs moderately to about 4.2 miles. After leveling out, it surmounts a final open, moderate slope to the lake.

AMOUNT OF USE
Heavy at the east end, decreases to light at the far end.

VIEWS

South Arapaho Peak is in full view from the top of the Ho-hum downhill ski slope near the start of the trail.

The bare knoll traversed by the railroad grade as it crosses the head of Jenny Creek on its way from East Portal to Yankee Doodle Lake and Rollins Pass is visible straight ahead on the steep descent into Jenny Creek at about 1.4 miles. The Jenny Creek-Forest Lakes Route (43B) crosses the saddle behind this knoll.

From Yankee Doodle Lake, a road sign marking where the Rollins Pass Route (45) joins the railroad grade is visible high above on the ridge to the northwest. The trace of the railroad may be followed south to Needle Eye tunnel. Unnamed peaks on the corniced continental divide above Forest and Arapaho Lakes are to the southwest. Standing alone to the south,

Yankee Doodle Lake, Needle Eye Tunnel

James Peak rises above the tundra slopes of Nebraska Hill.

PRIVATE PROPERTY AND OTHER RESTRICTIONS

Access through the Eldora ski area is on the Jenny Creek Trail only. Dogs are not allowed.

The area designated for overnight parking near the Eldora Ski Area is marked with a sign *Jenny Creek Trail Parking.* It's just outside the ski area, 0.2 miles from the trailhead.

* * * * *

TRAIL NO. 35A

DEADMAN GULCH TRAIL

SUMMARY

An alternative to the lower part of the Jenny Creek Trail to gain access to Jenny Creek and the National Forest land from the Eldora Ski Area. It climbs and descends less and avoids the not uncommon poor snow conditions on the south facing slope of the Jenny Creek Trail. It does however require an Eldora Nordic trail pass.

CLASSIFICATION Easy

ALTITUDE (feet)

Starting 9,360
Highest 9,540
Cumulative gain 290
Cumulative loss 110

TIME (hours)

Southwestbound 0.9
Eastbound 0.7

TRAIL MAP Side 2 (South)

MAP COORDINATES 47/20

PAGE-SIZE MAP No.17

USGS 7 ½' QUADRANGLES
Nederland (C3)

DISTANCE (one way)
1.8 miles

ACCESS
At Eldora Ski Area Trailhead (R).

ROUTE DESCRIPTION (southwestbound)
Climb up the left side of the downhill slope as for the Jenny Creek Trail (35). Cross behind the chairlift and in 70 yards turn left at a sign *Jenny Creek Ski Trail.* Continue straight at a junction where the Jenny Creek Trail turns right. Stay right through three more junctions on Eldora Nordic trails and descend Deadman Gulch to a broad meadow at the bend of Jenny Creek. Follow the trail up the valley bottom to the property boundary at a well at 0.9 miles. Cross the cable barrier and continue west up the valley bottom through Forest Service land to a junction with the Jenny Creek Trail at 1.8 miles.

ADDITIONAL CONNECTING TRAIL INFORMATION
The first 0.9 miles are part of the Eldora Ski Area trail system. See an Eldora Nordic trail map.

SKILLS RECOMMENDED
Skiing ability— Novice.

Endurance— Very easy.

Routefinding skill— Novice.

SNOW CONDITIONS
Medium, nearly always well packed.

WIND EXPOSURE
Moderate.

GRADIENT OR STEEPNESS
This alternate trail climbs the same moderate downhill slope as does the Jenny Creek Trail but descends a shorter and less steep moderate slope into Jenny Creek. Thereafter, the trail up Jenny Creek is nearly flat.

Heavy.

VIEWS
South Arapaho Peak is in full view from the top of the Ho-hum downhill ski slope near the start of the trail.

PRIVATE PROPERTY AND OTHER RESTRICTIONS
An Eldora Nordic trail pass ($10 for the 1994-5 season) is required for the first 0.9 miles. Dogs are not allowed on the trail.

* * * * *

TRAIL NO. 36

GUINN MOUNTAIN TRAIL

SUMMARY
Challenging for intermediate skiers, long and steep enough to give a good workout for all but the hardiest, the trail climbs out of Jenny Creek onto the upper slopes of Guinn Mountain to end at the Colorado Mountain Club's Arestua Hut. Situated at near optimum snow conditions of high altitude and the protection of tall trees, the hut is a favorite day and overnight shelter for up and down skiers as well as those continuing over Rollins Pass to Winter Park.

CLASSIFICATION Difficult

ALTITUDE (feet)
Starting 9,640
Highest 10,960
Cumulative gain 1,320
Cumulative loss 0

TIME (hours)
Westbound, up 1.5
Eastbound, down 0.7

TRAIL MAP Side 2 (South)

MAP COORDINATES 46/21

PAGE-SIZE MAP No.17

USGS 7 ½' QUADRANGLES
Nederland (C3)
East Portal (C2)

DISTANCE (one way)
2.1 miles

ACCESS
From the Eldora Ski Area (R), ski the Jenny Creek Trail (35), 1.9 miles to a sign-marked trail junction.

ROUTE DESCRIPTION (westbound)
The blue diamond-blazed and easily followed trail climbs moderately steeply for a half mile from the junction on the Jenny Creek Trail (35) before leveling out for

another half mile. It then climbs steeply on entering a gully to follow its steep right side to pass the ruins of a large cabin at 1.4 miles and 10,540 feet altitude.

Switchback as needed to climb the steep treeless slope at head of the gully 300 yards beyond the cabin. Turn left at the top and continue on a slight to moderate climb west through large trees. The trail here, with only widely spaced blue diamond blazes, is not easily followed if untracked.

The Arestua Hut at 2.1 miles and 10,960 feet altitude is visible 100 yards to the left front from where the trail enters a wind swept clearing. It is operated by the Boulder Group of the Colorado Mountain Club and is open to all. Not locked nor hosted, it can comfortably sleep about eight persons, and has a wood burning stove. The operation of other cooking stoves is not permitted because of the fire hazard.

Approaching Arestua Hut

In the event it is not possible to follow the trail above the steep head of the gully at 1.6 miles, a convenient landmark and route to the hut is provided by the natural gas pipeline that extends west from Eldora Ski Area along the ridge connecting Bryan Mountain, Point 10918, Guinn Mountain, and Rollins Pass. The swath cut through the trees is 20 yards wide and follows the crest of the ridge. It can be reached by skiing north through the moderately spaced trees from anywhere above the head of the gully.

To find the hut from the pipeline, ski west on the pipeline swath to the west end of a wide saddle where the ridge can be seen to climb westward continuously to the summit of Guinn Mountain. The remnant of a small cabin at the north side of the pipeline swath may be visible here in the deep snow. The Arestua Hut is visible from here, about 100 yards to the south in the second clearing. Only the front peak of the roof is visible.

ADDITIONAL CONNECTING TRAIL INFORMATION
A sign-marked junction with the Guinn Mountain-Jenny Creek Cutoff Trail (36B) is at 0.7 miles.

Connections with the North Gully Bryan Mountain Route (34), the Rollins Pass Route (45), and the Yankee Doodle Cutoff Route (36A) are at the Arestua Hut.

SKILLS RECOMMENDED
Skiing ability— Intermediate.

Endurance— Strenuous.

Routefinding skill— Intermediate.

SNOW CONDITIONS
Good on the lower section, excellent higher.

WIND EXPOSURE
The trail is generally well protected from wind by trees.

GRADIENT OR STEEPNESS

Steep sections are interspaced with more moderate. The steepest sections are where 400 feet altitude is gained in the first half mile, the lower part of the gully at 1.0 miles, and the headwall 300 yards beyond the ruins of a large cabin at 1.4 miles.

AMOUNT OF USE
Moderate.

VIEWS
From the lower part of the trail, the Moffat Route can be seen to the south across Jenny Creek as it climbs a twisting course from East Portal to Rollins Pass.

PRIVATE PROPERTY AND OTHER RESTRICTIONS
Abide by the posted rules for the Arestua Hut so as to not endanger it by fire and to insure that it will be clean and usable for the next group.

TRAIL NO. 36A

YANKEE DOODLE CUTOFF ROUTE

SUMMARY
This exhilarating off trail route descends through widely spaced trees from the summit of Guinn Mountain to Yankee Doodle Lake at the head of Jenny Creek. The steep descent is best done with good snow.

CLASSIFICATION Difficult

ALTITUDE (feet)
Starting 11,210
Highest 11,210
Cumulative gain 0
Cumulative loss 600

TIME (hours)
Down, Southwestbound 0.4
Up, northeastbound 0.8

TRAIL MAP Side 2 (South)

MAP COORDINATES 44/21

PAGE-SIZE MAP No.17

USGS 7 ½' QUADRANGLES
East Portal (C2)

DISTANCE (one way)
0.6 miles

ACCESS
North end. At Guinn Mountain summit. From Eldora Ski Area Trailhead (R), ski the Jenny Creek Trail (35) 1.9 miles, the Guinn Mountain Trail (36) 2.1 miles to the Arestua Hut, and the Rollins Pass Route (45) 0.4 miles to the Guinn Mountain summit. A total distance of 4.4 miles.

South end. On Jenny Creek 0.3 miles south of Yankee Doodle Lake. From Eldora Ski Area Trailhead (R), ski 4.3 miles west on the Jenny Creek Trail (35) to an unmarked locale at approximately 10,600 feet where the valley heading is north.

ROUTE DESCRIPTION (down, southwestbound)
From the summit of Guinn Mountain, ski south along the edge of the steep drop off to find a gradient of your liking. Pick a route through the trees down the steep slope to Jenny Creek at 0.6 miles.

ADDITIONAL CONNECTING TRAIL INFORMATION
None.
SKILLS RECOMMENDED
Skiing ability— Expert.

Endurance— Strenuous.

Routefinding skill— Advanced.

SNOW CONDITIONS
Medium, the open area near the top of Guinn Mountain can be blown free of snow.

WIND EXPOSURE
Exposed to wind near the top, but protected by trees lower on the slope.

GRADIENT OR STEEPNESS
Very steep, the gradient can be lessened by going further south.

AMOUNT OF USE
Nearly unused.

VIEWS
From the top of Guinn Mountain, South Arapaho Peak is visible to the north across the tributary valleys of Middle Boulder Creek. To the south, the corniced ridge of the continental divide at the head of South Boulder Creek leads south to James Peak. Needle Eye tunnel on the Moffat Route, and the present day passenger car summer route to it, is across the cirque of Yankee Doodle Lake at the head of Jenny Creek.

PRIVATE PROPERTY AND OTHER RESTRICTIONS
None.

* * * * *

TRAIL NO. 36B

GUINN MOUNTAIN-JENNY CREEK CUTOFF TRAIL

SUMMARY
A connecting trail between the Guinn Mountain and Jenny Creek Trails, it can offer some variety to the routes on Guinn Mountain and Jenny Creek. A short loop at the far end of a half day trip up Jenny Creek from Eldora Ski Area is one possibility.

CLASSIFICATION Moderate

ALTITUDE (feet)
Starting 9,810
Highest 10,060
Cumulative gain 250
Cumulative loss 0

TIME (hours)
Northbound, up 0.5
Southbound, down 0.3

TRAIL MAP Side 2 (South)

MAP COORDINATES 49/20

PAGE-SIZE MAP No.16

USGS 7 ½' QUADRANGLES
East Portal (C2)
Nederland (C3)

DISTANCE (one way)
0.7 miles

ACCESS

Southwest (Lower) End. From the Eldora Ski Area Trailhead (R), ski the Jenny Creek Trail (35) 2.6 miles to a junction at a corner where the westbound trail turns south to follow the creek at 2.6 miles. This is 300 yards west of the west end of a long meadow notorious for ice and a rocky roadbed. The sign for the trail to the north reads *Guinn Mountain.*

Northeast (Upper) End. From the Eldora Ski Area Trailhead (R), ski the Jenny Creek Trail (35) 1.9 miles to the Guinn Mountain Trail (36). Gain 450 feet skiing up this trail 0.7 miles to a junction. The sign here reads *Jenny Creek.*

ROUTE DESCRIPTION (northbound, up)

The blue diamond-blazed, easily followed trail climbs a minor drainage north from Jenny Creek. At about 400 yards it turns to the right to cross the drainage above an old cabin. Beyond here the trail is unblazed and if untracked, somewhat obscure. It traverses moderately steeply to the east, curves north, and again traverses east to join the Guinn Mountain Trail (36) in 0.7 miles at a sign-marked junction.

ADDITIONAL CONNECTING TRAIL INFORMATION

None

SKILLS RECOMMENDED

Skiing ability— Beginner

Endurance— Easy

Routefinding skill— Intermediate

SNOW CONDITIONS

Medium on the lower part where trail climbs directly up the south facing slope. Good higher up where it is more shaded. The   trail is likely to be untracked.

WIND EXPOSURE

The trail is well shielded from wind by medium to large trees.

GRADIENT OR STEEPNESS

Steep sections are interspersed with moderate.

AMOUNT OF USE

Light.

VIEWS

The Moffat Route railroad grade is visible to the south across Jenny Creek.

PRIVATE PROPERTY AND OTHER RESTRICTIONS

None.

TRAIL NO. 37

ANTELOPE CREEK TRAIL

SUMMARY

The Antelope Creek group of trails (37, 37A,B,C) form a network centered on Antelope Creek and extending north over Antelope Ridge to Jenny Creek. They also reach south to the switchbacks and loops of the Giants Ladder. These sheltered, unblazed, intermediate trails with generally good snow see little use due mainly to their remoteness from trailheads. They can be combined to form a relatively low altitude passage from South Boulder Creek to Eldora Ski Area.

The Antelope Creek Trail (37) starts at the first switchback of the Giants Ladder Railroad Grade (present summer automobile road) to approximately follow the loop of the old railroad into Jenny Creek. Where the old railroad completed the switchback with a now collapsed tunnel, the trail follows Antelope Creek upstream to end where the railroad grade makes a higher crossing of the creek.

CLASSIFICATION Moderate-difficult

ALTITUDE (feet)
Starting 9,400
Highest 9,950
Cumulative gain 600
Cumulative loss 50

TIME (hours)
Westbound 1.2
Eastbound 0.7

TRAIL MAP Side 2 (South)

MAP COORDINATES 49/19

PAGE-SIZE MAP No.17

USGS 7 ½' QUADRANGLES
Nederland (C3)

DISTANCE (one way)
1.8 miles

ACCESS

Southeast end. From the Giants Ladder Trailhead (U), ski the Giants Ladder Railroad Grade (41), 2.3 miles to the first switchback.

West end. From the Eldora Ski Area Trailhead (R), ski the Jenny Creek Trail (35), 2.6 miles to an unmarked junction with the West Antelope Ridge Trail (37B). Ski this 1.1 miles to the end at a junction with both the Antelope Creek Trail and the Giants Ladder Railroad Grade (41). The total distance is 3.7 miles.

ROUTE DESCRIPTION (westbound)

From the first switchback on the Giants Ladder Railroad Grade (41), ski a near level course north across the meadow past the ruins of a cabin at 300 yards. Locate the unblazed trail which contours northeast around a conical hill to an unmarked trail junction on the north side of Jenny Creek at 0.5 miles. The old railroad grade, higher on the hillside, does not offer a good route as the trestles are missing. Ski west up the creek, passing a square wooden railroad water tank (toppled in 1992-3) at 0.7 miles, and continue the moderate climb through dense timber to the railroad grade at 1.8 miles.

ADDITIONAL CONNECTING TRAIL INFORMATION
The South Antelope Creek Trail (37A) also heads north from the Giants Ladder switchback, but crosses the saddle west of the conical hill.

The trail at 0.5 miles (37D on the map) can be skied 0.4 miles east down Antelope Creek to the confluence with Jenny Creek and the groomed Eldora Nordic trails. Deadman Gulch is 0.4 miles north up Jenny Creek on Zarlengos Loop and Eldora Ski Area is an additional 0.8 miles.

At 1.2 miles an unmarked junction is reached with the East Antelope Ridge Trail (37C).

A junction with a forty yard connecting trail south across the creek to the South Antelope Creek Trail (37A) is 130 yards to the west from the above junction. It is marked by a three foot metal stake.

Eastbound skiers may find it difficult to locate the west end of the trail if it is untracked. From the Giants Ladder Railroad Grade (41), 320 yards north of the crossing of Antelope Creek, turn east at signs *Forest Service Road 149* and *One Way Road*. Bear right and downhill of a single blue diamond blaze. The West Antelope Ridge Trail (37B) goes to the left on a nearly level course. It is Forest Service Road 502.

SKILLS RECOMMENDED
Skiing ability— Intermediate.

Endurance— Easy.

Routefinding skill— Beginner.

SNOW CONDITIONS
Poor at the exposed southeast end, medium elsewhere.

WIND EXPOSURE
None.

GRADIENT OR STEEPNESS
Nearly flat around the conical hill, moderate climb up Jenny Creek.

AMOUNT OF USE
Light.

No distant views. The square wooden water tank at 0.7 miles and the Zarlengo cabin ruin at Ladora at 0.1 miles are relics of the Moffat Road.

PRIVATE PROPERTY AND OTHER RESTRICTIONS
The trail is on private property.

* * * * *

TRAIL NO. 37A

SOUTH ANTELOPE CREEK TRAIL

SUMMARY
From the first switchback on the Giants Ladder, this trail crosses the saddle above the collapsed Tunnel 31 on the Moffat Road, and contours into Antelope Creek. There, the south bank is followed upstream to reach the railroad grade again where it crosses the creek.

CLASSIFICATION Moderate

ALTITUDE (feet)
    Starting 9,400
    Highest 9,920
    Cumulative gain 560
    Cumulative loss 40

TIME (hours)
    Westbound 1.2
    Eastbound 0.9

TRAIL MAP Side 2 (South)

MAP COORDINATES 48/19

PAGE-SIZE MAP No. 17

USGS 7 ½' QUADRANGLES
    Nederland (C3)

DISTANCE (one way)
    1.3 miles

ACCESS
Southeast end. From the Giants Ladder Trailhead (U), ski 2.3 miles on the Giants Ladder Railroad Grade (41) to the first switchback.

West end. From the Eldora Ski Area Trailhead (R), ski 2.6 miles on the Jenny Creek Trail (35) to an unmarked junction with the West Antelope Ridge Trail (37B). Follow it to its end at the railroad grade at 1.1 miles. Ski south on the railroad grade 0.2 miles to cross Antelope Creek. A total distance of 3.9 miles.

The west end may also be reached from the Moffat Road Trailhead (U), by skiing 5.3 miles on the Giants Ladder Railroad Grade (41).

ROUTE DESCRIPTION (westbound)
From the switchback at 2.3 miles on the Giants Ladder Railroad Grade (41), cross the 300 yard clearing to the north, passing above the ruins of the Zarlengo Cabin at Ladora. A faint route climbs steeply just west of the collapsed tunnel toward the

saddle. Near the top, a straight, better defined trail leads to the west, crosses the ridge, and continues on a near level course to reach the bottom of Antelope Creek.

The trail continues up the south side of the creek to a 100 yard clearing and immediately beyond, at 1.3 miles, the Giants Ladder Railroad Grade (41).

ADDITIONAL CONNECTING TRAIL INFORMATION
At 0.8 miles an unmarked junction with a 40 yard connecting trail across the creek to the Antelope Creek Trail (37) is passed.

SKILLS RECOMMENDED
Skiing ability— Beginner.

Endurance— Easy.

Routefinding skill— Intermediate.

SNOW CONDITIONS
Medium on the south facing slope to the saddle at 0.3 miles, good thereafter on the north facing slope of Antelope Creek.

WIND EXPOSURE
Well protected by dense trees except for the 300 yard clearing at the southeast end.

GRADIENT OR STEEPNESS
Moderate, the steepest is a short climb to the saddle.

Rest stop

AMOUNT OF USE
Nearly unused.

VIEWS
The collapsed remnant of Tunnel 31 on the Moffat Road is visible south of the saddle near mile 0.3.

The clearing at the west end of the trail is the site of Antelope station on the Moffat Road.

PRIVATE PROPERTY AND OTHER RESTRICTIONS
As with the Antelope Creek Trail, the trail is on private property.

156

TRAIL NO. 37B

WEST ANTELOPE RIDGE TRAIL

SUMMARY
A short, easily followed jeep road on the good snow of a north facing slope, it makes a gentle climb out of Jenny creek to cross the wind swept treeless ridge. It then contours into Antelope Creek to a common junction with both the railroad grade and the Antelope Creek Trail.

CLASSIFICATION Moderate

ALTITUDE (feet)
Starting 9,820
Highest 9,970
Cumulative gain 150
Cumulative loss 0

TIME (hours)
Southeastbound 0.9
Northwestbound 0.7

TRAIL MAP Side 2 (South)

MAP COORDINATES 47/19

PAGE-SIZE MAP No.17

USGS 7 ½' QUADRANGLES
Nederland (C3)

DISTANCE (one way)
1.1 miles

ACCESS
Northwest end. From the Eldora Ski Area Trailhead (R), ski the Jenny Creek Trail 2.6 miles to a junction marked with a sign giving distances on that trail and a disfigured post *FS 502*.

Southeast end. From the Giants Ladder Trailhead (U), ski the Giants Ladder Railroad Grade 5.3 miles to the end of that route as described here. This is 300 yards north of Antelope Creek.

ROUTE DESCRIPTION (southeastbound)
From the junction at mile 2.6 on Jenny Creek Trail (35), cross the bridge over Jenny Creek which may not be recognizable because of snow bridging of the creek. Enter the trees on an easily recognized jeep road that traverses the side of the valley to the east southeast, climbing only slightly, to gain Antelope Ridge just below the tree cleared swath of the railroad grade.

Continue on a level course through a treeless area, reenter the trees and continue below the railroad 400 yards on a distinct trail to the junction at 1.1 miles with the railroad grade.

For travel in the opposite direction, it may be easier to ski the railroad grade an additional 450 yards north to where it curves to cross the ridge. Go about 30 yards east to a wood post and contour north through sparse trees to find the steep side slope of a narrow corridor through more dense trees.

ADDITIONAL CONNECTING TRAIL INFORMATION
The southeast end of the trail connects with both the Giants Ladder Railroad Grade (41), and the Antelope Creek Trail (37).

SKILLS RECOMMENDED
Skiing ability— Novice.

Endurance— Easy.

Routefinding skill— Beginner.

SNOW CONDITIONS
Good.

WIND EXPOSURE
Protected by trees except at the ridge crossing.

GRADIENT OR STEEPNESS
Nearly flat.

AMOUNT OF USE
Very light.

VIEWS
Bryan and Guinn Mountains are across Jenny Creek to the north.

PRIVATE PROPERTY AND OTHER RESTRICTIONS
None.

* * * * *

TRAIL NO. 37C

EAST ANTELOPE RIDGE TRAIL

SUMMARY
Similar to the parallel West Antelope Ridge Trail, it is a short easily followed jeep road on the good snow of a north facing slope. In the shelter of dense trees it climbs gently out of Jenny creek to cross Antelope Ridge. It then contours into Antelope Creek and a junction near the midsection of the Antelope Creek Trail.

CLASSIFICATION Moderate   **TRAIL MAP** Side 2 (South)

ALTITUDE (feet)		MAP COORDINATES 48/19

ALTITUDE (feet)
Starting 9,600
Highest 9,710
Cumulative gain 110
Cumulative loss 70

MAP COORDINATES 48/19

PAGE-SIZE MAP No.17

USGS 7 ½' QUADRANGLES
Nederland (C3)

TIME (hours)
Southeastbound 0.6
Northwestbound 0.5

DISTANCE (one way)
0.7 miles

ACCESS

Northwest end. From the Eldora Ski Area Trailhead (R), ski the Jenny Creek Trail (35), 1.8 miles to an unmarked junction. See *ADDITIONAL CONNECTING TRAIL INFORMATION.*

Southeast end. From the Giants Ladder Trailhead (U), ski 2.3 miles on the Giants Ladder Railroad Grade (41) to the first switchback. Ski 1.2 miles on the Antelope Creek Trail (37).

ROUTE DESCRIPTION (southeastbound)

From the unmarked junction at mile 1.8 on the Jenny Creek Trail (35), descend south about 40 feet in 100 yards on an indistinct route to cross Jenny Creek. Turn southeast to enter trees as the well defined trail climbs to the top of the ridge, and descends the south side past a cable suspended on trees. It then switchbacks southwest and continues to an unmarked junction with the Antelope Creek Trail (37) at 0.7 miles.

ADDITIONAL CONNECTING TRAIL INFORMATION

The junction with the Jenny Creek Trail (35) is 220 yards west of the second clearing along Jenny Creek and 100 yards east of the junction with the Guinn Mountain Trail (36). A sign *Dead End*, visible to eastbound traffic, identifies the junction.

SKILLS RECOMMENDED

Skiing ability— Novice.

Endurance— Easy.

Routefinding skill— Intermediate.

SNOW CONDITIONS

Good.

WIND EXPOSURE

Protected by dense trees.

GRADIENT OR STEEPNESS

Slight.

Nearly unused.

VIEWS
Bryan and Guinn Mountains are visible through the trees to the north across Jenny Creek.

PRIVATE PROPERTY AND OTHER RESTRICTIONS
None.

* * * * *

TRAIL NO. 38

JENNY LIND GULCH TRAIL

SUMMARY
A short easy trail up the valley bottom, it gradually steepens enroute to a six hundred foot bowl where only an occasional tree restricts telemark descents of the moderate to steep slopes. Try to ski this bowl in midwinter or after a good snowfall as the relatively low altitude and exposure to sun and wind preclude consistently good snow conditions.

CLASSIFICATION Moderate

ALTITUDE (feet)
Starting 8,800
Highest 10,470
Cumulative gain 1,670
Cumulative loss 0

TIME (hours)
Southbound, up 1.4
Northbound, down 1.0

TRAIL MAP Side 2 (South)

MAP COORDINATES 52/15

PAGE-SIZE MAP No.17

USGS 7 ½' QUADRANGLES
Nederland (C3)

DISTANCE (one way)
2.6 ,miles

ACCESS
At Jenny Lind Gulch Trailhead (S).

ROUTE DESCRIPTION
(southbound, up)
From the small parking area at the trailhead on the Rollinsville-East Portal road, ski south up the valley bottom on the jeep road. Keep to the right at 300 yards where a posted road angles to the left. At 0.7 miles, pass the first of three gullies draining into Jenny Lind Gulch from the west. The first, in a 30 yard clearing is short, steep, brushy, and without a trail. The second gully at 1.0 miles is at the far end of a 150 yard clear corridor. Beyond here, the trail climbs more steeply.

The valley and trail curve to the right to reach the bottom of the bowl at 2.2 miles. Climb 650 feet to reach the nearly level section of ridge at the top of the bowl at 10,470 feet and 2.6 miles.

ADDITIONAL CONNECTING TRAIL INFORMATION

The West Fork Loop Route (38A) branches off at the unmarked junction at 1.0 miles to climb the second gully. The routes rejoin on top of the ridge at 2.6 miles.

At 1.4 miles, opposite the third gully, an alternative route, usually tracked, drops left and continues up the creek bottom paralleling the jeep road main route which climbs slightly onto the west side of the valley.

SKILLS RECOMMENDED

Skiing ability— Intermediate overall. Novice at the beginning, intermediate to advanced in the bowl.

Jenny Lind bowl

Endurance— Moderate.

Routefinding skill— Novice.

SNOW CONDITIONS

Poor at the beginning, improving to medium in the bowl.

WIND EXPOSURE

Well protected by trees in the valley bottom, more exposed on the treeless slopes of the bowl.

GRADIENT OR STEEPNESS

Increases gradually from nearly flat to moderate further up the valley. Slopes in the bowl are moderate to steep.

AMOUNT OF USE

Moderate.

VIEWS
Abandoned mine workings on Dakota Hill are visible to the east.

PRIVATE PROPERTY AND OTHER RESTRICTIONS
None.

*****

TRAIL NO. 38A

WEST FORK LOOP ROUTE

SUMMARY
The route follows a short steep gully branching off from Jenny Lind Gulch and climbs 1300 feet to cross a ridge. Here the broad expanse of the ski bowl at the head of Jenny Lind Gulch lies below.

CLASSIFICATION Difficult

ALTITUDE (feet)
Starting 9,150
Highest 10,470
Cumulative gain 1,320
Cumulative loss 0

TIME (hours)
Up, southwestbound 1.5
Down, northeastbound 1.0

TRAIL MAP Side 2 (South)

MAP COORDINATES 50/15

PAGE-SIZE MAP No.17

USGS 7 ½' QUADRANGLES
Nederland (C3)

DISTANCE (one way)
1.6 miles

ACCESS
From Jenny Lind Gulch Trailhead (S), ski 1.0 miles south on the Jenny Lind Gulch Trail (38) to an unmarked junction at the second gully from the right. This is at the far end of a 150 yard clear corridor.

ROUTE DESCRIPTION (up, southwestbound)
The route up this gully changes from a jeep road cut through trees at the bottom to a wider open snow gully higher. A mine dump is passed at 9,920 feet. At 10,100 feet where the main gully curves slightly to the right, turn to the left to climb a smaller drainage up a moderately steep slope. Continue climbing south southeast through an area of thinned trees as the slope lessens to cross the ridge at 10,470 feet and 1.6 miles. This is the top of the bowl above Jenny Lind Gulch.

ADDITIONAL CONNECTING TRAIL INFORMATION
None.

Skiing ability— Advanced.

Endurance— Moderate.

Routefinding skill— Advanced.

SNOW CONDITIONS
Medium.

WIND EXPOSURE
Protected from wind until the ridge is approached.

GRADIENT OR STEEPNESS
Very steep.

AMOUNT OF USE
Nearly unused.

VIEWS
From the ridge top, the switchbacks of Giants Ladder on the Moffat Route, the downhill runs at Eldora Ski Area, and South Arapaho Peak are visible to the north, across the valley of South Boulder Creek.

PRIVATE PROPERTY AND OTHER RESTRICTIONS
None.

* * * * *

TRAIL NO. 39

BLACK CANYON TRAIL

SUMMARY
A little used trail up a low altitude, forested, north facing canyon, it is reached by a short cutoff route from Jenny Lind Gulch.

CLASSIFICATION Moderate

ALTITUDE (feet)

Starting	8,840
Highest	9,710
Cumulative gain	870
Cumulative loss	0

TRAIL MAP Side 2 (South)

MAP COORDINATES 49/16

PAGE-SIZE MAP No.17

USGS 7 ½' QUADRANGLES
Nederland (C3)

TIME (hours)

Southwestbound, up . . . . 1.9   **DISTANCE** (one way)

Northeastbound, down . . . . 1.2   2.3 miles

ACCESS

From the Jenny Lind Gulch Trailhead (S), ski 200 yards up the Jenny Lind Gulch Trail (38) to an indefinite junction.

ROUTE DESCRIPTION (southwestbound, up)

From the above indefinite junction, bushwack west across the stream on a level course near the base of the hill to the south. Continue to a barbed wire fence and staying on the left (south) side, follow it west to where a poorly defined jeep road can be seen heading up a shallow drainage to the left. Follow this jeep road past the several cabins and ruins of buildings, including the old city hall that make up Baltimore at 0.6 miles.

From Baltimore, Black Canyon is visible up the drainage to the southwest. Pass three cabins, about 300 yards beyond Baltimore on the right side of the creek. The easily followed jeep road stays on the right side of the creek, but sometimes climbs as much as a hundred feet above it. At 1.1 miles pass the weathered sign of the Henry Toll Ranch, *Toll Ranch 3,000 acres, 9,000 feet.*

At 1.5 miles the jeep road/trail crosses the creek, then recrosses in 230 yards. At 1.7 miles it turns sharply to the right, away from the creek, to climb 50 feet in about 50 yards to pass a boiler and two cabin ruins. Above here the trail climbs a steep 80 feet, levels off and returns to creek level. Now more difficult to follow, it crosses the creek three times and ends in a 70 yard diameter clearing at 2.3 miles. A large dead tree draped with wire is near the center of this clearing.

ADDITIONAL CONNECTING TRAIL INFORMATION

The Baltimore Ridge Route (39A) continues on from the end of this trail.

SKILLS RECOMMENDED

Skiing ability— Beginner.

Endurance— Moderate.

Routefinding skill— Intermediate.

SNOW CONDITIONS

Medium.

WIND EXPOSURE

Generally well protected by trees except for clearings and aspen groves in the creek bottom.

GRADIENT OR STEEPNESS
Moderate.

AMOUNT OF USE
Nearly unused.

VIEWS
None.

**PRIVATE PROPERTY AND
OTHER RESTRICTIONS**

The trail is on the Henry Toll ranch.
Private cabins are passed at Baltimore.

* * * * *

TRAIL NO. 39A

BALTIMORE RIDGE
ROUTE

Baltimore city hall

SUMMARY

This unmarked route bushwhacks 550 feet up a timbered drainage from the end of
the Black Canyon Trail to cross Baltimore Ridge and descend the open slopes to the
Mammoth Gulch Road.

CLASSIFICATION Difficult

ALTITUDE (feet)
Starting 9,710
Highest 10,260
Cumulative gain 550
Cumulative loss 510

TIME (hours)
Westbound 2.0
Eastbound 1.8

TRAIL MAP Side 2 (South)

MAP COORDINATES 48/15

PAGE-SIZE MAP No.17

USGS 7 ½' QUADRANGLES
Nederland (C3)

DISTANCE (one way)
2.5 miles

ACCESS

East end. From the Jenny Lind Gulch Trailhead (S), ski 200 yards on the Jenny
Lind Gulch Trail (38), then 2.3 miles on the Black Canyon Trail (39) to its end.

West end. From the Tolland Trailhead (T), ski the Mammoth Gulch Road (40) 1.6

miles to the sign-marked jeep road junction. Take the upper (toward Apex townsite) of the three choices.

ROUTE DESCRIPTION (westbound)

From the dead tree clearing at the end of the Black Canyon Trail (39), climb through the moderately spaced trees, following the east fork of the drainage on an off trail route to 10,000 feet altitude. Angle to the right to cross the knoll between the forks at 10,220 feet and contour across the head of the west fork, to Baltimore Ridge at 1.0 miles. Follow the jeep road down the open slope to a sign-marked junction with the Mammoth Gulch Road (40) at 2.5 miles.

ADDITIONAL CONNECTING TRAIL INFORMATION
None.

SKILLS RECOMMENDED
Skiing ability— Advanced.

Endurance— Strenuous.

Routefinding skill— Advanced.

Windy conditions on Baltimore Ridge

SNOW CONDITIONS

Medium in Black Canyon, poor on the exposed west side of Baltimore Ridge.

WIND EXPOSURE
Protected by trees in Black Canyon, very exposed on the ridge and west side.

GRADIENT OR STEEPNESS
Steep.

AMOUNT OF USE
Nearly unused.

VIEWS
From the ridge, the rugged east face of James Peak (13,294) is at the head of Mammoth Gulch to the southwest. To the north, the giants ladder switchbacks on the Moffat Road traverse the slopes across South Boulder Creek. South Arapaho Peak is visible ten miles distant.

Access to the east end of this route is through the Toll Ranch. Look for posted signs.

* * * * *

TRAIL NO. 40

MAMMOTH GULCH ROAD

SUMMARY

The wide U-shaped glacial valley of Mammoth Gulch is followed from Tolland up its gently curving course toward its source at the base of the rugged east face of James Peak.

CLASSIFICATION Moderate

ALTITUDE (feet)

Starting 8,920
Highest 10,340
Cumulative gain 1,420
Cumulative loss 0

TIME (hours)

Southwestbound, up 2.5
Northeastbound, down 1.5

TRAIL MAP Side 2 (South)

MAP COORDINATES 46/16

PAGE-SIZE MAP No.17

USGS 7 ½' QUADRANGLES
East Portal (C2)
Nederland (C3)
Empire (D2)
Central City (D3)

DISTANCE (one way)
4.8 miles

ACCESS
At Tolland Trailhead (T).

ROUTE DESCRIPTION (southwestbound, up)
Follow the obvious wide road as it climbs from Tolland on a steady diagonal course, out of the valley of South Boulder Creek, to the hanging valley of Mammoth Gulch. At a sign-marked junction of jeep roads at 1.6 miles, take the middle of three choices, *Forest Service Road 176*. After a short passage through woods, the road enters an open area on a gentle climb. Follow the course of the jeep road by maintaining a gentle climb while watching for road cuts and marker posts.

At 2.4 miles, enter the trees as the now well defined road climbs up valley on the south side. At 3.4 miles where a cable is across the road, pass a cabin and steam boiler on the left side and a mine dump on the right. At 3.8 miles, pass a cabin on the right. At 4.1 miles, a road with a sign *No Trespassing* branches left uphill to a mine.

A barbed wire fence, gate, and *No Trespassing* signs at 4.8 miles bar further travel

167

on the road. A substantial two story building and outbuildings are about 150 yards beyond. Remains of an ore processing table are near the gate.

James Peak east face from Mammoth Gulch

ADDITIONAL CONNECTING TRAIL INFORMATION
A junction with the Baltimore Ridge Route (39A) is at the sign-marked jeep road junction at 1.6 miles.

SKILLS RECOMMENDED
Skiing ability— Beginner.

Endurance— Moderate.

Routefinding skill— Beginner.

SNOW CONDITIONS
Poor on the lower part, good on the upper.

WIND EXPOSURE
Except for a short tree protected section above the junction at 1.6 miles, the lower 2.4 miles are exposed to the wind.

GRADIENT OR STEEPNESS
Below the junction at 1.6 miles the gradient is moderate, above it is generally slight.

Light.

VIEWS

From the open area beyond the junction at 1.6 miles, South Arapaho Peak is visible to the north and the east face of James Peak is visible at the head of Mammoth Gulch.

PRIVATE PROPERTY AND OTHER RESTRICTIONS

Posted mining operations are at the end of the road and on a side road along the way.

* * * * *

TRAIL NO. 41

GIANTS LADDER RAILROAD GRADE

SUMMARY

A low altitude link from South Boulder Creek to Antelope and Jenny Creeks, it can be followed in darkness or poor visibility. With a constant gradient of 0.8 percent the track can be fast if packed by snowmobiles. The wide road is however, very exposed to wind.

This ski trail follows the first 5.3 miles of the Moffat Road, the route of the Denver and Rio Grande Railroad over the continental divide used prior to the completion of the Moffat Tunnel in 1928. The Rollins Pass Ski Route (45), partly follows this same road further on, enroute to Winter Park. Although closed at Needle Eye Tunnel, the road is open in the summer to vehicles and the lower sections are popular with snowmobilers.

CLASSIFICATION Moderate

ALTITUDE (feet)
Starting 9,190
Highest 9,950
Cumulative gain 760
Cumulative loss 0

TIME (hours)
Northbound 2.5
Southbound 2.1

TRAIL MAP Side 2 (South)

MAP COORDINATES 47/17

PAGE-SIZE MAP No.16

USGS 7 ½' QUADRANGLES
East Portal (C2)
Nederland (C3)

DISTANCE (one way)
5.3 miles

ACCESS

South end. At Giants Ladder Trailhead (U).

North end. From Eldora Ski Area Trailhead (R), ski Jenny Creek Trail (35) 2.6 miles to the West Antelope Ridge Trail (37 B), which is skied 1.1 miles to its end. A total of 3.7 miles.

ROUTE DESCRIPTION
(northbound)

From the trailhead on the Rollinsville-East Portal road, follow the wide railroad grade on a steady climb out of the valley. Switchback sharply at 2.3 miles and continue on the road to the crossing of Antelope Creek at 5.1 miles and 300 yards more, to a jeep road junction marked with signs *One Way Road, Forest Service Road 149* and *502*, at 5.3 miles. Although the railroad grade continues west up Jenny Creek, this is the end of the route described here.

ADDITIONAL CONNECTING TRAIL INFORMATION

An unmarked junction with both the Antelope Creek Trail (37) and the South Antelope Creek Trail (37A) is at the switchback at 2.3 miles. A junction with the Antelope Creek Trail (37), and the West Antelope Ridge Trail (37B), is at the road signs at 5.3 miles.

Giants Ladder railroad grade

SKILLS RECOMMENDED

Skiing ability— Novice

Endurance— Easy.

Routefinding skill— Novice.

SNOW CONDITIONS

Poor to medium, usually packed by snowmobiles but may be blown clear in places.

WIND EXPOSURE

Very exposed due to the wide roadbed.

GRADIENT OR STEEPNESS

Slight, a constant 0.8 percent.

AMOUNT OF USE

Light, mainly by snowmobiles.

From the switchbacks, one can look across South Boulder Creek and up Mammoth Gulch. James Peak is to the right, behind the long ridge of Nebraska Hill.

PRIVATE PROPERTY AND OTHER RESTRICTIONS
None.

* * * * *

TRAIL NO. 42

SOUTH BOULDER CREEK TRAIL

SUMMARY
One of the more popular trails in the area, it climbs 1900 feet from East Portal in little over three and a half miles to end near the timberline site of the former CMC Pfiffner Hut at Rogers Pass Lake. Almost the entire trail is in the shelter of tall trees, the snow is excellent, and the gradient steep enough for a rapid and stimulating descent. Routes (42 A, B, C, D) continue beyond this trail to gain access to the continental divide where one can continue to Winter Park or descend another route on a high altitude loop.

CLASSIFICATION Difficult

ALTITUDE (feet)
Starting 9,210
Highest 11,100
Cumulative gain 1,890
Cumulative loss 0

TIME (hours)
Southwestbound, up 2.8
Northeastbound, down 1.4

TRAIL MAP Side 2 (South)

MAP COORDINATES 43/16

PAGE-SIZE MAP No.16

USGS 7 ½' QUADRANGLES
East Portal (C2)
Empire (D2)

DISTANCE (one way)
3.6 miles

ACCESS
At East Portal Trailhead (W).

ROUTE DESCRIPTION (southwestbound, up)
Cross the railroad tracks near the Moffat Tunnel entrance and scale the padlocked gate at the bridge over the concrete ditch. The trail into the shelter of trees is about 100 yards to the south, across a meadow and near a small building. Ski past several ranch buildings on the obvious, near level trail and continue 350 yards past a stream crossing to a junction with the Forest Lakes Trail (43) at 1.0 miles, in a 300 yard diameter clearing. Continue across the clearing, passing above the ruins of a log cabin, to again enter the trees on a well defined, steeper trail.

The trail is generally easy to follow, but is marked only occasionally with arrow and skier symbol signs and flagging. In places, it can be difficult to follow if untracked. It climbs the main, more southerly drainage rather than the tributary drainage followed by the summer trail shown on the USGS map. As it curves right to the west, it passes close under the steep rocky northern slopes of James Peak. After climbing a short steep headwall requiring switchbacks, more moderate and open slopes are reached. The drainage is then followed west across open wind swept meadows, to Rogers Pass Lake at the base of Haystack Mountain at 3.6 miles.

East portal of the Moffat Tunnel

ADDITIONAL CONNECTING TRAIL INFORMATION
An unmarked and probably untracked junction with the Clayton Lakes Route (42D) is at 1.9 miles.

The Rogers Pass (42A), Heart Lake (42B), and Iceberg Lake (42C) Routes continue from Rogers Pass Lake to separate crossings of the continental divide ridge.

The Pfiffner Hut of the Boulder Group of the Colorado Mountain Club was located about 100 yards east of Rogers Pass Lake. It became unserviceable after many years of use and was removed in 1988.

SKILLS RECOMMENDED
Skiing ability— Advanced.

Endurance— Strenuous.

Routefinding skill— Intermediate.

SNOW CONDITIONS
Medium to good for the first mile, excellent thereafter.

WIND EXPOSURE
The terrifying winds which seem to continuously sweep the East Portal trailhead area are left behind on entering the shelter of the trees in a hundred yards. The trail is well sheltered by tall trees until the more open area of scattered clumps of trees is reached, above the steep headwall at 3.2 miles.

GRADIENT OR STEEPNESS
The gradient is slight for the first mile and moderate to steep thereafter except for the very steep headwall at 3.2 miles.

AMOUNT OF USE
Usage for the first mile is moderate and decreases to light thereafter.

VIEWS
The slopes of massive James Peak tower above the trail as it curves to the west on nearing Rogers Pass Lake. From the lake, a minor peak, Haystack Mountain, is immediately to the south in front of James Peak. To the west, switchbacks climb the windblown slope to Rogers Pass.

PRIVATE PROPERTY AND OTHER RESTRICTIONS
Approximately the first mile and a half of the trail crosses the Henry Toll Ranch. Please respect their consideration in allowing access by staying on the established trail.

Bracing against wind on the continental divide

TRAIL NO. 42A

ROGERS PASS ROUTE

SUMMARY

The Rogers Pass, Heart Lake, Iceberg Lakes, and Clayton Lake Routes are all steep, above timberline routes branching from the South Boulder Creek Trail above East Portal. After climbing to the crest of the continental divide ridge, they descend the tundra slopes west to join the Rollins Pass Route at Riflesight Notch. All are shorter than the Rollins Pass Route, thereby reducing the exposure to the wind for a divide crossing, but are more difficult and exposed to possible avalanche.

Other routes (42 B, C, D) offer better terrain for skiing than the Rogers Pass Route. On this route the steep ascent of the east side is best done when the switchbacked trail above the lake is blown free of snow, carrying skis.

CLASSIFICATION Very difficult

ALTITUDE (feet)
Starting 11,100
Highest 11,910
Cumulative gain 910
Cumulative loss 900

TIME (hours)
Westbound 2.2
Eastbound 2.2

TRAIL MAP Side 2 (South)

MAP COORDINATES 41/14

PAGE-SIZE MAP No.18

USGS 7 ½' QUADRANGLES
East Portal (C2)
Empire (D2)

DISTANCE (one way)
3.2 miles

ACCESS
From the East Portal Trailhead (W), ski the South Boulder Creek Trail (42), 3.6 miles to its end at Rogers Pass Lake.

ROUTE DESCRIPTION (westbound)
From Rogers Pass Lake climb the switchbacks of the trail 900 feet to the pass at 11,910 feet and 1.0 miles. Follow the road north on an moderate descending traverse of the tundra slope to the trestle at Riflesight Notch at 3.2 miles and 11,107 feet.

ADDITIONAL CONNECTING TRAIL INFORMATION
An indefinite, above timberline junction with the Jim Creek Headwall Route (44) is at Rogers Pass.

Above Iceberg Lakes, James Peak in background

SKILLS RECOMMENDED
Skiing ability— Expert.
Endurance— Very strenuous.
Routefinding skill— Advanced.

SNOW CONDITIONS
Poor, the route may be blown clear.

WIND EXPOSURE
The entire route is exposed to the high winds and blowing snow common above timberline.

GRADIENT OR STEEPNESS
Very steep on east side, moderate on the west.

AMOUNT OF USE
Nearly unused.

VIEWS
The corniced ridge of the continental divide extends north to the Arapaho Peaks. James Peak looms nearby to the south. In the west, the distant peaks of the Gore Range are on the horizon beyond the Williams Fork Mountains. The ski runs of Winter Park and Mary Jane, cut into the forested slopes beyond the Fraser Valley, are visible down Jim Creek.

PRIVATE PROPERTY AND OTHER RESTRICTIONS
None.

TRAIL NO. 42B

HEART LAKE ROUTE

SUMMARY

Like the Rogers Pass, Iceberg Lakes, and Clayton Lake Routes, this is an above timberline route branching from the South Boulder Creek Trail above East Portal. It ascends a steep but skiable ridge immediately north of Hart Lake and descends the tundra slope west to join the Rollins Pass Route at Riflesight Notch.

CLASSIFICATION Very difficult

ALTITUDE (feet)

Starting 11,100
Highest 12,050
Cumulative gain 950
Cumulative loss 940

TIME (hours)

Westbound 2.2
Eastbound 2.2

TRAIL MAP Side 2 (South)

MAP COORDINATES 41/14

PAGE-SIZE MAP No.15

USGS 7 ½' QUADRANGLES
East Portal (C2)
Empire (D2)

DISTANCE (one way)
2.9 miles

ACCESS

From the East Portal Trailhead (W), ski the South Boulder Creek Trail (42), 3.6 miles to its end at Rogers Pass Lake.

ROUTE DESCRIPTION (westbound)

From Rogers Pass Lake, ski north up the moderate, above timberline slope to the bench of Heart Lake. Climb the steep eastern end of the ridge north of the lake which may be blown clear of snow. Follow the crest of this ridge west with little gain in altitude as it becomes more bench-like, with a steep south side. Ascend the right side of the sharp ridge, southwest to the divide at 1.1 miles and 12,050 feet.

Descend the tundra slope northwest to intercept the jeep road which can be followed to Riflesight Notch and the Rollins Pass Route (45) at 2.9 miles.

ADDITIONAL CONNECTING TRAIL INFORMATION

None.

SKILLS RECOMMENDED

Skiing ability— Expert.

Endurance— Very strenuous.

Routefinding skill— Advanced.

SNOW CONDITIONS
Poor, the east end of the ridge northeast of Heart Lake may be clear of snow and the slope up the east side of the divide medium. The slopes on the west side of the divide are likely to be bare or wind packed.

WIND EXPOSURE
The entire route is exposed to the high winds and blowing snow common above timberline.

GRADIENT OR STEEPNESS
Very steep on the east side, moderate on the west.

AMOUNT OF USE
Nearly unused.

VIEWS
Similar to those for the Rogers Pass Route (42A).

PRIVATE PROPERTY AND OTHER RESTRICTIONS
None.

* * * * *

TRAIL NO. 42C

ICEBERG LAKES ROUTE

SUMMARY
Like the Rogers Pass, Heart Lake, and Clayton Lake Routes, this is an above timberline route which continues on from the South Boulder Creek Trail above East Portal. All climb the steep east side of the continental divide and descend the tundra slope west to join the Rollins Pass Route at Riflesight Notch.

Climbing steep windslab above Iceberg Lakes

This route follows the Heart Lake Route to ascend the ridge north of Heart Lake. It departs from that route to cross the wide basin to the north and climb an easier ridge to the continental divide south of Iceberg Lakes.

CLASSIFICATION Very difficult

ALTITUDE (feet)
Starting 11,100
Highest 12,120
Cumulative gain 1,020
Cumulative loss 1,010

TIME (hours)
Westbound 2.0
Eastbound 2.0

TRAIL MAP Side 2 (South)

MAP COORDINATES 40/15

PAGE-SIZE MAP No.15

USGS 7 ½' QUADRANGLES
East Portal (C2)
Empire (D2)

DISTANCE (one way)
2.4 miles

Open slopes above timberline

ACCESS
From the East Portal Trailhead (W), ski the South Boulder Creek Trail (42), 3.6 miles to its end at Rogers Pass Lake.

ROUTE DESCRIPTION (westbound)
As for the Heart Lake Route, from Rogers Pass Lake ski north up the moderate, above timberline slope, to the bench of Heart Lake. Climb the steep eastern end of the ridge north of the lake which may be blown clear of snow. Depart from the Heart Lake Route here and cross the basin to the north without loosing any significant altitude. Continue north up the steepening but moderate slope to gain the top of a subsidiary east-west ridge. Follow this ridge west as it steepens to join the continental divide at 1.2 miles and 12,120 feet. Avoid the wind slab on the steep

178

drop off to the north. Descend the tundra slope northwest to intercept the jeep road which can be followed to Riflesight Notch and a junction with the Rollins Pass Route (45) at 2.4 miles.

ADDITIONAL CONNECTING TRAIL INFORMATION
None.

SKILLS RECOMMENDED
Skiing ability— Expert.

Endurance— Very strenuous.

Routefinding skill— Advanced.

SNOW CONDITIONS
Poor, the east end of the ridge northeast of Heart Lake may be clear of snow, the basin medium, the ridge leading to the divide can be hard wind slab near the top, and the slopes on the west side wind scoured.

WIND EXPOSURE
The entire route is exposed to the high winds and blowing snow common above timberline.

GRADIENT OR STEEPNESS
Very steep on the ascent of the ridges of the east side, slight to moderate in the basin, and moderate on the west side.

AMOUNT OF USE
Nearly unused.

VIEWS
In addition to those described for the Rogers Pass and Heart Lake Routes, the view of the cornices on the eastern side of the continental divide ridge above Iceberg Lakes is extraordinary.

PRIVATE PROPERTY AND OTHER RESTRICTIONS
None.

* * * * *

TRAIL NO. 42D

CLAYTON LAKE ROUTE

SUMMARY
Like the Rogers Pass, Heart Lake, and Iceberg Lakes Routes, this is an above timberline route branching from the South Boulder Creek Trail above East Portal.

All climb the steep east side of the continental divide and descend the tundra slope west to join the Rollins Pass Route at Riflesight Notch.

This is the most direct of the routes. It branches off the South Boulder Creek Route less than two miles from East Portal and crosses the divide nearly directly above Riflesight Notch. Enroute to the divide, it climbs steeply through forested slopes to timberline at Clayton Lake, then up a moderate open bowl to a rocky ramp, generally free of snow, which leads to the continental divide north of Iceberg Lakes.

James Peak from slopes above Clayton Lake

CLASSIFICATION Very difficult

ALTITUDE (feet)
Starting 10,080
Highest 11,950
Cumulative gain 1,870
Cumulative loss 850

TIME (hours)
Westbound 3.4
Eastbound 2.8

TRAIL MAP Side 2 (South)

MAP COORDINATES 41/16

PAGE-SIZE MAP No.16

USGS 7 ½' QUADRANGLES
East Portal (C2)

DISTANCE (one way)
2.4 miles

ACCESS

From the East Portal Trailhead (W), ski the South Boulder Creek Trail (42), 1.9 miles to an indefinite junction at about 10,100 feet altitude. The location is difficult

Ascending boulders to continental divide above Clayton Lake

to specify as there are no obvious landmarks and an altimeter reading is of limited usefulness due to the nearly level terrain in the vicinity. The best indicator of the approximate location is the view of two steep rocky knobs through sparse trees uphill to the northwest.

ROUTE DESCRIPTION (westbound)
Bushwhack northwest through trees on a steep route up into the gap between the two rocky knobs described above. Turn west at 10,400 feet and ascend a steep drainage to gain the bench above and north of Clayton Lake at 0.8 miles.

Climb west up the moderate slopes of the above timberline bowl toward a gap in the cornice along the divide. It may be best to carry skis on the final ascent as fierce winds often scour the ramp like corridor free of snow to expose boulders underfoot. The divide is at 1.7 miles and 11,950 feet.

Descend directly down the fall line to the trestle at Riflesight Notch and the Rollins Pass Route (45) at 2.4 miles.

ADDITIONAL CONNECTING TRAIL INFORMATION
None.

SKILLS RECOMMENDED
Skiing ability— Expert.

Endurance— Very strenuous.

Routefinding skill— Expert.

SNOW CONDITIONS

Good to excellent untracked snow is usually found in the trees leading to Clayton Lakes, hard windpacked snow can be expected above timberline on the slopes leading to the ramp. The ramp is likely to be blown free of snow, and the steep tundra slopes on the west side of the divide may be blown clear.

WIND EXPOSURE

Protected by trees as far as Clayton Lake, exposed thereafter.

GRADIENT OR STEEPNESS

Very steep on the ascent through trees to Clayton Lake, moderate to steep for the remainder of the climb to the divide. The descent to Riflesight Notch is steep.

AMOUNT OF USE

Nearly unused.

VIEWS

James Peak dominates the skyline to the south. The Gore Range, Williams Fork Mountains, and the downhill ski runs of Winter Park and Mary Jane are visible to the west. As from the Heart Lake Route, the view of the corniced ridge of the continental divide, this time looking south, is spectacular.

PRIVATE PROPERTY AND OTHER RESTRICTIONS

None.

* * * * *

TRAIL NO. 43

FOREST LAKES TRAIL

SUMMARY

After switchbacking north from the South Boulder Creek Trail a mile above East Portal, this moderately steep unblazed trail climbs through stands of towering trees to Forest Lakes and then a steep two hundred feet more to the drainage divide of Jenny and South Boulder Creeks. The up and back trip makes a fine tour, or with a car shuttle one can continue north into the Jenny Creek drainage and down to Eldora Ski Area, a total distance of 9.3 miles.

CLASSIFICATION Difficult   **TRAIL MAP** Side 2 (South)

Corniced ridge of continental divide

ALTITUDE (feet)
Starting 9,590
Highest 10,820
Cumulative gain 1,230
Cumulative loss 0

TIME (hours)
Northbound, up 2.0
Southbound, down 0.9

MAP COORDINATES 44/17·

PAGE-SIZE MAP No.16

USGS 7 ½' QUADRANGLES
East Portal (C2)

DISTANCE (one way)
2.0 miles

ACCESS
South end. From East Portal Trailhead (W), ski 1.0 miles on the South Boulder Creek Trail (42) to a junction in a large clearing.

North end. From Eldora Ski Area Trailhead (R), ski 4.2 miles on the Jenny Creek Trail (35) to an indefinite junction with the Jenny Creek-Forest Lakes Route (43B). Ski this route 2.1 miles to its end. Total distance is 6.3 miles.

ROUTE DESCRIPTION (northbound, up)
Switchback sharply to the right from the junction at mile 1.0 on the South Boulder Creek Trail (42) and begin a moderate climbing traverse north into the trees. At 0.7 miles, cross Arapaho Creek and climb a short steep section to gain entry into the hanging tributary valley.

At 1.2 miles and 10,080 feet altitude (840 yards beyond the creek crossing), find the unmarked junction where this trail forks to the right onto a faint unblazed trail, which climbs diagonally up the valley side.

The trail to the left is the Arapaho Creek-Forest Lakes Gully Route (43A) which continues up valley, without climbing appreciably, onto the sidehill. Either trail may be tracked. The junction is about 20 yards short of a rounded gray stump, which stands about 2 feet above snow line on the uphill side of the upper trail. Leave some challenge for others by not marking this with flagging.

Further on, our trail is marked by tree slashes as it climbs steadily, leveling out only when near the easternmost of the Forest Lakes at 1.8 miles and 10,630 feet altitude.

Pick a route northeast past the lake 200 feet more up the steep slope to the drainage divide of South Boulder Creek and Jenny Creek at 2.0 miles where this route ends. Avoid going too far west, as it means extra climbing to clear the ridge. The railroad grade is 200 feet too high.

ADDITIONAL CONNECTING TRAIL INFORMATION
The route to Eldora Ski Area may be continued on the Jenny Creek-Forest Lakes Route (43B) or South Fork Jenny Creek Route (43C).

SKILLS RECOMMENDED
Skiing ability— Advanced.

Endurance— Strenuous.

Routefinding skill— Advanced.

SNOW CONDITIONS
Excellent.

WIND EXPOSURE
Exposed only while crossing the easternmost of the Forest Lakes.

GRADIENT OR STEEPNESS
Moderate to the turn off from Arapaho Creek at 1.2 miles, except for a short steep section above the creek crossing. Beyond the turn off, the gradient is steep and unrelenting with only a short respite at the lake before the final very steep 200 feet to the ridge top.

AMOUNT OF USE
Light.

Lunch stop near Forest Lakes

VIEWS

The view to the south from above Forest Lakes is dominated by the imposing bulk of James Peak. The cirques on the continental divide above Forest and Arapaho Lakes form a dramatic curtain to the west.

PRIVATE PROPERTY AND OTHER RESTRICTIONS
None.

* * * * *

TRAIL NO. 43A

ARAPAHO CREEK-FOREST LAKES GULLY ROUTE

SUMMARY

An alternate to the Forest Lakes Trail, it continues up the valley bottom of Arapaho Creek from where the Forest Lakes Trail angles more steeply up the forested hillside. At the abrupt head of the gradual valley, it climbs a steep gully to Forest Lakes.

CLASSIFICATION Difficult   **TRAIL MAP** Side 2 (South)

185

ALTITUDE (feet)
Starting 10,120
Highest 10,820
Cumulative gain 720
Cumulative loss 0

TIME (hours)
Northbound, up 1.2
Southbound, down 0.7

MAP COORDINATES 43/18

PAGE-SIZE MAP No.16

USGS 7 ½' QUADRANGLES
East Portal (C2)

DISTANCE (one way)
1.3 miles

ACCESS

South end. From East Portal Trailhead (W), ski 1.0 miles on the South Boulder Creek Trail (42) to a junction with the Forest Lakes Trail (43). Follow it 1.2 miles to where it climbs right from an unmarked junction. A total distance of 2.2 miles.

North end. The access is identical to that for the north end of the Forest Lakes Trail (43). A total distance of 6.3 miles from Eldora Ski Area Trailhead (R).

ROUTE DESCRIPTION (northbound, up)

Continue on the trail near the valley bottom from where the Forest Lakes Trail (43) angles north more steeply from an unmarked junction. The recognizable trail ends in a steep walled basin at 0.6 miles where a steep open gully descends the forested slope to the north. Climb the curving course of this gully to the middle Forest Lake at 0.9 miles. Climb northeast to cross the ridge as low as possible at 1.4 miles and 10,820 feet altitude.

ADDITIONAL CONNECTING TRAIL INFORMATION

The north end of the route joins the Forest Lakes Trail (43), the Jenny Creek-Forest Lakes Route (43B), and the South Fork Jenny Creek Route (43C) at an indefinite junction on the ridge above Forest Lakes, approximately a half mile southeast of the railroad grade.

SKILLS RECOMMENDED

Skiing ability— Advanced.

Endurance— Strenuous.

Routefinding skill— Advanced.

SNOW CONDITIONS

Excellent.

WIND EXPOSURE

Moderate.

GRADIENT OR STEEPNESS

Slight along the valley bottom, very steep in the gully.

Light along the valley bottom, very light in the gully.

VIEWS

The corniced ridge of the continental divide above the glacial cirque settings of Arapaho and Forest Lakes, is a mile to the west.

PRIVATE PROPERTY AND OTHER RESTRICTIONS

None.

* * * * *

TRAIL NO. 43B

JENNY CREEK-FOREST LAKES ROUTE

SUMMARY

This route offers the freedom of untracked skiing over moderate terrain. Heavily timbered slopes, as well as the mix of open slopes and isolated tree stands common near timberline, are traversed. Out and back skiers from Eldora Ski Area and trekers from East Portal to Eldora Ski Area both use this off trail route.

CLASSIFICATION Difficult

TRAIL MAP Side 2 (South)

ALTITUDE (feet)
Starting 10,820
Highest 10,820
Cumulative gain 20
Cumulative loss 220

MAP COORDINATES 44/20

PAGE-SIZE MAP No.16

USGS 7 ½' QUADRANGLES
East Portal (C2)

TIME (hours)
Northbound, down 1.4
Southbound, up 1.5

DISTANCE (one way)
2.1 miles

ACCESS

South end. From East Portal Trailhead (W), ski 1.0 miles on the South Boulder Creek Trail (42) to a junction with the Forest Lakes Trail (43). Follow it 2.0 miles to its end on the ridge above Forest Lakes. A total distance of 3.0 miles.

North end. From Eldora Ski Area Trailhead (R), ski 4.2 miles on the Jenny Creek Trail (35) to an indefinite junction where the valley and trail turn north at 10,600 feet as Yankee Doodle Lake is approached.

ROUTE DESCRIPTION (northbound, down)

From the unmarked junction on the ridge above Forest Lakes, descend about 50 feet to more gentle terrain and traverse with only a slight loss of altitude past scattered clumps of trees to enter the continuous forest. Cross the saddle on the minor ridge dividing the forks of Jenny Creek and descend the moderate slope north to the curve of the railroad grade at its base.

Cross the valley bottom east northeast toward the treeless slopes of Guinn Mountain without gaining altitude, to intercept the Jenny Creek Trail (35) at an unmarked and untracked junction at 2.1 miles.

ADDITIONAL CONNECTING TRAIL INFORMATION
The south end joins the Forest Lakes Trail (43), the Arapaho Creek-Forest Lakes Gully Route (43A), and the South Fork Jenny Creek Route (43C). This junction is unmarked and only generally located on the ridge above Forest Lakes.

SKILLS RECOMMENDED
Skiing ability— Intermediate.

Endurance— Strenuous.

Routefinding skill— Advanced.

SNOW CONDITIONS
Excellent.

WIND EXPOSURE
Exposed where the route skirts the open slopes at timberline.

GRADIENT OR STEEPNESS
After a short moderate descent from the ridge, the traverse is near level until ending with a moderate descent to Jenny Creek.

AMOUNT OF USE
Nearly unused.

VIEWS
The route of the Moffat Road making its sinuous way across the tundra slopes at the head of Jenny Creek is visible northwest toward the continental divide.

PRIVATE PROPERTY AND OTHER RESTRICTIONS

None.

James Peak from near Yankee Doodle Lake

* * * * *

TRAIL NO. 43C

SOUTH FORK JENNY CREEK ROUTE

SUMMARY

An alternate to the Jenny Creek-Forest Lakes Route, it also connects Jenny Creek and the Eldora Ski Area with East Portal. Shorter and with good telemark skiing at the upper end, one must bushwhack through dense timber in the creek bottom at the lower end.

CLASSIFICATION Difficult

ALTITUDE (feet)

Starting 10,820
Highest 10,820
Cumulative gain 0
Cumulative loss 660

TIME (hours)

Northeastbound, down 0.8
Southwestbound, up 1.8

TRAIL MAP Side 2 (South)

MAP COORDINATES 44/19

PAGE-SIZE MAP No.16

USGS 7 ½' QUADRANGLES
East Portal (C2)
Nederland (C3)

DISTANCE (one way)
1.4 miles

ACCESS

Southwest end. From East Portal Trailhead (W), ski 1.0 miles on the South Boulder Creek Trail (42) to a junction with the Forest Lakes Trail (43). Follow it 2.0 miles to its end on the ridge above Forest Lakes. A total distance of 3.0 miles.

Northeast end. From Eldora Ski Area Trailhead (M), ski 3.5 miles on the Jenny Creek Trail (35) to an indefinite junction at 10,160 feet, 300 yards past the roofless cabin at 3.2 miles.

ROUTE DESCRIPTION (northeastbound, down)

From the ridge above Forest Lakes, descend the fall line to the north through scattered clumps of trees and then continuous forest. Pick up an unmarked trail for a few hundred yards (an arm of the railroad "wye" turnaround) to cross the railroad grade as it curves to cross the creek at 0.8 miles .

Continue down through the thicket of dense small trees in the steep walled drainage to about 10,200 feet where you are below the steep treeless knob crossed by the railroad grade to the north.

Bushwhack north across the near level terrain to the Jenny Creek Trail (35) on the north side of the creek at 1.4 miles.

ADDITIONAL CONNECTING TRAIL INFORMATION

The southwest end joins the Forest Lakes Trail (43), the Arapaho Creek-Forest Lakes Gully Route (43A), and the Jenny Creek-Forest Lakes Route (43B), all at an indefinite junction on the ridge above Forest Lakes.

SKILLS RECOMMENDED

Skiing ability— Advanced.

Endurance— Strenuous.

Routefinding skill— Advanced.

SNOW CONDITIONS

Excellent upper part, good lower.

WIND EXPOSURE

Moderate exposure on the higher open slopes, well protected lower in the trees.

GRADIENT OR STEEPNESS

Moderate, the upper slopes offer good telemarking.

AMOUNT OF USE

Nearly unused.

Distant views are shielded by the dense trees and terrain of the route except at the crossing of the railroad grade and on the open slopes near the upper end.

PRIVATE PROPERTY AND OTHER RESTRICTIONS
None.

* * * * *

TRAIL NO. 44

JIM CREEK HEADWALL ROUTE

SUMMARY
This is a very steep descent route from the continental divide near Rogers Pass into Jim Creek and on to Winter Park. It can be linked with the Rogers Pass, Heart Lake, or Iceberg Lakes Routes for a divide crossing from East Portal. The two thousand foot descent of open slope at the head of Jim Creek should not be attempted unless snow conditions are stable.

CLASSIFICATION Very difficult

ALTITUDE (feet)
Starting 11,860
Highest 11,860
Cumulative gain 0
Cumulative loss 2,760

TIME (hours)
Down, westbound 1.4
Up, eastbound 4.0

TRAIL MAP Side 2 (South)

MAP COORDINATES 39/14

PAGE-SIZE MAP No.18

USGS 7 ½' QUADRANGLES
East Portal (C2)
Empire (D2)
Fraser (C1)

DISTANCE (one way)
3.8 miles

ACCESS
East or top end, on the continental divide. From the East Portal Trailhead (W), ski the South Boulder Creek Trail (42), 3.6 miles to its end at Rogers Pass Lake. Climb or ski either the Rogers Pass Route (42A) 1.0 miles, the Heart Lake Route (42 B) 1.1 miles, or the Iceberg Lakes Route 1.2 miles to the ridge top and continental divide. A total distance of 4.6 to 4.8 miles.

West or bottom end, at Jim Creek Trailhead, 0.4 miles south of Winter Park on Highway 40.

ROUTE DESCRIPTION (Down, westbound)
From the top of the continental divide, descend the very steep slope, past scattered clumps of trees, two thousand feet to the bottom of Jim Creek at 1.1 miles and

10,050 feet. Follow the jeep road trail down the valley to the highway at 3.8 miles.

ADDITIONAL CONNECTING TRAIL INFORMATION
None.

SKILLS RECOMMENDED
Skiing ability— Expert.

Endurance— Very strenuous.

Routefinding skill— Advanced.

SNOW CONDITIONS
Good conditions are likely on the steep open slope for the descent to Jim Creek. Excellent conditions should prevail for the remainder of the route.

WIND EXPOSURE
Exposed to wind on the steep open slope, protected by trees thereafter.

GRADIENT OR STEEPNESS
Very steep descent to Jim Creek, slight descent thereafter.

AMOUNT OF USE
Nearly unused.

VIEWS
Similar to that from Rogers Pass Route (42A). The drop into Jim Creek is awesome.

PRIVATE PROPERTY AND OTHER RESTRICTIONS
None.

* * * * *

TRAIL NO. 45

ROLLINS PASS ROUTE

SUMMARY
One of the classic routes of Front Range skiing, it crosses the continental divide at the historic Corona station site on Rollins Pass where the Moffat Railroad route once crossed prior to the 1928 completion of the Moffat tunnel. This is the easiest of the divide crossings from the eastern slope to Winter Park but has a long exposure, about five miles, to the high winds and ground blizzards common above timberline. An overnight stay at the Arestua Hut permits an early start on the crossing. The

Early morning departure of Eldora for Rollins Pass

complexities of car shuttling can be avoided by using the metropolitan area RTD bus service from Denver or Boulder to Eldora Ski Area and returning from Winter Park village (Hideaway Park on USGS maps) to Denver by train or regularly scheduled bus service. See the section *Public Transportation*.

CLASSIFICATION Difficult

ALTITUDE (feet)
Starting 10,960
Highest 11,760
Cumulative gain 910
Cumulative loss 2,770

TIME (hours)
Westbound 6.0
Eastbound 8.0

TRAIL MAP Side 2 (South)

MAP COORDINATES 42/20

PAGE-SIZE MAP No.12

USGS 7 ½' QUADRANGLES
Fraser (C1)
East Portal (C2)
Nederland (C3)

DISTANCE (one way)
9.2 miles

ACCESS

East end. At Arestua Hut. From Eldora Ski Area Trailhead (R), ski the Jenny Creek Trail (35), 1.9 miles to the Guinn Mountain Trail (36), and 2.1 miles to its end at the Arestua Hut. A total distance of 4.0 miles.

West end. At Winter Park Ski area.

Guinn Mountain above Arestua Hut

ROUTE DESCRIPTION (westbound)

From Arestua Hut, climb 250 feet to the top of Guinn Mountain at 0.4 miles, either by heading north to the pipeline swath and following it to the summit or by skiing uphill and west through a series of clearings. Ski west along the top of the narrow ridge and climb the wider steep wind packed slope to the sign at the railroad grade at 0.9 miles. Stay near the crest of the ridge to avoid the steeper slopes on either side that could avalanche.

Following the trace of a road if possible, climb the gentle tundra slope to the west. Stay on the north side and as much as 200 feet below the crest of the long ridge leading to Rollins Pass to avoid unnecessary climbing above the pass, but at the same time, keep high above the railroad trestles to avoid the steep side slopes above Middle Boulder Creek.

From the gentle pass at 2.4 miles and 11,671 feet, follow the railroad grade on a steady descent of about four percent to the south as it drops lower on the broad ridge of the divide. Telegraph poles are occasionally helpful to indicate the location of the railroad. Care should be taken in poor visibility to not mistake minor ridges to the west at BM 11382 and at the Corona Range Study Plot for the knob at Riflesight Notch. Visibility permitting, Riflesight Notch at 5.6 miles and 11,107 feet is identifiable by the railroad trestle.

Follow the road to the south from the top of the trestle and switchback north in 300 yards to arrive at the base of the trestle. With good snow conditions, the steep

Climb to railroad grade above Yankee Doodle Lake

descent from here of the South Fork of Ranch Creek is a delight. On reaching the railroad grade again in a level clearing at 6.8 miles, follow the wide roadbed on a near level course to where the slope changes so that the left side is downhill at 7.4 miles. Turn left off the road here down Buck Creek. Find the wagon road on the left side of the drainage, 0.7 miles and 400 feet below the turn off. Follow the road down Buck Creek drainage to the level aqueduct at 8.9 miles, turn right on it and go 500 yards to where a road downhill leads to Highway 40 and Winter Park ski area, at 9.7 miles and 9100 feet.

ADDITIONAL CONNECTING TRAIL INFORMATION
The Upper Railroad Switchback Road (45A) branches off at the bottom of Riflesight Notch at 6.0 miles and rejoins the route at 6.8 miles.

The Lower Railroad Switchback Road (45B) continues on the railroad grade at 7.4 miles.

SKILLS RECOMMENDED
Skiing ability— Advanced.

Endurance— Very strenuous.

Routefinding skill— Expert.

SNOW CONDITIONS
Medium overall, the snow is generally good from the hut to the saddle above Yankee

Rollins Pass on foot in a ground blizzard

Doodle Lake at 0.7 miles. The climb to the railroad grade at 0.9 miles is likely on hard windslab. The ridge leading to Rollins Pass and the descent to Riflesight Notch at 5.6 miles is all above timberline. Normally it has wind packed snow drifted into the road cut, however a significant part may be blown clear, necessitating walking. It is important to have a pack with slots or some arrangement to carry skis.

The snow from Riflesight Notch to Winter Park is protected by trees and is frequently excellent.

WIND EXPOSURE
The five mile section above timberline is exposed to high winds out of the west and subsequent ground blizzards. Adequate clothing for extreme conditions, including face protection, is essential. The wind is less of a problem for eastbound travel.

GRADIENT OR STEEPNESS
Generally moderate, but with a steep climb from the saddle above Yankee Doodle Lake at 0.7 miles to the railroad grade, a steep descent of the South Fork of Ranch Creek where the route leaves the railroad grade below Riflesight Notch, and again where Buck Creek is followed in preference to the railroad at 7.4 miles.

AMOUNT OF USE
Very light.

VIEWS

Outstanding views abound along the route. From Guinn Mountain, James Peak to the south and South Arapaho Peak to the north loom larger than all others. At the saddle at 0.7 miles, Yankee Doodle Lake is nestled in the bowl immediately below to the south, at the head of Jenny Creek. Middle Boulder Creek and the King Lake Trail are below, to the north. From Rollins Pass south, the distant serrated peaks of the Gore Range can be seen beyond Byres Peak and the Williams Fork Mountains. The downhill slopes of Winter Park and Mary Jane are across the Fraser Valley. If all other views are obscured by weather, the nearby rugged face of Mt. Epworth to the west can be seen in passing, a mile south of Rollins Pass.

PRIVATE PROPERTY AND OTHER RESTRICTIONS

None.

* * * * *

TRAIL NO. 45A

UPPER RAILROAD SWITCHBACK ROAD

SUMMARY

This alternative ski trail is a loop of railroad grade which gradually looses 800 feet altitude in 3.2 miles. It can be used as an alternative to the 0.8 mile steep section of the Rollins Pass Route, which shortcuts the railroad grade by following the South Fork of Ranch Creek below Riflesight Notch. This alternative is useful when spring or otherwise uncommon poor snow conditions make skiing the shorter route difficult. Descent of the gradual incline of the loop can be rapid if packed by snowmobile traffic.

CLASSIFICATION Moderate-difficult

ALTITUDE (feet)
Starting 11,100
Highest 11,100
Cumulative gain 0
Cumulative loss 800

TIME (hours)
Down, westbound 0.8
Up, eastbound 1.4

TRAIL MAP Side 2 (South)

MAP COORDINATES 38/17

PAGE-SIZE MAP No.15

USGS 7 ½' QUADRANGLES
East Portal (C2)

DISTANCE (one way)
3.2 miles

ACCESS

Upper end. At the Riflesight Notch trestle, mile 6.0 of the Rollins Pass Route (45).

Lower end. At mile 6.8 on the Rollins Pass Route.

ROUTE DESCRIPTION
(down, westbound)

From below and on the south side of the trestle at Riflesight Notch, ski the road west as it contours across the slope. Pass through a maze of snowmobile tracks near the ridge top at 0.7 miles and switchback sharply to the left at 1.6 miles after descending a steeper section. Follow the wide roadbed as it traverses back into the South Fork of Ranch Creek to the junction at 3.2 miles with the Rollins Pass Route (45). This is at a nearly level clearing where the road turns right to cross the creek.

ADDITIONAL CONNECTING TRAIL INFORMATION
None.

SKILLS RECOMMENDED
Skiing ability— Novice.

Endurance— Strenuous because of the access.

Routefinding skill— Novice.

Rollins Pass ogre

SNOW CONDITIONS
Medium overall, the snow is generally packed by snowmobile traffic.

WIND EXPOSURE
The upper leg of the switchback is exposed to wind, the lower is less exposed.

GRADIENT OR STEEPNESS
Constant and slight, except moderate above the switchback at 1.6 miles.

AMOUNT OF USE
Moderate, used by snowmobiles.

VIEWS
The downhill slopes of Winter Park Ski Area are visible to the west, across the Fraser valley.

PRIVATE PROPERTY AND OTHER RESTRICTIONS
None.

Mary Jane, Winter Park, Riflesight Notch

* * * * *

TRAIL NO. 45B

LOWER RAILROAD SWITCHBACK ROAD

SUMMARY

The off trail steep descent of Buck Creek of the Rollins Pass Route is bypassed by following the gradual incline of the railroad grade on a long meandering alternate route to Winter Park. This bypass adds 4.1 miles and its junction with Highway 40 is 0.6 miles north of the ski area. A variation of the bypass descends cross country trails to Ski Idlewild, 0.7 miles north of town. Here, one can ride the free shuttle bus to town or Winter Park Ski Area.

CLASSIFICATION Moderate

ALTITUDE (feet)
Starting 10,180
Highest 10,180
Cumulative gain 0
Cumulative loss 1,080

TIME (hours)
Down, westbound 2.0
Up, eastbound 2.5

TRAIL MAP Side 2 (South)

MAP COORDINATES 35/18

PAGE-SIZE MAP No.15

USGS 7 ½' QUADRANGLES
Fraser (C1)
East Portal (C2)
DISTANCE (one way)
6.4 miles

ACCESS
Upper end. At mile 7.4 of the Rollins Pass Route (45).

Lower end. At a road junction on Highway 40, 0.6 miles north of Winter Park Ski Area, or alternatively at Ski Idlewild.

ROUTE DESCRIPTION
(westbound, down)

Continue descending the road at mile 7.4 of the Rollins Pass Route (45) where that route leaves the road. At 2.6 miles, go straight through the crossroads near half-section marker 9666, and on to the junction at 6.4 miles with Highway 40, 0.6 miles north of the ski area.

ADDITIONAL CONNECTING TRAIL INFORMATION
To descend the cross country trails to Ski Idlewild, turn right off the Lower Railroad Switchback Road where it turns left (south) at a junction at 4.1 miles. The USGS map shows this junction near half-section marker 9427. It is 2.0 miles to Ski Idlewild base.

Descent from Riflesight Notch

SKILLS RECOMMENDED
Skiing ability— Novice.
Endurance— Moderate.
Routefinding skill— Novice.

SNOW CONDITIONS
Medium, packed by snowmobilers.

WIND EXPOSURE
Moderate.

GRADIENT OR STEEPNESS
Nearly flat.

AMOUNT OF USE
Moderate, used frequently by snowmobilers.

VIEWS
None.

PRIVATE PROPERTY AND OTHER RESTRICTIONS
None.

TRAIL SUMMARY TABLE

TRAIL NUMBER		PAGE-SIZE MAP	MAP COORDINATES	USGS QUADRANGLES	TRAILHEAD	CLASSIFICATION	MILES
1	SANDBEACH LAKE	3	52/52	A3	A	4	4.2
2	THUNDER LAKE	3	48/31	A3,A2	B	4	7.1
2A	CALYPSO CASCADES	2	51/49	A3	B	3	1.5
3	ALLENS PARK-FINCH LK-PEAR RESERVOIR	3	48/47	A3,A2	C	4	5.8
4	ROCK CREEK	6	53/45	A3	D	3	3.1
4A	EAST RIDGE ST. VRAIN MOUNTAIN	5	52/45	A3	D	4	1.5
5	ST. VRAIN MOUNTAIN	6	53/46	A3	D	4	3.5
5A	NORTH GULLY ST. VRAIN MOUNTAIN	5	50/47	A3	D	5	1.3
6	MIDDLE ST. VRAIN ROAD	6	55/42	A3	E	2	4.7
7	BUCHANAN PASS	6	55/42	A3	E	3	6.3
7A	ST. VRAIN GLACIER	5	47/45	A3,A2	F,E	4	2.4
8	PARK CREEK	6	56/43	A3	E	3	3.3
8A	LOGGING ROAD SPUR	6	56/43	A3	E	2	1.0
8B	ROCK CREEK SADDLE	6	54/44	A3	E,D	4	1.8
9	NORTH SOURDOUGH	6	56/41	A3,B3	E,G	3	2.0
9A	BEAVER RESERVOIR CUTOFF	8	56/41	A3,B3	E,F	2	0.8
10	CONEY FLATS	8	53/42	A3,B3	F	2	3.2
10A	FOUR WHEEL DRIVE	6	52/41	A3,B3	F	3	1.8
10B	CONEY FLATS-MIDDLE ST. VRAIN	5	51/43	A3	F,E	3	0.6
11	SOUTH ST. VRAIN	9	57/38	B3,B4	H,K	3	5.6
12	MIDDLE SOURDOUGH	8	55/38	B3	J,G	3	6.3
12A	BEAVER RESERVOIR ROAD CUTOFF	8	56/40	B3	H	1	0.7
12B	CHURCH CAMP CUTOFF	8	55/38	B3	J,H	3	0.3
12C	BAPTISTE-WAPITI	8	54/39	B3	G,J	3	2.2
13	WALDROP (NORTH)	8	53/37	B3	J	3	2.8
13A	BRAINARD BRIDGE CUTOFF	7	52/37	B3	J	1	0.5
14	BRAINARD LAKE ROAD	8	52/37	B3	J	1	2.1
14A	BRAINARD LAKE LOOP	7	51/36	B3	K	1	1.0
14B	MITCHELL LAKE ROAD SPUR	7	50/37	B3	K	1	0.4
14C	LONG LAKE ROAD SPUR	7	50/36	B3	K	1	0.4
15	CMC SOUTH	8	53/36	B3	J	1	2.3
16	LITTLE RAVEN	8	53/36	B3	J	3	2.7
17	LEFT HAND PARK RESERVOIR ROAD	8	53/36	B3	J	2	1.7
18	SOUTH SOURDOUGH	8	54/34	B3	J,L	3	5.5
19	NIWOT RIDGE ROAD	11	52/32	B3	L	3	2.7
19	NIWOT RIDGE TRAVERSE	10	51/34	B3	L,J	4	2.4
20	MITCHELL LAKE	7	50/37	B3,B2	K	4	2.3
21	BEAVER CREEK	7	50/39	B3,A3	K,F	5	4.4
21A	AUDUBON CUTOFF	7	50/38	B3	K,J	5	2.0
21B	FIREBREAK CUTOFF	8	52/41	B3	F	4	1.6
22	PAWNEE PASS	7	49/36	B3,B2	K	3	1.9
23	JEAN LUNNING	7	49/35	B3,B2	K	3	1.5
24	LONG LAKE CUTOFF	7	50/36	B3	K	2	0.5
25	RAINBOW LAKES ROAD	11	54/29	B3	M	2	4.0
26	GLACIER RIM	10	51/30	B3	M	4	1.9

TRAIL SUMMARY TABLE

DIRECTION OF TRAVEL	ALTITUDE GAIN, FEET	ALTITUDE LOSS, FEET	HOURS, OUTBOUND	HOURS, RETURN	ALTITUDE, STARTING	ALTITUDE, HIGHEST	SNOW QUALITY	AMOUNT OF USE	PERCENT OF TRAIL EXPOSED TO WIND	GRADIENT, FREQUENT	GRADIENT, MAXIMUM	SKIING ABILITY	ENDURANCE	ROUTE FINDING	MOUNTAINEERING
W	2010	40	3.2	1.7	8360	10330	5	2	10	3	4	3	4	3	4
W	2200	0	4.4	2.4	8380	10600	5	3	2	3	3	4	5	3	4
E	570	0	0.7	0.5	9150	9720	3	1	0	3	3	3	2	1	2
W	1950	250	3.4	2.0	8900	10600	4	2	2	3	4	3	5	4	4
SW	2100	0	2.4	1.2	8580	10680	3	3	2	3	3	2	3	2	2
NW	650	130	1.2	0.8	10680	11330	3	1	70	3	4	4	5	4	5
W	2620	0	3.0	1.4	8580	11200	2	2	70	4	4	4	4	3	4
NW	0	1100	2.0	0.7	11200	11200	4	1	5	5	5	5	5	4	5
W	1080	0	2.0	1.5	8520	9600	3	4	10	2	3	1	3	1	1
W	1390	0	3.4	2.7	8520	9910	2	3	10	2	3	2	3	2	2
W	990	0	2.4	1.2	9910	10900	4	1	10	2	3	2	5	4	5
NW	1200	0	2.7	1.4	8560	9760	3	1	0	2	3	2	3	4	2
S	350	0	0.7	0.4	8870	9220	2	1	5	2	3	2	1	2	2
NW	380	460	1.5	1.5	9760	10140	2	1	7	3	4	4	3	4	4
S	540	0	1.3	1.0	8600	9160	3	2	0	3	4	3	2	2	2
SW	300	0	0.6	0.4	9190	9190	3	1	2	2	3	2	1	2	2
W	600	0	1.9	1.3	9190	9790	3	4	10	1	2	2	3	2	3
W	290	100	1.2	0.9	9590	9880	4	1	0	2	3	3	4	3	3
N	30	230	0.5	0.3	9790	9820	3	2	10	2	3	2	4	2	3
W	1730	70	3.0	2.0	8740	10480	3	3	5	2	3	3	4	3	2
N	600	1620	3.5	3.1	10060	10120	3	3	7	2	3	3	4	3	3
SW	240	0	0.4	0.3	8920	9160	1	1	10	2	2	1	1	1	1
N	80	0	0.3	0.2	9640	9720	2	1	0	2	3	3	3	2	2
CCW	580	200	1.5	1.0	9400	9920	3	2	0	3	4	3	3	3	3
W	510	230	1.4	1.0	10120	10420	3	4	5	2	4	3	2	1	2
SW	80	40	0.3	0.3	10300	10380	4	2	10	1	1	1	2	2	2
W	290	50	1.2	1.0	10120	10360	2	5	90	1	1	1	1	1	1
W	40	40	0.5	0.5	10340	10370	2	5	70	1	1	1	2	1	1
W	110	0	0.2	0.2	10370	10480	3	5	70	1	1	1	2	1	1
W	130	0	0.2	0.2	10370	10500	2	5	70	1	1	1	2	1	1
W	360	60	1.0	0.9	10120	10420	4	5	5	1	3	1	1	1	1
W	540	200	1.5	0.9	10040	10580	4	3	7	2	4	3	2	1	2
SW	550	0	1.0	0.6	10070	10620	2	4	50	2	3	2	2	1	2
S	450	1260	3.1	2.5	10060	10260	2	3	0	2	3	2	4	1	2
W	1140	0	1.9	1.0	9800	11000	3	3	30	3	3	2	3	2	2
N	440	840	2.0	1.7	11000	11440	2	1	100	3	4	3	4	4	5
W	840	0	1.7	1.0	10480	11320	5	3	30	3	3	3	4	3	4
N	820	1540	4.0	4.0	10500	11320	5	1	30	4	5	5	5	5	5
N	540	590	2.1	2.1	10450	10970	4	1	50	3	5	5	5	5	5
W	670	140	1.4	1.0	9360	10160	3	1	20	3	4	3	4	4	4
W	380	0	1.2	0.9	10500	10880	5	3	10	1	4	3	4	2	3
W	130	40	0.9	0.9	10520	10650	5	2	7	1	1	1	3	3	2
W	170	0	0.4	0.3	10360	10530	3	2	50	2	3	2	3	3	2
W	740	70	2.0	1.5	9290	9960	1	2	50	1	2	1	3	1	2
W	1070	0	1.9	1.0	9960	11030	5	1	7	3	3	3	5	3	5

TRAIL SUMMARY TABLE

TRAIL NUMBER		PAGE-SIZE MAP	MAP COORDINATES	USGS QUADRANGLES	TRAILHEAD	CLASSIFICATION	MILES
26A	RAINBOW LAKES BOWL	10	50/29	B3	M	4	1.9
27	CARIBOU CREEK	11	51/27	B3,C3	M,N	2	2.3
28	CARIBOU FLAT	13	50/24	C3	P,N	4	2.6
29	KING LAKE	13	45/22	C2,C3	P	4	6.1
30	DEVILS THUMB	13	45/25	C2,C3	P	5	4.2
30A	JASPER CREEK	12	45/24	C2	P	5	2.2
31	WOODLAND LAKE	12	45/23	C2	P	5	1.9
31A	WOODLAND MOUNTAIN OVERLOOK	12	43/23	C2	P	5	0.3
32	FOURTH OF JULY ROAD	13	47/26	C2,C3,B2	P	3	4.3
33	LOST LAKE	13	47/22	C3	P	2	0.5
34	NORTH GULLY BRYAN MOUNTAIN	13	46/21	C3,C2	P,R	5	2.1
34A	LOWER GULLY BRYAN MOUNTAIN	13	48/22	C3	R,P	4	0.8
35	JENNY CREEK	17	47/20	C3,C2	R	3	4.6
35A	DEADMAN GULCH	17	50/20	C3	R	1	1.8
36	GUINN MOUNTAIN	17	46/21	C3,C2	R	4	2.1
36A	YANKEE DOODLE CUTOFF	12	44/21	C2	R	4	0.6
36B	GUINN MTN-JENNY CREEK CUTOFF	16	49/20	C2,C3	R	2	0.7
37	ANTELOPE CREEK	17	49/19	C3	U,R	3	1.8
37A	SOUTH ANTELOPE CREEK	17	48/19	C3	U,R	2	1.3
37B	WEST ANTELOPE RIDGE	17	47/19	C3	R,U	2	1.1
37C	EAST ANTELOPE RIDGE	17	48/19	C3	R,U	2	0.7
38	JENNY LIND GULCH	17	52/15	C3	S	2	2.6
38A	WEST FORK LOOP	17	50/15	C3	S	4	1.6
39	BLACK CANYON	17	49/16	C3	S	2	2.3
39A	BALTIMORE RIDGE	17	48/15	C3	S,T	4	2.5
40	MAMMOTH GULCH	17	46/16	C3,C2,D3,D2	T	2	4.8
41	GIANTS LADDER	16	47/17	C2,C3	U	2	5.3
42	SOUTH BOULDER CREEK	16	43/16	C2,D2	W	4	3.6
42A	ROGERS PASS	18	41/14	C2,D2	W	5	3.2
42B	HEART LAKE	18	41/14	C2,D2	W	5	2.9
42C	ICEBERG LAKES	15	40/15	C2,D2	W	5	2.4
42D	CLAYTON LAKE	16	41/16	C2	W	5	2.4
43	FOREST LAKES	16	44/17	C2	W	4	2.0
43A	ARAPAHO CREEK-FOREST LAKES	16	43/18	C2	W	4	1.3
43B	JENNY CREEK-FOREST LAKES	16	44/20	C2	W,R	4	2.1
43C	SOUTH FORK JENNY CREEK	16	44/19	C2	W,R	4	1.4
44	JIM CREEK HEADWALL	18	39/14	C2,C1,D2	W	5	3.8
45	ROLLINS PASS	12	42/20	C2,C1,C3	R	4	9.2
45A	UPPER RAILROAD SWITCHBACK	15	38/17	C2	R	3	3.2
45B	LOWER RAILROAD SWITCHBACK	15	35/18	C1,C2	R	2	6.4

TRAIL SUMMARY TABLE

DIRECTION OF TRAVEL	ALTITUDE GAIN, FEET	ALTITUDE LOSS, FEET	HOURS, OUTBOUND	HOURS, RETURN	ALTITUDE, STARTING	ALTITUDE, HIGHEST	SNOW QUALITY	AMOUNT OF USE	PERCENT OF TRAIL EXPOSED TO WIND	GRADIENT, FREQUENT	GRADIENT, MAXIMUM	SKIING ABILITY	ENDURANCE	ROUTE FINDING	MOUNTAINEERING
E	0	1070	2.0	1.7	11030	11030	4	1	30	4	4	5	5	4	5
S	280	110	1.1	1.1	9820	9990	1	1	90	1	1	1	2	2	3
N	1010	330	2.2	1.7	9320	10330	2	1	70	4	5	4	5	4	5
W	2090	0	3.8	2.3	8810	10900	5	2	7	3	3	2	5	3	4
W	1660	0	3.6	2.0	9620	11280	5	2	15	3	4	5	5	4	5
E	0	990	1.7	0.8	11280	11280	5	2	20	3	4	5	5	4	5
W	1270	0	1.7	1.2	9710	10980	4	1	30	4	5	5	4	4	5
SW	280	0	0.5	0.3	10980	11260	5	1	5	5	5	5	4	4	5
N	1170	0	2.5	1.7	8990	10160	3	4	30	2	3	2	3	1	2
S	160	0	0.5	0.3	9620	9780	3	2	30	2	2	2	2	2	2
S	1240	60	2.0	1.4	9780	10960	2	1	70	5	5	5	4	4	5
NE	0	820	1.0	0.5	9940	9940	5	1	20	5	5	5	3	3	4
W	1600	240	2.5	1.3	9360	10720	3	5	5	2	3	3	4	2	3
SW	290	110	0.9	0.7	9360	9540	3	5	10	2	3	1	1	1	1
W	1320	0	1.5	0.7	9640	10960	5	4	2	4	4	3	4	3	4
SW	0	600	0.8	0.4	11210	11210	3	1	30	5	5	5	4	4	4
N	250	0	0.5	0.3	9810	10060	4	3	3	3	4	2	2	3	2
W	600	50	1.2	0.7	9400	9950	3	3	0	3	4	3	2	2	2
W	560	40	1.2	0.9	9400	9920	3	1	0	3	3	2	2	3	2
SE	150	0	0.9	0.7	9820	9970	4	2	10	1	2	1	2	2	2
SE	110	70	0.6	0.5	9600	9710	4	1	0	2	3	1	2	3	2
S	1670	0	1.4	1.0	8800	10470	2	4	30	3	4	3	3	1	1
SW	1320	0	1.5	1.0	9150	10470	3	1	10	5	5	4	3	4	4
SW	870	0	1.9	1.2	8840	9710	3	1	5	3	3	2	3	3	2
W	550	510	2.0	1.8	9710	10260	3	1	50	4	4	4	4	4	4
SW	1420	0	2.5	1.5	8920	10340	3	3	20	2	3	2	3	2	2
N	760	0	2.5	2.1	9190	9950	2	3	70	1	1	1	2	1	2
SW	1890	0	2.8	1.4	9210	11100	5	4	5	4	5	4	3	4	
W	910	900	2.2	2.2	11100	11910	2	1	100	5	5	5	5	4	5
W	950	940	2.2	2.2	11100	12050	2	1	100	5	5	5	5	4	5
W	1020	1010	2.0	2.0	11100	12120	2	1	100	5	5	5	5	4	5
W	1870	850	3.4	2.8	10080	11950	3	1	70	5	5	5	5	5	5
N	1230	0	2.0	0.9	9590	10820	5	3	3	4	5	4	4	4	4
N	700	0	1.2	0.7	10120	10820	5	2	5	4	5	4	4	4	4
N	20	220	1.5	1.4	10820	10820	5	1	20	2	3	3	4	4	4
NE	0	660	1.0	0.8	10820	10820	4	1	10	3	3	4	4	4	5
W	0	2760	4.0	1.4	11860	11860	4	1	50	5	5	5	5	4	5
W	910	2770	8.0	6.0	10960	11760	3	2	50	3	4	4	5	5	5
W	0	800	1.4	0.8	11100	11100	3	4	50	2	3	1	4	1	4
W	0	1080	2.5	2.0	10180	10180	3	4	30	2	2	1	3	1	2

TRAIL SUMMARY TABLE EXPLANATIONS

PAGE-SIZE MAP— Page-size map for the beginning of a trail. Maps 1-20 are on pages 208-227. Each map is a quarter of a USGS 7 ½' quadrangle. The configuration is shown in figure 3, page 207.

MAP COORDINATES— Refer to blue labeled ticks at 1 km intervals on the folded trail map. Read RIGHT UP. Trails 1-24 are on Side 1 (North) and 25-45B on Side 2 (South).

USGS QUADRANGLES— See figure 2, page 8, for 7 ½' quadrangle names corresponding to abbreviations.

TRAILHEAD—See table of contents, page 4, for trailhead names corresponding to abbreviations.

CLASSIFICATION—See page 12 for the correspondence of numerical ratings on a scale of 1 to 5, to descriptive terms. These are given for the classification for overall difficulty, trail characteristics, and specific skills. A rating of 5 means the most difficult, best snow, most use, steepest gradient, and the highest skill.

GRADIENT FREQUENT—The gradient or steepness that will often be encountered. It is not the average gradient.

GRADIENT MAXIMUM—The steepest gradient that will be encountered.

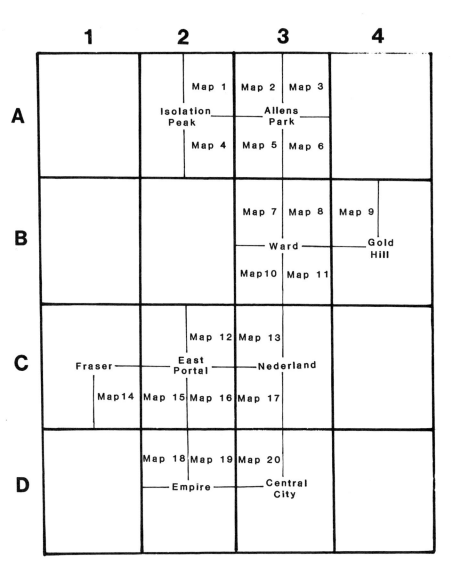

Figure 3. Page-size trail maps (numbered) shown on a mosaic of USGS 7 ½' quadrangle maps. Each is a quarter of a quadrangle. Letters and numbers along margins are combined to give abbreviations used in trail summary table for USGS quadrangle names, i.e. Ward is abbreviated B3.

207

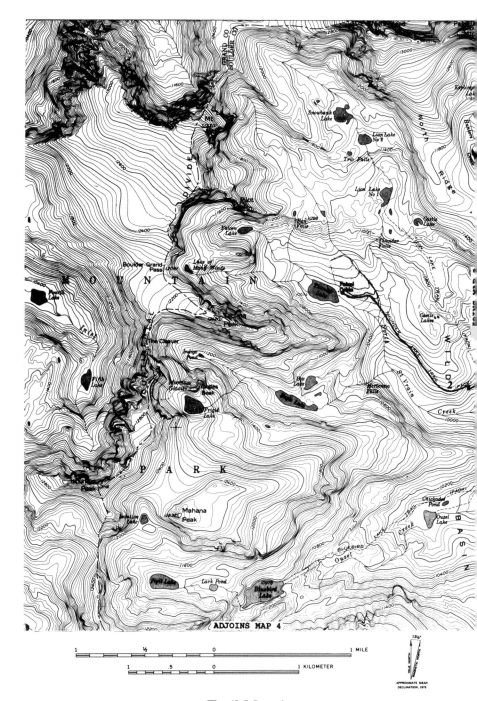

Trail Map 1

Northeast quarter of USGS Isolation Peak 7 ½' quadrangle

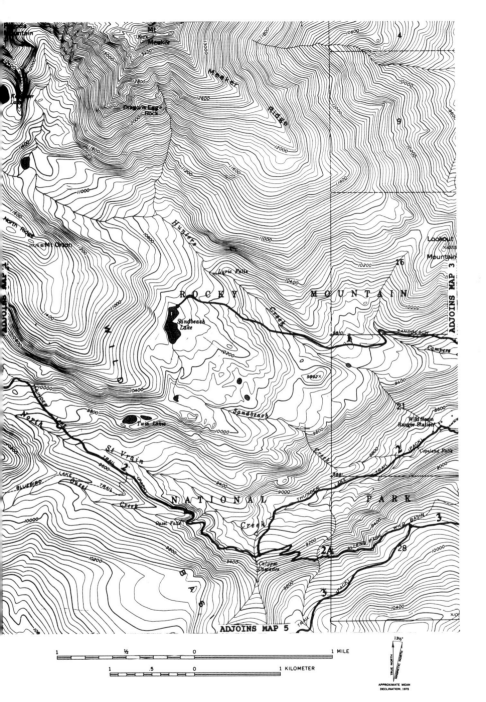

Trail Map 2
Northwest quarter of USGS Allens Park 7 ½' quadrangle

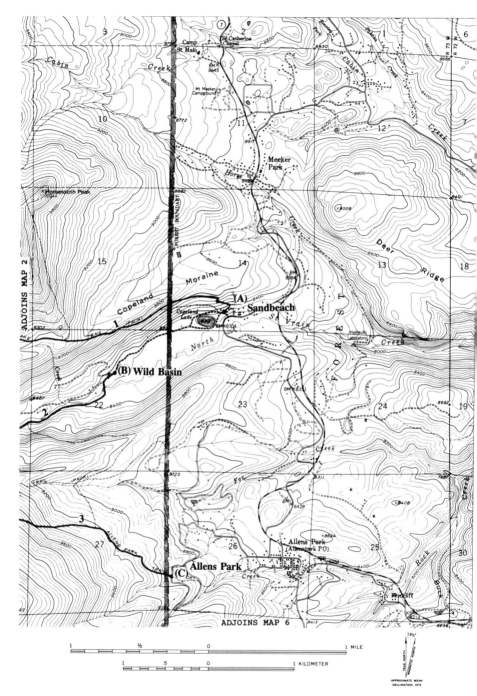

Trail Map 3
Northeast quarter of USGS Allens Park 7 ½' quadrangle

210

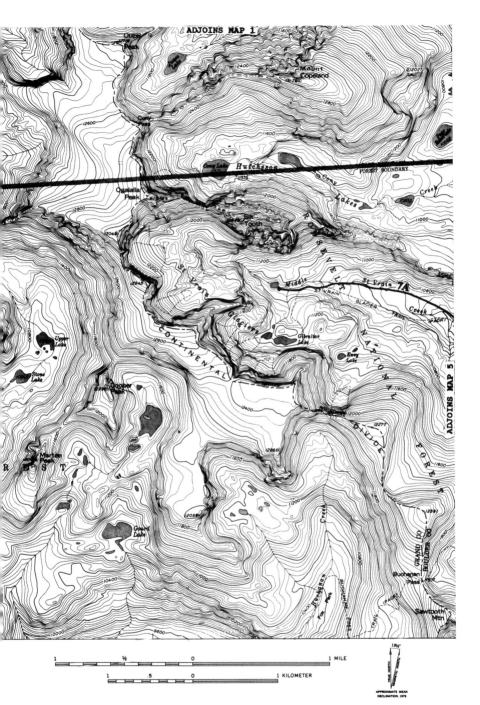

Trail Map 4
Southeast quarter of USGS Isolation Peak 7 ½' quadrangle

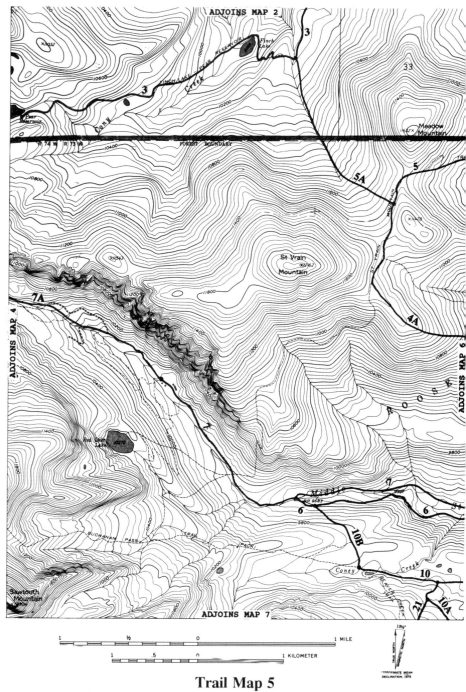

Trail Map 5
Southwest quarter of USGS Allens Park 7 ½' quadrangle

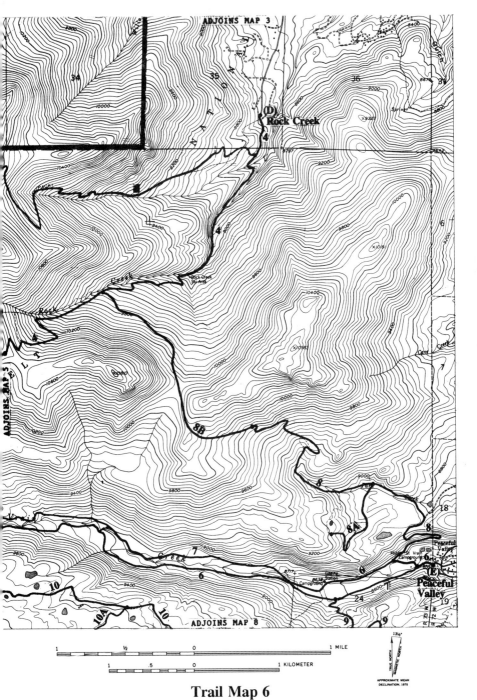

Trail Map 6
Southeast quarter of USGS Allens Park 7 ½' quadrangle

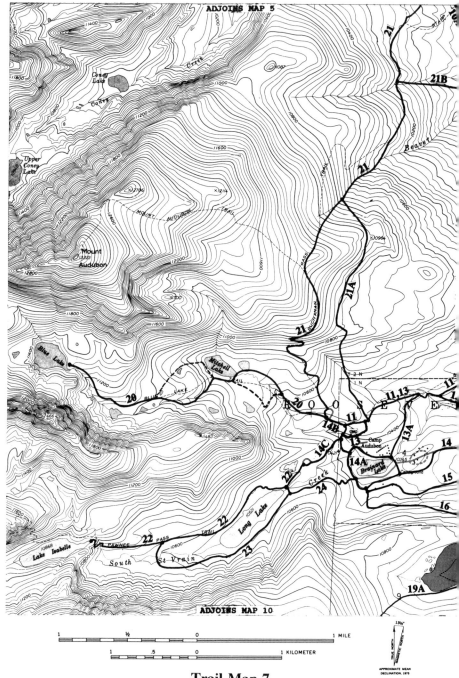

ADJOINS MAP 10

Trail Map 7
Northwest quarter of USGS Ward 7 ½' quadrangle

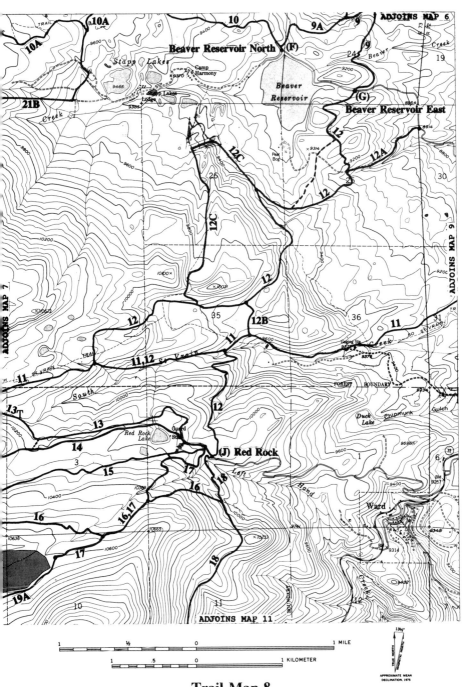

Trail Map 8
Northeast quarter of USGS Ward 7 ½' quadrangle

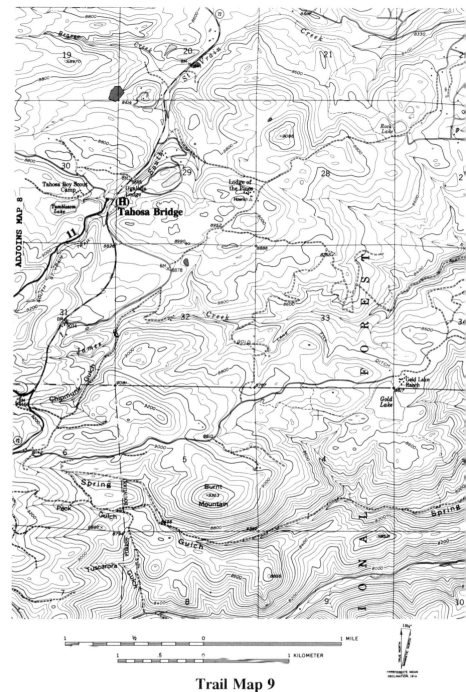

Trail Map 9

Northwest quarter of USGS Gold Hill 7 ½' quadrangle

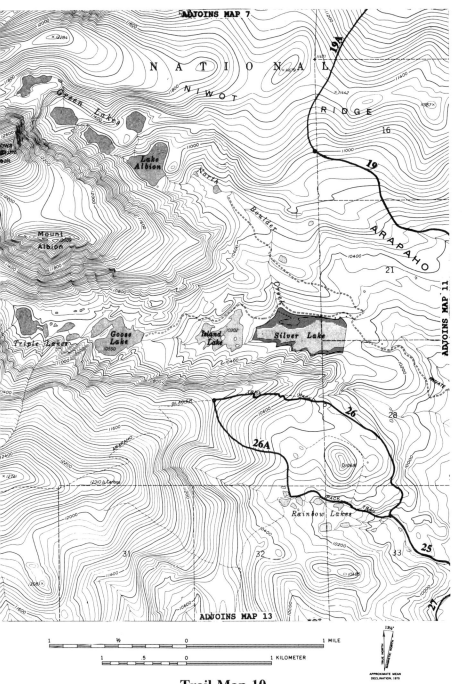

NATIONAL

NIWOT

RIDGE

ARAPAHO

Green Lakes

Lake
Albion

North

Boulder

Creek

16

19A

19

21

Mount
Albion

Triple Lakes

Goose
Lake

Island
Lake

Silver Lake

GLACIER

ARAPAHO

TRAIL

26

26A

28

PRIVATE

Rainbow Lakes

PACK

TRAIL

25

31

32

33

27

1   ½   0   1 MILE

1   .5   0   1 KILOMETER

TRUE NORTH

MAGNETIC NORTH

APPROXIMATE MEAN
DECLINATION, 1975

Trail Map 10
Southwest quarter of USGS Ward 7 ½' quadrangle

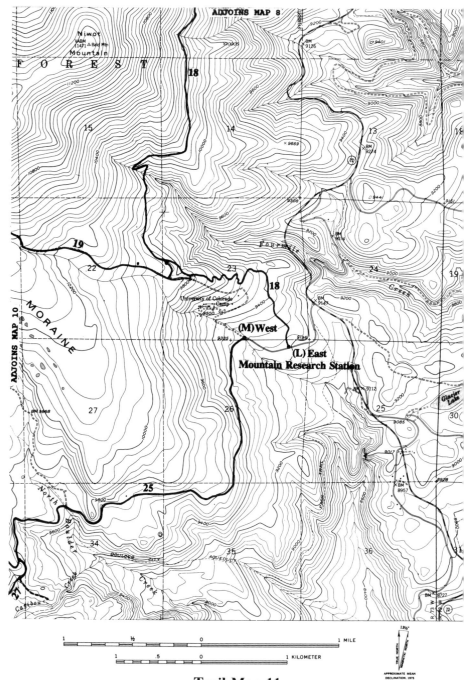

Trail Map 11

Southeast quarter of USGS Ward 7 ½' quadrangle

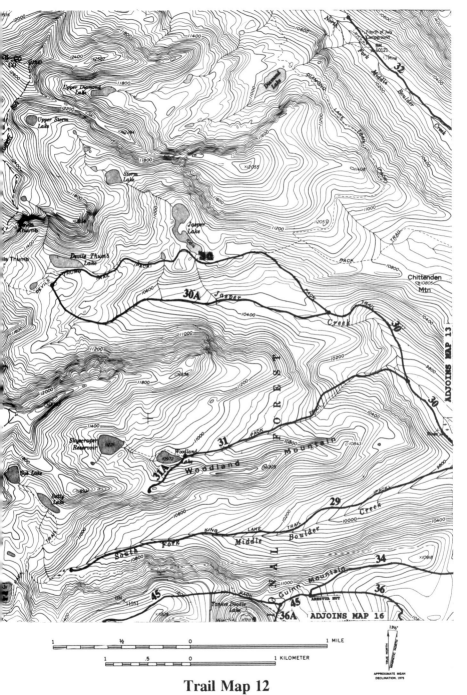

Trail Map 12
Northeast quarter of USGS East Portal 7 ½' quadrangle

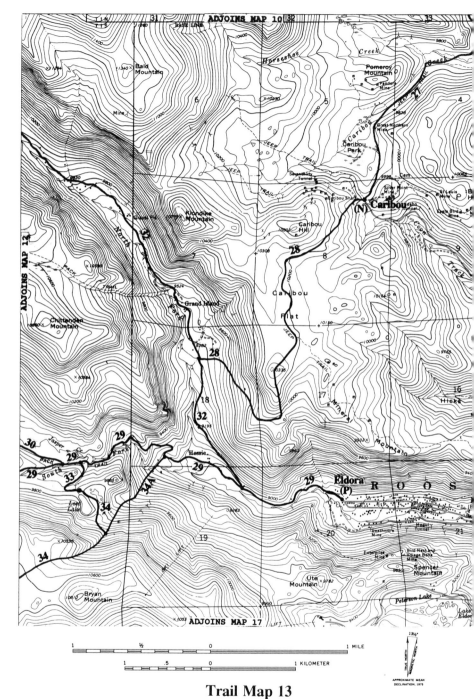

Trail Map 13

Northwest quarter of USGS Nederland 7 ½' quadrangle

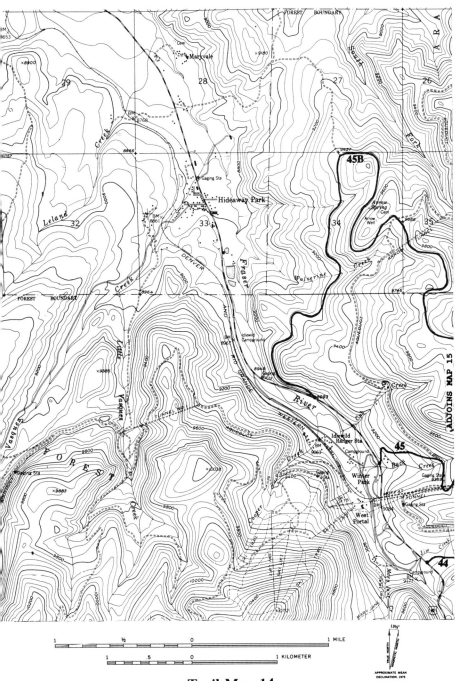

Trail Map 14
Southeast quarter of USGS Fraser 7 ½' quadrangle

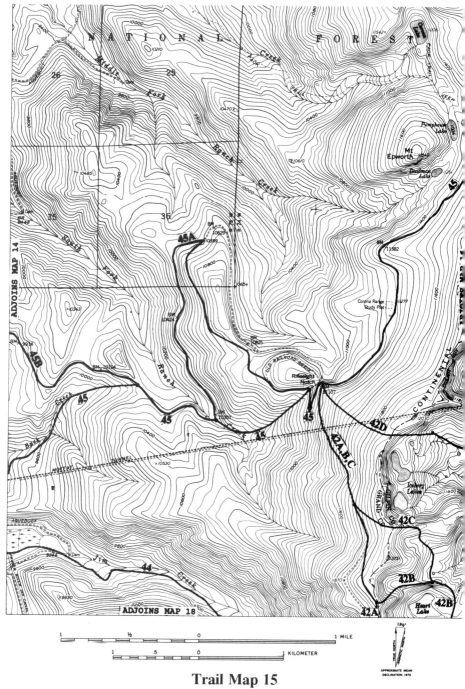

Trail Map 15
Southwest quarter of USGS East Portal 7 ½' quadrangle

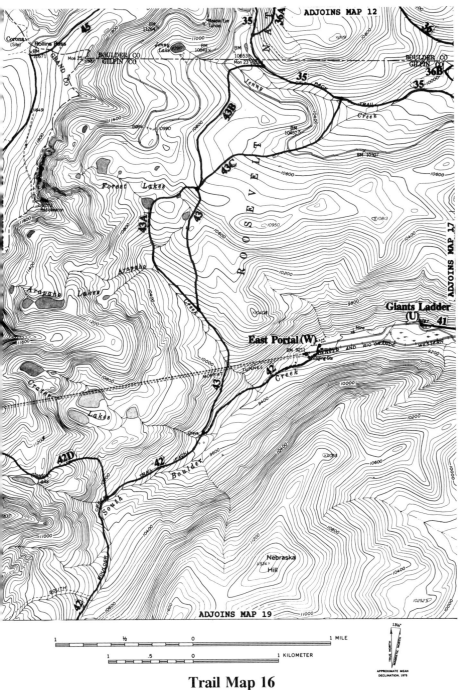

ADJOINS MAP 19

Trail Map 16
Southeast quarter of USGS East Portal 7 ½' quadrangle

223

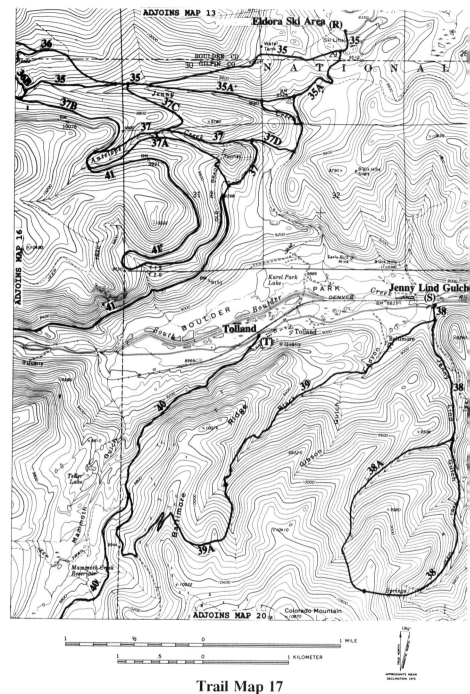

Trail Map 17
Southwest quarter of USGS Nederland 7 ½' quadrangle

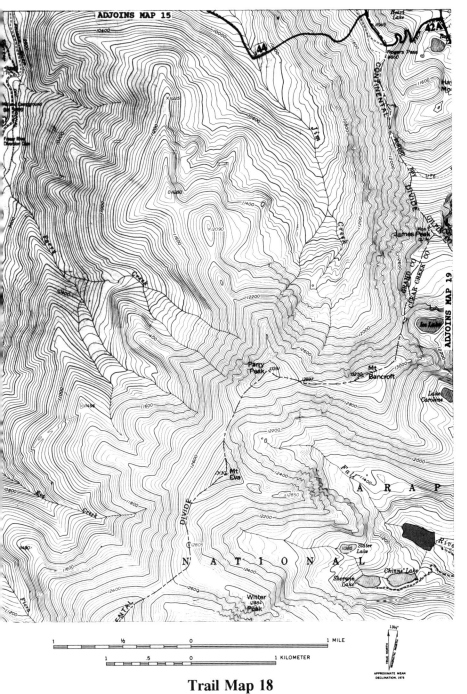

Trail Map 18
Northwest quarter of USGS Empire 7 ½' quadrangle

225

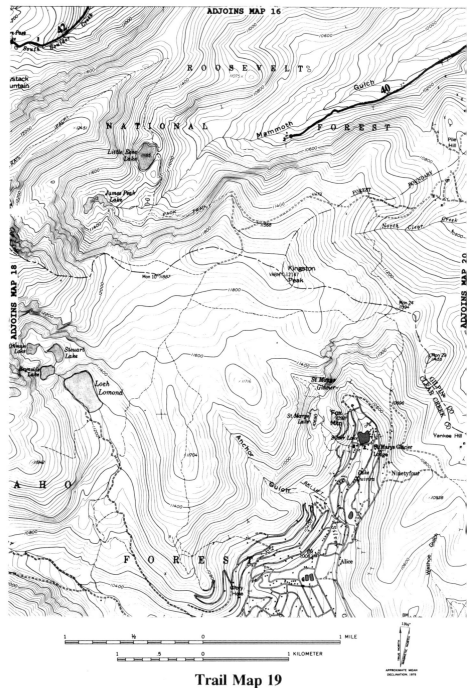

ADJOINS MAP 18

ADJOINS MAP 20

ROOSEVELT

NATIONAL

Mammoth

Gulch

FOREST

40

Pile
Hill

FOREST
BOUNDARY

North Clear Creek

Little Echo
Lake

James Peak
Lake

PACK TRAIL

Mon 10 11887

Kingston
Peak

VABM 12147

Mon 24
7394

GILPIN
CLEAR CREEK

Mon 29
1455

Ohman
Lake

Steuart
Lake

Reynolds
Lake

Loch
Lomond

St Marys
Glacier

St Marys
Lake

Fox
Mtn

Yankee Hill

Silver Lake

Anchor

Gulch

St Marys Glacier
Lake

Silver
Creek

SKI LIFT

Ninetyfour

Idaho
Springs

Alice

Glory
Hole

FOREST

Westoe Gulch

1/2   0   1 MILE

1   .5   0   1 KILOMETER

13¾°

TRUE NORTH

APPROXIMATE MEAN
DECLINATION, 1975

Trail Map 19
Northeast quarter of USGS Empire 7 ½' quadrangle

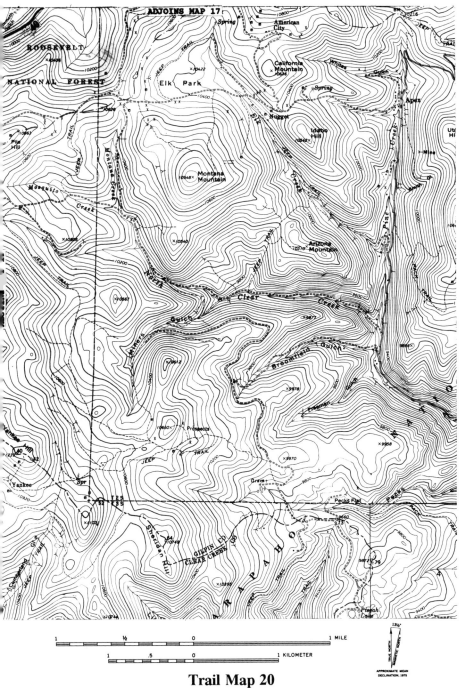

Trail Map 20

Northwest quarter of USGS Central City 7 ½' quadrangle

BIBLIOGRAPHY

Avalanche

The ABC of Avalanche Safety, E. R. LaChapelle, The Mountaineers

Avalanche Handbook, Agriculture Handbook 489, U. S. Department of Agriculture, Forest Service

The Avalanche Book, Betsy Armstrong & Knox Williams, Fulcrum Inc.

The Avalanche Handbook, David McClung & Peter Schaerer, The Mountaineers

Ski technique and equipment

Mountain Skiing, Vic Bein, The Mountaineers

Backcountry Skiing, Lito Tejada-Flores, Sierra Club Books

Cross Country Skiing, Ned Gillette & John Dostal, The Mountaineers

Wilderness Skiing and Winter Camping, Chris Townsend, Ragged Mountain Press

Cross-Country Downhill, Steve Barnett, Pacific Search Press

Free-Heel Skiing, Paul Parker, Chesla Green Publishing Co.

The Telemark Movie, Dick Hall & John Fuller, North American Telemark Organization (70 minute videotape)

Mountaineering

Mountaineering The Freedom of the Hills, Fifth Edition, Ed Peters Editor, The Mountaineers

Wilderness Mountaineering, Phil Powers, National Outdoor Leadership School

First aid

Medicine for Mountaineering, Fourth Edition, James A. Wilkerson, The Mountaineers

NOLS Wilderness First Aid, Second Edition, Tod Schimelpfenig and Linda Lindsey, National Outdoor Leadership School

Advanced First Aid & Emergency Care, The American National Red Cross

Emergency Care and Transportation of the Sick and Injured, American Academy of Orthopaedic Surgeons

Hypothermia, Frostbite and other Cold Injuries, James A. Wilkerson, Cameron C. Bangs, and John S. Hayward, The Mountaineers

Hiking trail guidebooks for area

The Indian Peaks Wilderness Area guide, J. Murray, Pruett

Rocky Mountain National Park Hiking Trails, K. & D. Dannen, East Woods

Colorado's Indian Peaks Wilderness Area-Classic Hikes and Climbs, Gerry Roach, Fulcrum

Fifty Front Range Hiking Trails, Richard DuMais, High Peak Books

Rocky Mountain National Park Trail Guide, E. Nilsson, Anderson World

Trails of the Front Range, L. Kenofer, Pruett Publishing Company

Skiing guidebooks for area

Colorado Front Range Ski Tours, Tom and Sanse Sudduth, The Touchstone Press

Fifty Colorado Ski Tours, Richard Du Mais, High Peak Publishing

Ski Trail Map, Brainard Lake-Middle St Vrain, Harlan Barton, Colorado Mountain Club

Tree identification

Rocky Mountain Tree Finder, Tom Watts, Nature Study Guild

Map reading

A Comprehensive Guide to Land Navigation, Noel J. Hotchkiss, Alexis Publishing

Geology of area

Geology of National Parks, Ann Harris and Esther Tuttle, Kendall/Hunt

Roadside Geology of Colorado, Halka Chronic, Mountain Press

Prairie Peak and Plateau, John and Halka Chronic, Colorado Geological Survey Bulletin 32

History of area

Red Rocks to Riches, Silvia Pettem, Stonehenge Books

Rails that Climb, Edward T. Bolinger, Colorado Railroad Historical Foundation

The Moffat Road, Edward T. Bolinger and Frederick Bauer, Sage Books

INDEX

ABOUT THE AUTHOR Harlan N. Barton

A fascination with maps was first piqued as a field artillery forward observer during the Korean War. It continued with the challenge of navigating, often with only rudimentary maps or aerial photos, while doing geologic field work in remote areas of Alaska and the West. This has been combined with a long standing enthusiasm for exploring new areas for cross country skiing to make him uniquely qualified to produce this comprehensive guide to cross country skiing on the eastern slope of the Front Range.

Living in Boulder, he is a trip leader for the Colorado Mountain Club and a past member of the Rocky Mountain Rescue Group. A ski trail map of the Brainard Lake and Middle St. Vrain area published by the Colorado Mountain Club and the first edition of this book are earlier products of his ski trail mapping. He is retired from the U. S. Geological Survey, where he did field studies of proposed wilderness areas. In addition to Colorado and other contiguous states, he has hiked and climbed in British Columbia, Mexico, Ecuador, Patagonia, the Brooks Range, Himalayas and Karakoram.